VOLUME 476   NOVEMBER 1984

THE ANNALS

of The American Academy *of* Political
and Social Science

RICHARD D. LAMBERT, *Editor*
ALAN W. HESTON, *Associate Editor*

CHINA IN TRANSITION

Special Editor of this Volume

MARVIN E. WOLFGANG
President
American Academy of Political
and Social Science
Professor of Social Systems Sciences,
Sociology, and Law
University of Pennsylvania
Philadelphia, Pennsylvania

SAGE PUBLICATIONS   *BEVERLY HILLS   LONDON   NEW DELHI*

Framingham State College
Framingham, Massachusetts

THE ANNALS

© 1984 *by* The American Academy *of* Political *and* Social Science

ERICA GINSBURG, *Assistant Editor*

All rights reserved. No part of this volume may be reproduced or utilized in any form or by any means, electronic or mechanical, including photocopying, recording or by any information storage and retrieval system, without permission in writing from the publisher.

Editorial Office: 3937 Chestnut Street, Philadelphia, Pennsylvania 19104.

For information about membership* (Individuals only) and subscriptions (institutions), address:

SAGE PUBLICATIONS, INC.
275 South Beverly Drive
Beverly Hills, CA 90212 USA

From India and South Asia,
write to:
SAGE PUBLICATIONS INDIA Pvt. Ltd.
P.O. Box 3605
New Delhi 110 024
INDIA

From the UK, Europe, the Middle
East and Africa, write to:
SAGE PUBLICATIONS LTD
28 Banner Street
London EC1Y 8QE
ENGLAND

**Please note that members of The Academy receive THE ANNALS with their membership.*

Library of Congress Catalog Card Number 84-071048
International Standard Serial Number ISSN 0002-7162
International Standard Book Number ISBN 0-8039-2363-5 (Vol. 476, 1984 paper)
International Standard Book Number ISBN 0-8039-2362-7 (Vol. 476, 1984 cloth)
Manufactured in the United States of America. First printing, November 1984.

The articles appearing in THE ANNALS are indexed in *Book Review Index; PAIS Bulletin; Social Sciences Index; Monthly Periodical Index; Current Contents; Behavioral, Social Management Sciences;* and *Combined Retrospective Index Sets.* They are also abstracted and indexed in *ABC Pol Sci, Historical Abstracts, Human Resources Abstracts, Social Sciences Citation Index, United States Political Science Documents, Social Work Research & Abstracts, Peace Research Reviews, Sage Urban Studies Abstracts, International Political Science Abstracts,* and/or *America: History and Life.*

Information about membership rates, institutional subscriptions, and back issue prices may be found on the facing page.

Advertising. Current rates and specifications may be obtained by writing to THE ANNALS Advertising and Promotion Manager at the Beverly Hills office (address above).

Claims. Claims for undelivered copies must be made no later than three months following month of publication. The publisher will supply missing copies when losses have been sustained in transit and when the reserve stock will permit.

Change of Address. Six weeks' advance notice must be given when notifying of change of address to insure proper identification. Please specify name of journal. Postmaster: Send address changes to: THE ANNALS, c/o Sage Publications, Inc., 275 South Beverly Drive, Beverly Hills, CA 90212.

DS
706
C497
1984

The American Academy of Political and Social Science

3937 Chestnut Street   Philadelphia, Pennsylvania 19104

Board of Directors

ELMER B. STAATS	COVEY T. OLIVER
MARVIN E. WOLFGANG	THOMAS L. HUGHES
LEE BENSON	LLOYD N. CUTLER
RICHARD D. LAMBERT	RANDALL M. WHALEY
REBECCA JEAN BROWNLEE	

Officers

President
MARVIN E. WOLFGANG

Vice-Presidents
RICHARD D. LAMBERT, *First Vice-President*
STEPHEN B. SWEENEY, *First Vice-President Emeritus*

Secretary	Treasurer	Counsel
REBECCA JEAN BROWNLEE	ELMER B. STAATS	HENRY W. SAWYER, III

Editors, THE ANNALS

RICHARD D. LAMBERT, *Editor*   ALAN W. HESTON, *Associate Editor*

THORSTEN SELLIN, *Editor Emeritus*

Business Manager
INGEBORG HESSLER

Origin and Purpose. The Academy was organized December 14, 1889, to promote the progress of political and social science, especially through publications and meetings. The Academy does not take sides in controverted questions, but seeks to gather and present reliable information to assist the public in forming an intelligent and accurate judgment.

Meetings. The Academy holds an annual meeting in the spring extending over two days.

Publications. THE ANNALS is the bimonthly publication of The Academy. Each issue contains articles on some prominent social or political problem, written at the invitation of the editors. Also, monographs are published from time to time, numbers of which are distributed to pertinent professional organizations. These volumes constitute important reference works on the topics with which they deal, and they are extensively cited by authorities through-out the United States and abroad. The papers presented at the meetings of The Academy are included in THE ANNALS.

Membership. Each member of The Academy receives THE ANNALS and may attend the meetings of The Academy. Membership is open only to individuals. Annual dues: $26.00 for the regular paperbound edition (clothbound, $39.00). Add $9.00 per year for membership outside the U.S.A. Members may also purchase single issues of THE ANNALS for $6.95 each (clothbound, $10.00).

Subscriptions. THE ANNALS (ISSN 0002-7162) is published six times annually—in January, March, May, July, September, and November. Institutions may subscribe to THE ANNALS at the annual rate: $45.00 (clothbound, $60.00). Add $9.00 per year for subscriptions outside the U.S.A. Institutional rates for single issues: $10.00 each (clothbound, $15.00).

Second class postage paid at Philadelphia, Pennsylvania, and at additional mailing offices.

Single issues of THE ANNALS may be obtained by individuals who are not members of The Academy for $7.95 each (clothbound, $15.00). Single issues of THE ANNALS have proven to be excellent supplementary texts for classroom use. Direct inquiries regarding adoptions to THE ANNALS c/o Sage Publications (address below).

All correspondence concerning membership in The Academy, dues renewals, inquiries about membership status, and/or purchase of single issues of THE ANNALS should be sent to THE ANNALS c/o Sage Publications, Inc., 275 South Beverly Drive, Beverly Hills, CA 90212. *Please note that orders under $20 must be prepaid.* Sage affiliates in London and India will assist institutional subscribers abroad with regard to orders, claims, and inquiries for both subscriptions and single issues.

THE ANNALS

of The American Academy *of* Political *and* Social Science

RICHARD D. LAMBERT, *Editor*
ALAN W. HESTON, *Associate Editor*

——————— **FORTHCOMING** ———————

See page 3 for information on Academy membership and
purchase of single volumes of **The Annals.**

CONTENTS

BOOK DEPARTMENT CONTENTS

SOCIOLOGY

ECONOMICS

OPENING REMARKS AT THE
EIGHTY-SEVENTH ANNUAL MEETING

Welcome to the eighty-seventh annual meeting of the American Academy of Political and Social Science, founded in 1889 and incorporated in 1891.

One of my functions as president of the academy is to prepare for and to organize these annual meetings. The board of directors and I regularly try to plan a meeting around a topic that will be important and timely, but we must plan it nearly a year in advance. Traditionally, the topic one year is international, and the next year it is domestic. Two years ago our topic was international terrorism, an equally viable topic today, considering bombings in Israel and a United States officers' club and the firing from the Libyan embassy in London.

This year our topic, China in transition, is obviously international, and we were fortunate to choose it, not knowing how newsworthy it would be at the end of April. Indeed, this week *Time* magazine is featuring on its cover "China's New Face" and *Newsweek* is featuring on its cover "The Terms of Endearment," a study of President Reagan's visit to Beijing. Yesterday the president landed in Beijing. We are today and tomorrow talking about China, a country in which the United States has a major interest.

We have an interesting and informative program. Some of the most illustrious members of the academic and political science community will present new and fascinating papers on the internal politics of China, population control, migration, the relationships among China, the USSR, and the United States, rural agriculture and modernization, and the development of legal education.

Approximately 130 American firms now have offices in Beijing, and trade between our two countries amounts to about $5.5 billion, a fiftyfold increase since our last annual meeting dealt with the topic of China, in 1972. Moreover, 10 years ago only a handful of Chinese were allowed to study overseas, while today there are 12,000 students in the United States alone.

I am excited by this meeting because it concerns a people that represents 1 billion of the world's population. More people speak Chinese as their native tongue than any other language on earth. If one combines both native and second languages, English is the most commonly used language. Together we rule the linguistic world.

China is huge in space and people. China is significant in size and for future development, far beyond any part of the globe.

Ethical issues of population control and migration control, legal issues of criminal justice and civil rights, even copyright issues of printed ownership, and investment of capital in hotels, in high technology, and in nuclear power are all of major concern as the United States and China together move through the 1980s and 1990s. On the population issue, we note that there has been a significant rise in life expectancy in China, from age 40 in 1950 to over 60 in 1983. China's population has increased by more than 500 million since World War II. "That is roughly," says

Time magazine, "the equivalent of moving all the people of Western Europe and the U.S. into the already overcrowded Middle Kingdom."[1]

The problem of Hong Kong is important from an investment viewpoint, but it is minuscule compared to electrical energy, nuclear power, industrial development, and general modernization. No country in the world has the problems China has in controlling and planning families. Limitations of food, space, and educational facilities are crucial. Rural versus urban population control policies are critical. We in the West can hardly stand in a posture of severe criticism of what the Chinese government may do or devise. I suggest that our political, social, and scientific perspective should be one of tolerant understanding. We are two cultures and need to study and understand one another while we seek more social, scientific, and educational interrelationships.

I wish to thank my colleagues Allyn Rickett, professor of Chinese and Oriental studies at the University of Pennsylvania, and Professor Chong-Sik Lee, chairman of that university's Graduate Program in International Relations, for their help in making suggestions for topics and speakers to this novice in Chinese studies. I wish also to thank Kenneth Lieberthal, for he was one of the first persons contacted to develop this meeting.

Many Chinese experts—both American and Chinese—are in China today accompanying the president. But many who have worked, lived, taught, and researched in China are here today. We are indeed fortunate and grateful for their presence and contributions here. Moreover, the deputy of the Chinese mission in Washington, Mr. Hu, will be our luncheon speaker. You may have seen the photograph of him in last Sunday's *New York Times,* waving good-bye to President Reagan. Mr. Hu will be with us tomorrow.

This is our marvelous program. The excellent and exciting papers presented here today and tomorrow will be published in *The Annals* in the November issue.

27 April 1984   MARVIN E. WOLFGANG

---

1. *Time*, 30 Apr. 1984, p. 28.

ANNALS, *AAPSS*, **476**, November 1984

China Today

By HU DINGYI

ABSTRACT: Since the founding of the People's Republic of China, the country has made considerable strides forward. Recently its modernization program coupled with a series of reforms has registered success. The record of 1983 is a good illustration. A careful study of China's achievements and challenges shows that the country will move ahead in the years to come. The main points of China's foreign policy are to develop relations with all countries on the basis of the Five Principles of Peaceful Coexistence; to strengthen solidarity with the other Third World countries and to promote friendship with the people of all countries; and to oppose hegemony and safeguard world peace. The steady and sustained development of friendly relations between China and the United States is not only in the interests of the two peoples, but also of great benefit to the maintenance of world peace and the promotion of human progress. The potential is great, but obstacles such as the Taiwan question need to be removed.

Hu Dingyi graduated from the Central University, Chongqing, to prepare for a diplomatic career. Currently minister at the Embassy of the People's Republic of China in Washington, D. C., he has held numerous responsible diplomatic positions, including consul general in San Francisco, counselor at the Chinese embassy in London, and division chief in the African Department of the Ministry of Foreign Affairs in Beijing.

T HE current international situation is a fluid one. Many forces are at work to determine the level of political cohesion, military balance, and economic development in different regions. Though the whole is so much more than the sum of its parts, the study of individual countries is a basic building block for a proper understanding of the various contributing factors to the state of the world today.

China covers 9.6 million square kilometers with a population of 1 billion. It has the oldest uninterrupted civilization in the world, and is a very active member of the international community. Therefore its past and present and its internal development and external relaions deserve a careful look.

1949—THE WATERSHED

Ancient China is the birthplace of, among other things, the compass, gunpowder, movable type, and paper. At one time or another, it led the world in science, technology, art, and literature.

However, toward the middle of the nineteenth century, China started to go downhill fast. Feudalism increasingly obstructed social development. Foreign powers grabbed Chinese territory and carved China into their spheres of influence, riding roughshod over the Chinese. The corrupt, repressive regimes at home pursued a traitorous foreign policy while bleeding its own people white. This combination made the Chinese economy extremely backward, and life was an agony for my people. Millions died of war, hunger, disease, and natural calamities each year.

Never giving up hope under the worst of conditions, the Chinese people rose up in revolution. Countless patriots went through fire to save the nation.

Such heroism culminated in the founding of a socialist, new China in 1949. Since then, the country has gradually come to occupy its rightful place in the world community. The Chinese people are now basically free from shortages of food and clothing. Their personal safety is assured. A nationwide, comprehensive industrial base has been established. We are approaching or even have arrived at the level of the advanced world in some fields of science and technology.

Of course, the People's Republic of China, being a young country, has had its own share of setbacks. The so-called Cultural Revolution, between 1966 and 1976, plunged the country into great chaos. The Chinese people have become all the wiser from that costly experience and will not permit its repetition. Bold measures have since been taken to put China back on the right track.

THE MODERNIZATION PROGRAM

The nation's goal is the modernization of its industry, agriculture, national defense, and science and technology by the end of the century. Specifically, the total value of industrial and agricultural production is to be quadrupled between the years 1980 and 2000. This goal requires ingenuity, sustained efforts, and consistency of purpose of the whole nation, and it cannot afford any vacillation or deviation from the set course.

The stage has been set for the successful execution of the modernization program. Politically, unity and stability are here to stay. The program is enshrined in China's constitution. The legislative process is being pushed forward with a view to promoting the rule of law and enhancing the democratic rights of the people. Political leadership has been strengthened and rejuvenated. A small core of trusted founding fathers of the People's Republic forms the top echelon. Day-to-day affairs of the state are left to the second echelon of well-experienced and active leaders. A new infusion of competent, younger, and better-educated persons makes up the third echelon at both the national and local levels. The three-echelon leadership structure will ensure a smooth transition of power and continuity of policies.

Economically, China has been implementing the principles of readjustment, restructuring, consolidation, and improvement as well as the policy of opening itself to the outside world and invigorating the domestic economy. This approach has paid off handsomely.

Many Chinese view economic restructuring and reform of the existing economic management system as a main factor in improving the overall performance of the national economy. The national consensus is that while the economy remains a planned one, room should be given to market regulation to play a supplementary role.

In agricultural production, a new responsibility system has been installed. Nowadays, within the general framework of the state plan, each farming family may decide what crops to plant and enter into a contract for fixed quotas of production. All production over and above the quota goes to the family for its own consumption or for sale at the free market. Tremendous vigor has thus been injected into a diverse rural economy.

In the industrial sector, things are more complicated, yet the principles concerning reform are basically the same. A management responsiblity system has come into being. Within the overall framework of the state plan,

enterprises now have more decision-making power so as to be responsive to market needs. Before, enterprises handed over all profits to the state, which provided them with all the funds needed for production and other purposes. Now they are beginning to become tax-paying entities, retaining profits and investing them or distributing them as bonuses for all the employees, as they see fit. Consequently, the enterprises and their employees have incentives to improve their managerial skills, and better economic results are sure to emerge.

In addition to these reforms in the state-owned enterprises, the government also encourages the setting up of cooperatives as well as an appropriate development of individual businesses as necessary and useful supplements to the public sector.

Thanks to the measures of reform and the hard work of the Chinese people, in recent years the national economy has been able to maintain a fairly high rate of growth, averaging over 7 percent annually.

Success in 1983

The year 1983 was the third year of China's Sixth Five-Year Plan (1981-85) and also one of the best since the founding of the People's Republic. The gross output value for industry and agriculture as well as the output for more than 30 industrial and agricultural products—including grain, cotton, crude oil, pig iron, rolled steel, and motor vehicles—reached the goal set in the Sixth Five-Year Plan for 1985, two years ahead of schedule.

In 1983, the total grain output was about 380 million tons, 26 million tons more than in 1982, which itself was a year of bumper harvests. Cotton output reached 4.5 million tons, an increase of 25 percent from 1982, when it rose 21.2 percent. The annual agricultural output value exceeded $130 billion U.S., 5 percent more than in 1982, based on 1980 constant prices.

The total industrial output value reached $295.7 billion U.S., an increase of 10.2 percent over that in 1982. The economic consequences of industry also improved. In 1983, profit and taxes handed over to the state by state industrial enterprises rose by 6.2 percent over that in 1982.

Total investment for capital construction increased as well. In terms of investment structure, the proportion of state budgetary investment increased. The proportion of total investment for energy, transport and communications, and postal services and telecommunications—all key areas for economic development—increased from 30 percent in 1982 to 38 percent in 1983. This is a satisfactory achievement in implementing the principle of concentrating funds to guarantee key projects.

Meanwhile, China has strengthened the technical transformation of its existing enterprises. Last year, the state spent $14.4 billion U.S. on the technical transformation and equipment renewal of old enterprises. This expenditure has played a positive role in increasing production, cutting costs, raising the level of technology, and improving transportation and communications.

Foreign trade also performed well last year. The total volume of imports and exports was $43.66 billion U.S., an increase of 4.9 percent over 1982, and there was a trade surplus of $1 billion U.S.

Progress has also been made in absorbing foreign funds and advanced technology. In 1982 China had 83 ventures that combined Chinese with foreign investment. In 1983 the number increased to 188. The Regulations for the Implementation of the Law of the People's Republic of China on Joint Ventures Using Chinese and Foreign Investment, which was promulgated on 20 September 1983, contains some stipulations regarding favorable treatment for such ventures in marketing, taxation, and foreign-exchange control. Last year the Chinese government signed loan contracts with foreign governments or international financial organizations to the tune of $1.33 billion U.S.

At present, China has established 42 companies to undertake projects in more than 40 foreign countries and regions. They have signed contracts for the construction of power stations, highways, bridges, and houses.

While mainly relying on our own efforts in the modernization drive, we in China are fully aware of the importance and value of expanding mutually beneficial trade and economic cooperation with foreign countries. The door of China will never close again.

Challenge and prospect

Though the Chinese economy was moving forward at a fast clip and the people's living standards were rapidly improving, there were still many unsolved problems in 1983.

The scale of capital construction was still too big. The growth of the energy industry still fell behind that of the manufacturing industry, and this condition has aggravated the shortage of energy and raw materials that appeared in 1982. The contradiction between economic development and insufficient transport facilities became more acute. Consumption funds increased too rapidly. Some enterprises issued excessive bonuses and various kinds of subsidies that have had an adverse effect on state finance. The economic results of some enterprises still left much to be desired.

All these problems have adversely affected the balance between material supply and demand, between incomes and expenditures, and between credit receipts and payments. Therefore, China is still faced with an arduous task if it wants to produce a fundamental turn for the better in its financial and economic situation.

What can be said for 1984? I believe that, despite the problems, the trend will continue to be favorable. Economic development in the countryside is on the rise, and there is still great potential. Moderate growth will be maintained in industrial production. As the construction of some big and medium-sized projects moves into full swing, investment in capital construction will be slightly higher than in 1983. Trade and economic cooperation with foreign countries will see fairly big increases. The national economy will be on a path of steady and healthy development.

FOREIGN POLICY

In order to attain the goal of modernization, it is essential to ensure a peaceful international environment. In this sense, China's future is closely linked with world peace and security.

The current world situation remains turbulent. Local wars have never stopped since the end of World War II. A fierce arms race, particularly in nuclear arms, has aggravated the tension. Foreign forces occupying Kampuchea and Afghanistan have thus far refused to withdraw. War flames keep burning in the Middle East. The situation in Central America is tense. Racists are still running amok in southern Africa. Worldwide economic recession has brought troubles to North-South relations and has also increased the contradictions among developed countries. Tensions and turbulence pose a serious threat to world peace, causing untold suffering to many countries. How can a country concentrate on economic development when its own security, independence, and sovereignty are in danger?

Bearing in mind the great sacrifice the Chinese people made to win their national independence, it is no surprise that China attaches great importance to its independence. To be exact, independence is the fundamental principle of China's foreign policy. We do not attach ourselves to any big power and are not subject to any big power's will.

It is in accordance with the fundamental interests of the people of China and of the world that we have determined our foreign policy, which includes the following points:

—to develop relations with all countries on the basis of the five principles of (1) mutual respect for sovereignty and territorial integrity, (2) mutual nonaggression, (3) noninterference in each other's internal affairs, (4) equality and mutual benefit, and (5) peaceful coexistence;

—to strengthen solidarity with the other Third World countries and to promote friendship with the people of all countries, and

—to oppose hegemony and safeguard world peace.

Major approach and issues

China is a developing socialist country. We share similar historical experiences with the other Third World countries and face the same task of economic development. We firmly support them in their just cause of safeguarding national independence and developing their national economies. We are in favor of increased South-South cooperation, improving North-South relations, and establishing a new international economic order through global negotiations.

On the basis of the Five Principles of Peaceful Coexistence, China wishes to develop friendly relations and cooperation with all other countries. China has established diplomatic relations with 129 countries and has settled boundary questions leftover from the past with most of its neighbors, such as Burma, Nepal, Pakistan, Korea, and Mongolia. In spite of the difference in social systems, China has maintained good relations with Japan and many other developed countries, and its cooperation with them has assumed new dimensions both in depth and in scope.

We are working hard for the normalization of Sino-Soviet relations, which requires the removal of three obstacles. China's position is that, first, the Soviet Union must stop supporting Vietnam in its aggression against Kampuchea; second, it must withdraw its troops from Afghanistan; and third, it must withdraw its forces from the Sino-Soviet border and Mongolia.

China and the Soviet Union have already held several rounds of consultations. However, the Soviet side has thus far evaded discussion of these three questions, which pose a threat to China's security and the security of the other countries concerned. Although Sino-Soviet relations have improved somewhat in recent years, greater effort by the two sides is called for if the relations are to be really normalized.

Sino-U.S. relations

China attaches great importance to Sino-U.S. relations. The two countries have different social systems, and each has its own foreign policy to pursue and national interests to protect. Naturally, they differ in their views and approaches in certain areas. However, in the turbulent world today, the two countries have common interests on a number of major international issues. The steady and sustained development of friendly relations between our two countries is not only in the interest of the two peoples, but also of great benefit to the maintenance of world peace and the promotion of human progress.

Since the reopening of the lines of communication between our two countries in 1972, and particularly since the establishment of diplomatic relations in 1979, the winter of estrangement has yielded to a springtime of burgeoning ties in various fields.

In 1971 the Chinese and Americans were virtually cut off from each other, and the two governments had little contact. In 1983 about 100,000 Americans visited China, and many Chinese delegations came to the United States. Chinese and American government officials are engaged in a meaningful dialogue, encompassing political, economic, and many other areas.

In 1971 there was hardly any trade between the two countries, but in the last few years the annual trade volume has been around $5 billion. Equally important, over 100 contracts and agreements have been signed concerning economic and technological cooperation. Our scientists have joined hands in about 300 projects under 20 government protocols, ranging from seismology to medicine.

Sino-U.S. cultural exchanges have also broadened from a trickle to a strong current. Today, there are about 10,000 Chinese visiting scholars and students in the United States. For its part, the United States has 250 scholars and students on Chinese campuses, not counting the 1700 who have left after taking short-term courses in China in the last year.

Remarkable as this progress has been, our bilateral relations have also experienced ups and downs and twists and turns. Many people realize that there are two possibilities ahead for these relations. One is a steady and continuous development of our friendship and cooperation on the basis of equality and mutual benefit, with differences being ironed out and obstacles removed. The other is stagnation of our relations at the present level with frequent friction and even setbacks. To be specific, the Taiwan question is the main obstacle to the development of Sino-U.S. relations.

Sino-U.S. diplomatic relations came about only after the U.S. government recognized, in the Sino-U.S. joint communiqué of 1 January 1979, the government of the People's Republic of China as the sole legal government of China and acknowledged China's position that there is but one China and that Taiwan is part of China.

Yet, up to this day the U.S. government still treats Taiwan as an independent political entity. It continues to sell large amounts of arms to Taiwan, thus infringing upon China's sovereignty and territorial integrity. Here I wish to stress that we are not asking the United States to help us reunify our country; we only ask the United States not to stand in the way of our efforts to bring about Taiwan's return to the motherland by peaceful means. We do ask the United States to observe strictly the mutually confirmed principles contained in the communiqué of 1 January 1979 and the communiqué of 17 August 1982 concerning U.S. arms sales to Taiwan. We hope that the United States will live up to its commitments and gradually reduce—and ultimately terminate—its arms sales to Taiwan. Only thus can the clouds hanging over Sino-U.S. relations be dispelled.

Sino-U.S. relations have already moved beyond the political domain to embrace many other activities, notably trade and economic and technological cooperation. We in China welcome the U.S. decision to liberalize its control on exports to China. We hope that, with this decision, the U.S. government will truly treat China as a friendly, non-allied country, thus helping to bring about a substantial growth in our mutually beneficial trade relations. In this regard, may I also say that the outdated U.S. trade legislation discriminating against China needs to be amended as well—or rescinded—so that a favorable setting may be created for such relations.

Although Sino-U.S. trade has grown rapidly, the scale of economic cooperation remains limited. Such moderation is quite incommensurate with the population, resources, and total productive capacity of China and the United States. The American business firms have abundant funds and are ahead of others in such fields as oil, coal, power stations, communications, and transportation. Therefore they are in a good position to expand economic and technical cooperation with China in many forms. Now it depends on whether China and the United States are good at making use of these opportunities. Of course, in so doing we should handle our political relations well; otherwise, they may work against the broadening of such opportunities.

The friendship between our two great peoples goes back a long way, and Sino-U.S. relations have come a long way. Facts through all these years prove that the significance of better Sino-U.S. relations goes far beyond the realm of ordinary bilateral relations and constitutes an important factor for world peace and stability. Recently Premier Zhao Ziyang paid a successful visit to the United States, the first trip ever made by a Chinese head of government to the United States. His visit increased mutual understanding and helped stabilize bilateral relations. President Reagan was the first incumbent U.S. president to visit China since the establishment of Sino-U.S. diplomatic relations. People in both countries hope that this exchange of visits will provide a fresh impetus to the development of Sino-U.S. relations.

CONCLUSION

A brief review of China's domestic situation and its interaction with the outside world shows that China has set for itself three major tasks in the 1980s and 1990s. They are (1) realizing modernization, (2) opposing hegemony and safeguarding world peace, and (3) bringing about Taiwan's return to the motherland so as to realize the country's peaceful reunification. Arduous as these tasks are, favorable conditions for their fulfillment do exist. More important, the Chinese government and people have the will and resourcefulness to face up to the challenge.

China's Political Reforms:
A Net Assessment

By KENNETH LIEBERTHAL

ABSTRACT: China's leaders since the death of Mao Zedong have tried to reform the political system so as to reduce the level of political coercion, increase the use of rational/legal processes, put talented individuals into responsible positions, enhance their capacity to base decisions on pragmatic criteria, and restore and strengthen the legitimacy of the polity. Their efforts to further these goals have produced important results, but the reforms still have not taken root. The reforms have been hedged in by fundamental untouchables, resisted by uncooperative cadres, and undercut by the inherent incompatibility of different components of the reform package itself. The prognosis for the various elements of the reform effort depends both on keeping the initiative in the hands of the reformers at the top of the Communist party and on achieving good results in the economic arena.

Kenneth Lieberthal is professor of political science and research associate at the Center for Chinese Studies of the University of Michigan. He frequently visits the People's Republic of China and has written many books, monographs, and articles on China's foreign policy, national and local politics, and decision making. He consults for the Department of State and various other organizations. Professor Lieberthal formerly taught at Swarthmore College and served on the social science staff of the Rand Corporation.

T HE Chinese have been trying to revamp their political system since 1977. Like related efforts in economics,[1] these political changes are a reaction to the enormous problems that Mao Zedong bequeathed his successors when he died in 1976.

Mao's gargantuan attempt in his last decade to steer China away from a "revisionist" course left a political shambles. The Cultural Revolution's encouragement of mass violence and factional conflict produced a radical de-institutionalization of the political system. Bureaucratic information channels became blocked or seriously distorted. Factional conflict affected both personnel appointments and policy outcomes. Political coercion within the governing bodies and toward the populace reached extraordinarily high levels. Fundamental disagreements divided even the highest-level leaders over such basic issues as the rules by which the system should be governed. The leadership's capacity to acquire good information, to base decisions on the substantive merits of issues, to have those decisions implemented in a prudent and conscientious way, and to elicit support from the population for this entire process had all seriously eroded between 1966 and 1976.

REFORM GOALS AND
INITIATIVES

In response to this situation, Deng Xiaoping and his colleagues launched a wide-ranging series of efforts to reform the political system. In broad terms,

1. Good overviews of the economic reform effort and its results are available in, for example, the symposium published in the *China Business Review*, pp. 8-27 (Nov.-Dec. 1983).

their policies seek to achieve the following goals:

—to reduce the level of political coercion throughout the system;

—to reduce the salience of patron-client relations, of factionalism, and of corruption while expanding the role of rational/legal processes in the polity and bringing into power successors with functional expertise;

—to enhance the capacity of the political organs to reach decisions based on pragmatic criteria; and

—to restore and strengthen the legitimacy of the polity.

The resulting political system will ideally be more capable of managing a wrenching evolution into modernity while maintaining the country's political stability. In more detail, the following reform initiatives have been taken to date.

Reducing coercion

There has been much attention devoted in the Western media to the vicissitudes of China's policy toward intellectual freedom. The "anti-pollution" campaign that flared up in the fall of 1983 raised the specter both domestically and abroad of another bout of radical know-nothingism. Although the line that defines the politically permissible continues to shift erratically, two basic changes have, on balance, made China significantly less coercive.

First, political labels on individuals have been removed step by step. China as of 1976 practiced severe discrimination against large groups of people based solely on political criteria. To have a bad label—as a landlord, capitalist, rightist, bad element, and so forth—severely limited one's opportunities for employment, marriage, and perhaps even freedom. This system has in the main been dismantled since 1978.

Virtually all of the approximately 150,000 remaining rightists have been restored to full citizenship. Landlords and capitalists have generally been proclaimed to be peasants and workers now that they have "adequately reformed." About 2.9 million Party members who were judged to be counterrevolutionaries during the Cultural Revolution have formally been rehabilitated. And countless thousands—indeed, probably millions—of others who bore one stigmatizing label or another have received relief via the efforts to redress past mistakes.[2]

The formal declaration that class struggle and political campaigns would no longer be the driving forces of China's revolution gave doctrinal underpinning to this substantial decline in the ranks of the pariah groups. Campaigns and struggles in the past had sometimes appeared from afar to involve fairly high-minded attempts to raise the populace to new levels of political purity. But in China the police and the labor camps were two of the key instruments of these so-called consciousness-raising efforts.

Second, the decline in coercion has been manifested in genuine encouragement of discussion and debate. During Mao's last decade, even top leaders found that almost anything they said might well be regarded primarily as an indicator of their political orthodoxy— at a time when unorthodox thoughts brought disaster. Since 1978, however, a wide range of views is solicited on many problems—although not on fundamental goals and priorities. Ministerial journals, technical periodicals, the general media, and private conversations are often spiced with relatively clear advocacy of competing positions. The reduction in political coercion, in short, has permitted a very substantial improvement in the quality of discourse on public policy.

Rational/legal processes and the succession

Much of the effort since 1978 has aimed at re-institutionalizing the polity and, relatedly, at putting people of talent in leadership positions so these strengthened institutions will produce good outcomes. As the Cultural Revolution undermined standard operating procedures and immersed individuals in a terror-filled environment, patron-client ties emerged as the major way to accomplish tasks and get ahead. Factions based on personal loyalties that extended across formal institutional boundaries became key combatants for the spoils of the political system. These factional ties were nurtured by exchanging favors that ranged from personnel appointments to procurement of scarce resources, provision of political support or protection, and other similar practices. In short, corruption based on political power became a defining characteristic of China's politics.[3]

This insidious development had many unhealthy ramifications for the

---

2. Richard Krauss analyzes this system of political labels in his *Class and Class Conflict in Chinese Socialism* (New York: Columbia University Press, 1981).

3. On Chinese factions, see, for example, Lucian Pye, *The Dynamics of Chinese Politics* (Cambridge, MA: Oelgeschlager, Gunn & Hain, 1981).

political system. It became very difficult to place the best-qualified people in executive positions because these positions were seen as part of the spoils of factional fighting. Rules on the books might affect forms and appearances, but they proved relatively weak in structuring actual behavior. Political discipline and the prestige of the political apparatus among the populace naturally suffered accordingly. Some political science literature notes that a little corruption can have beneficent effects on the politics of a developing country,[4] but the corruption in China grew to such an extent that it considerably harmed the polity.

Sharp divisions over substantive issues exacerbated the effects of corruption, as corrupt relationships shielded individuals who opposed and sabotaged current policy.[5] This lingering phenomenon still endangers the political and economic reforms because foot dragging by opponents makes it more difficult to produce the promised improvements in standards of living and personal security.

The pervasiveness and complexity of the intertwined problems of patron-client relations, factionalism and corruption sparked an appropriately wide-ranging mix of measures to improve the situation. At the end of 1978 the Party decided to estabish a hierarchy of Discipline Inspection Commissions to investigate and root out corruption and violations of rules within the Party. The new Party constitution, adopted in 1982, considerably stiffened the rules for membership and training. These measures were preparatory to the projected three-year Party rectification campaign that began in the winter of 1983-84. This campaign is supposed to be aimed especially at identifying and removing those Party members who still support a more leftist position than current policy dictates. The campaign is also intended to instill appropriate norms in the Party cadre.

Beyond the use of disciplinary bodies and related measures, a range of additional initiatives aims at buttressing the rational/legal elements in determining personnel appointments and policy outcomes. For example, elections in which candidates exceed posts have been held for key government positions up to the level of the county. These can be—and have been—manipulated by the authorities, but they have also to some limited extent reduced the ability of individuals to use political appointments as a way to build factional support.[6] Within both the Party and the government, moreover, the personnel rules are being changed so as to try to encourage the appointment of younger and better-educated people to executive positions.

A related initiative aims at reducing dramatically the multiple hat wearing of office holders. Before 1978 it was common for a high-ranking Party official, for example, to hold a corresponding executive position in the government and/or the military. This not only overly concentrated power; it also enhanced the potential for factional domination of individual offices and units, as one key person and his

4. See, for example, Samuel Huntington, *Political Order in Changing Societies* (New Haven, CT: Yale University Press, 1968), pp. 59-71.

5. This is confirmed, for example, by the Commentator article in *People's Daily*, 14 Feb. 1984, trans. in *Daily Report: People's Republic of China*, 15 Feb. 1984, pp. K1-3.

6. Barrett McCormick, of the University of Washington, provides a good analysis of this problem in his "Leninist Implementation: The Election Campaign," in *Policy Implementation in Post-Mao China*, ed. David M. Lampton (n.p., forthcoming).

followers could monopolize all the core positions. Between 1978 and 1983, in at least the most highly visible leadership positions down to the county level, this phenomenon was nearly abolished.

Personnel changes have aimed at more than reducing multiple hat wearing and breaking up factions. During the Cultural Revolution China recruited about 18 million new members into the Party, and many of these obtained official posts. After the Cultural Revolution, as already noted, about 3 million former officials were brought back to power. The new reform initiatives, however, required that many of the people from both these groups be removed—the former because they opposed current policy and the latter because they had become too old and lacked requisite skills. The attempts to remove these individuals have been combined with related efforts to slim down and rationalize the country's political institutions.

The numbers reflect the effects of these efforts. During 1983 about 70 percent of the 1400 provincial-level rehabilitees were removed and were replaced by a smaller number of better-educated officials. Overall, the number of provincial Party secretaries has dropped from 300 to 150, and the average age of these incumbents has declined from 63 to 56 years old. The percent with some college education has risen from 10 to 40 percent. Comparable changes have occured in the highest positions in the State Council. Comparable figures are lacking, however, on the mass of cadres below the top leadership positions at each level of the national hierarchy.

The reduction in multiple hat wearing and the replacement of older cadres by younger and better-educated counter-

parts is supposed to occur as much at the peak of the polity—in the politburo and its related organs—as in other units. China's media constantly tout the need to rejuvenate the leading organs and pass leadership on to a second and third generation. The object is both to avoid another debilitating succession struggle and to guide the country to modernization with technically qualified people in place of the old generals who survive from the early days of the revolution.

Enhancing decision-making capacities

Ever since Deng Xiaoping in the spring of 1978 declared that China must "seek truth from facts and make practice the sole criterion of truth," the authorities have taken many measures to improve the political system's capacity to make pragmatic decisions. The previously noted increased freedom of lower-ranking cadres to state their views has itself contributed significantly to a more pragmatic decision-making style. But the efforts in this sphere have gone well beyond loosening the ideological straitjacket.

Several bureaucratic initiatives merit attention. There is a renewed stress on rationally allocating responsibility among members of the Party and government committees; the head of each committee is now prohibited from simply imposing his views on the members. In addition, decision making has been somewhat decentralized. Many decisions previously had to be made by the central organs in Beijing, even though these organs lacked adequate information and cooperated only very poorly with each other. Now, by contrast, some of these decisions are made by lower-level, territorial Party and government committees that are close to the problems and better situated to coordinate the efforts of the relevant local specialized agencies.

Educated individuals are also being brought into executive positions. Many of those with a higher education who had been purged and vilified during Mao's last years have now been given responsible positions. As political agencies develop leading groups that are more educationally competent, the use of hard data as an element in decision making should increase.

There is also a more systematic effort to gather and disseminate pertinent data. The state statistical system was reduced to bureaucratic rubble during the Cultural Revolution. Substantial efforts have been made since the late 1970s to resuscitate this system and to increase its ability to withstand political pressures.[7] Numerous new publications, moreover, are transmitting the fruits of this and related data-gathering efforts to interested parties throughout the polity.

None of the foregoing measures is a panacea. All, though, contribute to the system's ability to reach good decisions and to respond quickly to changing circumstances.

*Restoring and
strengthening legitimacy*

Most reform initiatives help mitigate the crisis of legitimacy—or what the Chinese refer to as the crisis of confidence—that the system suffered by the late 1970s. Some measures, of course, have had a double edge, in that they actually decrease the legitimacy of the system for those individuals who rose rapidly when other priorities obtained during the Cultural Revolution. On balance, though, a more pragmatic, efficient, rational/legal, and less coercive regime is likely to win some favor from most Chinese, especially after the turmoil of the past.

But the hangover after the Cultural Revolution binge has proven prolonged and painful; millions of youths, especially, are severely disillusioned. Corruption and patriarchal behavior have raised charges about a new class of bureaucrats, while increased exposure to the outside world has created a revolution of rising material expectations. Modernization is itself a profoundly unsettling transition, no less in China than elsewhere.

Some reform policies seek specifically to cope with the legitimacy issue. Many of these have been economic, as the ability to deliver a rising standard of living has explicitly become one basis of the Chinese Communist party's rationale for governing.[8] But other measures have been political. These include the new election system up to the county level, mentioned earlier; strengthening the governmental representative bodies—the People's Congresses—and the various united front organizations; and the attacks on corruption by the Discipline Inspection Commissions.

On a broader level, the leaders are seeking a balance between greater freedom of thought and the promotion

7. At the height of the Cultural Revolution, the State Statistical Bureau had only 14 people left in its central office. On the rehabilitated statistical system, see the series of articles in *Daily Report: People's Republic of China,* 17 Feb. 1984, pp. K17-21.

8. See, for example, the speech given by General Secretary Hu Yaobang on a tour of Sichuan and Guizhou Provinces, where he said, "What do the people want the Communist Party to do? First, to gain liberation. Second, to get rich." Sichuan Radio, 8 Feb. 1984, trans. in *Daily Report: People's Republic of China,* 9 Feb. 1984, p. K11.

of an ideological orthodoxy to legitimize the system. The new orthodoxy is an uneasy amalgam of several elements: those parts of Mao Zedong's legacy that are most compatible with current policy; the *Selected Works of Deng Xiaoping*,[9] which gives definition to the new political priorities; and broad appeals based on the patriotic bonds that are supposed to unite all Chinese.

OBSTACLES TO REFORM

The efforts to reform the political system are wide ranging. Nevertheless, the reforms have been hedged in by fundamental untouchables, resisted by uncooperative cadres, and undercut by the very incompatibility of different elements in the reform package. While significant reforms have nevertheless taken hold, it is important to understand the factors that have limited—and will continue to circumscribe—the results of these initiatives.

First, there are sharp conceptual limits to the scope of the reforms. Even the leading reformers are basically still Leninists and will not tolerate a shift away from a patriarchal system toward a fundamentally more democratic and rational/legal polity.[10] Deng Xiaoping's "four basic principles" highlight this fact. They demand that the Communist party remain the sole leading party in China; that Marxism-Leninism-Mao Zedong Thought—including the "enrichment" of the latter by Deng and other top leaders—remain the sole permissible

ideological system; that the socialist path remain the sole legitimate path the country can follow; and that the people's democratic dictatorship remain the country's state system for the indefinite future.

These principles have themselves been subject to varying interpretations on specifics—for example, as to what, concretely, defines "the socialist path"—but they are in their entire thrust profoundly restrictive. The Communist Party will monopolize political power, but the Party in turn must be disciplined and led from the top down. While "practice is the sole criterion of truth" on concrete and limited matters, all fundamental truths must derive from, or at least be made compatible with, Marxism-Leninism-Mao Zedong Thought. Although economic reforms may permit foreign direct investment in China, de facto decollectivization of agriculture, and the encouragement of small-scale private industry, the bulk of the industrial, finance, and trade systems must remain publicly owned and operated. And the people's democratic dictatorship is a state form designed to oppress those who disagree over fundamentals.

This broad approach clearly penetrates into how the leaders think about everyday problems. For almost every issue, the path to improvement is still proclaimed to lie in having the leaders at each level properly understand the problem, commit themselves to it, and pay attention to it until it is solved. The key, in current Chinese thinking, thus remains always with the leaders, not with any autonomous bodies or staff.

Fundamentally, also, career success has continued to go primarily to those who carefully cultivate a bureaucratic base and then nurture that base as they

9. There have also been related publications of the selected works of Liu Shaoqi, Zhou Enlai, and Chen Yun.

10. These leaders are also influenced by China's long tradition of statecraft, which is likewise profoundly nondemocratic.

progress up the system.[11] This basic pattern of career mobility naturally strengthens the grip of patron-client relations on the polity and inhibits the selection of leading officials solely on the basis of talent.

Conceptually, in brief, the political reforms are the brain children of individuals who themselves are very much products of the Chinese system. While much significant tinkering may go on, therefore, more radical changes such as the creation of a truly multiparty system are not in the offing.

In the rough and tumble of Chinese politics, also, the reforms must contend with significant opposition. In some cases, those in charge of some specific reform are also the targets of that same initiative. This has been very much the case with local cadres who must oversee the nomination and election process to fill the offices that they themselves hold. Similarly, the Discipline Inspection Commissions were initially put under the leadership of the Party committee at their own bureaucratic level. But the primary targets of the Discipline Inspection Commissions were to be the very Party committees—and their subordinate organs—that had charge of them![12] The current three-year Party-rectification campaign suffers from the same problem, and these examples could be multiplied many times over. They reflect the tensions inherent in trying to pre-

11. This is the major lesson to be drawn from David M. Lampton's careful study of the careers of six major Chinese officials: *Paths to Power: Elite Mobility in Contemporary China* (Ann Arbor, MI: Michigan China Center, forthcoming).

12. See Lawrence Sullivan, "The Role of the Control Organs in the Chinese Communist Party, 1978-1982" (Paper delivered at the Conference of the New York State Political Science Association, 1983).

serve a patriarchal system while at the same time reforming it.

Balancing the political parts

The reform effort also presumes an altered balance among the basic territorial and bureaucratic building blocks of the Chinese system in a way that invites attempts from the losers to redress the balance. Territorially, the reforms—economic as well as political—should shift power and resources toward the coastal cities and away from the heartland. Bureaucratically, the reforms have important implications for the five basic building blocks of the system: economics, culture-propaganda, security, personnel, and the hierarchy of first secretaries of Party committees.

The economic bureaucracies are in charge of economic management and growth. Reform for them means enhancing efficiency and achieving a new sectoral balance that gives lower priority to development of the producer-goods industries. The cultural bureaucracies, by contrast, have responsibility for maintaining a political esprit while adapting to the demands of the economic development program. The reform program has given the cultural bureaucracies the twin tasks of freeing scientific and technological research from political constraints while bolstering a commitment to socialism and a spirit of patriotism throughout the populace.

The security bureaucracies cover everything from crime and fire fighting to political dissidence, counterespionage, and national defense. Reform to them means increasing adherence to law, lightening political repression, limiting foreign subversion, and modernizing the People's Liberation Army. The personnel bureaucracies control careers through the maintenance of personal dossiers and control over employment and promotion. While personnel units are embedded in economic enterprises and other organs, they in fact have their own sets of regulations independent of the host organs. Under the reform program, the personnel bureaucracies should cultivate and promote younger and better-educated individuals and weed out former leftists still in responsible positions.

Finally, the hierarchy of secretaries who lead the territorial Party committees reached a high point of power and influence as of the mid-1970s, when it was said that the "Party takes command of everything." The reforms, however, have forced these top Party executives to give up their concurrent posts in the government and/or military hierarchies. In addition, the watchword of the 1980s is to pull the Party out of detailed decision making in favor of having it concentrate on more general political tasks.

The reform program has thus had a complex effect on each of these bureaucracies. Some generalizations are, nevertheless, possible. First, the economic bureaucracies have to date gained the most, overall, from the program. They have greatly enhanced their control over economic decision making, allowing far less intrusion by the Communist Party than had previously been the case.

The power of the cultural-propaganda bureaucracies, by contrast, has been cut back. The reform program has played down the role of politics, when the raison d'être of these bureaucracies previously was to enforce political orthodoxy. Extensive contacts with overseas Chinese and with foreigners have simply

made the task of these bureaucracies more complex and difficult.

The security bureaucracies are in some ways in an even worse position. With the 2.9 million rehabilitations following the Cultural Revolution, numerous cadres who had been detained and abused by the security organs returned to positions of power. In addition, power within the security bureaucracies has now been divided somewhat. With the great increase in China's contacts abroad, moreover, the tasks of these bureaucracies have also become vastly more complex.

The military side of the security system has also had a mixed time with the reforms. Reportedly, high-ranking officers have been disgruntled over the denigration of Mao, have bridled at the greater political and cultural freedom allowed, and have chafed under the tight defense budgets that have accompanied the relegation of defense to fourth priority among the four modernizations.

The personnel system has been put in charge of cultivating and bringing into power a younger generation of better-educated cadres. Numerous reports indicate, however, that this bureaucracy had become a real stronghold of the leftists by the end of the Cultural Revolution.

Finally, as noted earlier, the leading secretaries in the territorial Party committees have had to yield both concurrent political positions and much decision-making authority.

The economic bureaucracies thus have clearly fared better than the cultural, security, personnel, and Party secretarial systems under the reforms. In the past, though, these other bureaucracies have time and again proven able to assert their interests vis-à-vis the economic organs. It will still be some years before a stable balance is struck among these sectors.[13]

There are, finally, structural contradictions among the various elements in the political reform effort itself. For example, initiatives have been taken to disperse and institutionalize authority. In Beijing, therefore, there is no longer a cult of personality that permits one individual to be the unquestioned arbiter of major policies. The position of Party chairman has been abolished, and four major organs—the politburo, State Council, Secretariat, and Central Advisory Commission—make policy; whereas in Mao's last years only the first two existed.[14] The degree of overlap of office holding has also diminished considerably. And the determination to prevent ruinous factional struggles and polarization of politics has meant that constant efforts have been made to fashion a consensus on issues in contention.[15]

The dispersion and only partial institutionalization of authority and the stress on consensus, while central components of the reform effort, also have the effect of attenuating other dimensions of that effort. Far-reaching change requires the centralization of authority in the hands of a reform group so that it can keep the effort on track even when the reforms are still too new and untried to produce the promised results. The notion of radical change in a patriarchal system simply does not conform easily to the political preference for seeking and maintaining a consensus among decision makers.

A NET ASSESSMENT

It is simply inappropriate to proclaim the success or failure of China's post-Mao political reforms. It is possible, though, to indicate to what extent various important dimensions of the system have changed. Even this effort inevitably requires drawing conclusions where some data are either impressionistic or inconclusive. On balance, then, to what extent have real reforms taken hold in the Chinese polity since the death of Mao?

There has been a real and marked reduction in the level of political coercion. The state has essentially declared that a considerably narrower band of thought and activity should be deemed political in the sense that the state should monitor and control it. China has, in this sense, become far less a totalitarian society, although it remains highly authoritarian.[16]

Several concrete changes that are part of the reform effort have taken hold. There has been a substantial change in the people who hold positions at the vice-ministerial level and above in Beijing, at the vice-governor level and above in the provinces, and at the vice-magistrate level and above in the counties, with for the most part comparable

13. This analysis draws from Kenneth Lieberthal, "Reform Politics," *China Business Review* 10(6):10-12 (Nov.-Dec. 1983).

14. Of these four, the Central Advisory Commission is clearly the least powerful. Nevertheless, it does to some extent further disperse authority at the apex of the Chinese system.

15. For an excellent discussion of consensus and reform, see Christopher M. Clarke, "Changing the Context for Policy Implementation: Organizational and Personnel Reform in Post-Mao China," in *Policy Implementation in Post-Mao China*, ed. Lampton; and David M. Lampton, "Water: Challenge to a Fragmented Political System," in ibid.

16. See Michel Oksenberg and Richard Bush, "China, 1972-1982: From Revolution to Reform," *Problems of Communism* (Sept. 1982).

changes occurring in the corresponding positions in the Party apparatus. Gross statistics, as noted previously, reveal that the new incumbents are generally younger and better educated and that the instances of multiple hat wearing have declined dramatically.

While these measures appear impressive, it is hard to gauge their real impact. New leaders appointed to provincial posts, for example, typically must work with an apparatus that remains loyal to their predecessors, who, more often than not, remain on the scene in some honorific post. Patterns of personal interaction will change only slowly, and in many cases clear institutional boundaries have yet to be drawn. China thus remains very much in a transitional stage, where some of the critical building blocks of a reformed polity have been put into place, but where they have not yet taken root. Current policies will have to be maintained for some years with constant attention devoted to making the reforms take hold before one can have real confidence in the permanence of the reform initiatives.

This issue of policy continuity focuses attention on the apex of the political system—the Party politburo and its related organs. While Deng Xiaoping has tried hard to put into place capable successors such as Hu Yaobang, Zhao Ziyang, Yao Yilin, and Wan Li, on balance what is impressive is the degree to which the old generals and aged revolutionaries still cling to power. The most powerful men currently, in terms of setting the broad outlines of policy, include Deng himself, who is 79 years old; Chen Yun, 79; Peng Zhen, 82; Li Xiannian, 78; and Ye Jianying, 86. The order in which these men leave the political stage can affect the thrust of the political-reform effort.

Nor is age a problem only at this highest level of decision making. Hu Yaobang is 69 and Zhao Ziyang is 66. The other sixteen members of the politburo average 73 years old; only four of them are under 70. Of the nine members of the Secretariat, eight are 68 to 71 years old. And the five leading members of the Military Affairs Commission average 82.5 years old; at 79, Deng is the youngest of them. When one considers that the Central Advisory Committee was to be the body to which older leaders would retire with honor, the problem with removing aged people from power stands out in even bolder relief.

Fundamentally, moreover, individuals remain more important than institutions in China, and the promulgation of new laws and administrative decrees alone will not change this in any serious way. To alter this situation substantially would require a very basic change in both ideology and psychology.

The question of legitimacy remains another difficult issue.[17] The reformers are trying to walk what may be a very thin line. They are pursuing a program that should encourage the development of pluralistic forces and have decried the kind of political fanaticism that characterized the Cultural Revolution era. But they are still determined to maintain a patriarchal system, where some combination of patriotism, commitment to socialism, material satisfaction, and fear of social instability binds the populace to the polity and legitimizes the system. Legitimacy is hard to measure, moreover, because no methodologically rigor-

17. Frederick Teiwes has wrestled with the legitimacy issue in his *Leadership, Legitimacy, and Conflict in China* (Armonk, NY: M. E. Sharpe, 1984), esp. pts. 2 and 3.

ous opinion surveys have been done. Also, the degree to which the current system enjoys legitimacy inevitably varies greatly among different population sectors.

Many peasants have benefited enormously in material terms from the recent reforms; former Red Guards, by contrast, have generally been shunted aside to make way for the better-educated younger generation. To the extent that proposed changes in labor policy are actually implemented, ambitious workers will benefit while others will lose the greatest benefit that the system had given them—total job security. The legitimacy of the system is unlikely to increase for these latter individuals. Numerous additional obstacles to enhancing the overall legitimacy of the system loom on the political horizon. Challenges will arise from the continuing exposure to foreign accomplishments, from increasing inequality in the distribution of domestic resources, from the inevitable tensions of the transition to an industrial society, and from myriad other sources.

Since 1977 China's leaders have proven willing to test an impressive range of political reform measures to try to cope with the new challenges confronting the largest polity in the world. This task is so daunting and complex that there is no way at this point to specify the degree to which each of these reform initiatives will succeed. Clearly, much will depend on the smoothness of the succession at the top during the coming years. Economic performance will also greatly affect the support that current policies engender, both among the populace and within the elite. On balance, the political reforms have not proceeded nearly as far as have their much heralded economic counterparts. In the future, political rejuvenation will likely continue to trail behind economic change, and the tensions between the two may at some point emerge as the central issue confronting the People's Republic of China.

*   *   *

QUESTIONS AND ANSWERS

Q (Ralph Goldberg, University of the District of Columbia): What is the present strength of regional influences in China, and how do such influences either help or hinder any of the efforts at central reform?

A: I believe that the current reform effort will, if it is carried through, significantly enhance regional inequality in China. The regions that will grow rapidly and that will become major economic forces throughout Asia are Southeast China, especially Guangdong Province, stretching into Guangxi, which will be primarily energy related; the eastern end of the Yangtze from Shanghai up to Nanjing and perhaps as far as Wuhan, which will be the center of China's entrepreneurial skills; and then the northern region around Beijing and southern Manchuria, which will be a heavy industrial base and also obviously the bureaucratic center.

People who currently staff leading organs in China in general come not from these regions but from the interior. There is a question of whether, over the longer run, the gradual redistribution of resources in the country will be sustained by a central leadership that largely hails from the areas that will be losing out in relative terms. I have asked some Chinese about this and one of the comments that I have heard is that, if the current reforms continue, over time we will see more and more people from the eastern regions moved into the top positions, because they are the technocrats in the bureaucracies in central ministries. These technocrats will be able to sustain this type of growing regional inequality.

COMMENT (Lee): One way the Chinese are going to deal with that problem is to centralize the party or parties so that the top level will maintain tight political authority over the provincial party, while at the same time allowing the decentralization of the operation of the government.

Q (Dr. Stikliorius, Wallingford, Pennsylvania): The reforms occurring in China do not change the fact that the government there is a brutal Communist dictatorship that has murdered millions more people than even Hitler and Stalin. The human-rights record of the Chinese regime is atrocious. We frequently condemn the Republic of South Africa for its bad record. Therefore, should we also boycott Communist China, or is our greed for profits from the Chinese market so big that we forget about the beautiful principles of human rights?

A: I would agree that the human-rights record has been pretty bad and that during the height of the Cultural Revolution and at the height of earlier campaigns in China, it reached truly dramatic proportions. It is also important to understand that that record has improved a great deal since the Cultural Revolution.

The United States is always caught, to a degree, in a dilemma when it deals with governments that do not have our political system and that do not respect human rights to the degree we do; and these are the vast majority of governments of the world, as you well know.

The question is, How much can be accomplished by condemning those governments and using U.S. public resources to try to isolate them in the world arena, versus trying to work with those governments and potentially in some indirect and obviously limited way improving the chances of a more tolerant political system? I think that in the Chinese case we have opted for the latter. My own sense is that that is a more productive approach, and therefore it is one I would support. I do not think that we should totally neglect human rights in China. If repression were to increase again, I think we should certainly take note of that and make representations privately to the Chinese about it. But I believe that the public condemnation should be done by private groups. On a government-to-government level, all sides, including the Chinese people, are better served by a cooperative, reasonable, and non-vituperative bilateral relationship.

Q (Stikliorius): The Chinese Communists are friendly to us because they are eager to get our advanced technology, nuclear plants, computers, and so on. What assurances do we have that they, after having received all our most advanced technology, will not turn back to their old friends in Moscow?

A: I think the simple answer is we have no assurances. We have no credible assurances in part because the current leaders will not still be on the political stage 20 or so years from now, which is the period that you are looking at. I think instead what we have to ask ourselves is, What kind of China do we want to see 20 years from now, and how do we want to position ourselves with relation to that country. What I fear, frankly, over the next 20 years is not so much a strong China, allied with the Soviet Union, as a weak China that invites aggression from the Soviet Union. I think that will be highly destabilizing, and that is a concern that I think should be high on our political agenda.

I suspect that 20 years from now, if China's modernization proceeds in a reasonably smooth and consistent way, that it will be a country that we find uncomfortable to deal with. It will be more assertive in the international arena, and it will still have values and priorities that are not totally in line with our own. But I do not see any reason for assuming that the Soviets will be any more comfortable with the Chinese or that Soviet and Chinese values will be any closer than our values are to either of theirs.

You are dealing with different cultures, with significantly different political systems. They share a long border, and I do not think that that is a situation that will be conducive to future close cooperation or future alliance simply because the Chinese have managed to develop their economy with reasonable speed and efficiency.

Q (Marc Blecher, Oberlin College, Ohio): How would one characterize the Maoist system in terms of combinations of patron-client, patriarchal, bureaucratic, totalitarian, and authoritarian elements?

A (Lee): I have been trying to avoid using any particular labels for the Maoist system and the political system that existed in China after the Cultural Revolution up to the fall of the Gang of Four. My feeling is that that was a transitional period where the power balance among the factions characterized the system. No faction was in a dominant position to impose one ideological view.

COMMENT (Lieberthal): Let me just draw a couple of distinctions around the terms that you used, Marc. I referred to China as a patriarchal society. By that I did not mean patron-client. To me a patriarchal society is one in which the top leadership presumes that it essentially monopolizes the wisdom on what policies are correct. Decisions therefore flow downward, rather than being developed by a range of reasonably autonomous bodies that compete with each other in some way. In that sense I think China under Mao was patriarchal. China under Deng Xiaoping is, I think, equally patriarchal in that fundamental way. I also noted that China under Mao was totalitarian. In fact, in a strict sense, there are all kinds of problems with that classification, but in relative terms, "totalitarian" to me means that a society has an extremely wide range of things considered to be political. In other words, the boundary between politics and society is not strong; politics pervades almost everything. And while, as all China specialists know, those boundaries shifted at different times under Mao, fundamentally China was a society in which an extraordinarily wide range of things was considered political. I think that has changed very substantially since Mao died; and China is now a more authoritarian society, in which essentially there are a lot of things that the state really does not care about. If a person wants to raise canaries and walk along the street with them, that is not a political statement. If a scientist wants to advocate a particular theory in nuclear physics, that is not a political statement. Those things were political before.

The patron-client ties, I think, became important because under Mao there was a de-institutionalization of the system. While the level of political coercion was high during the Cultural Revolution, it was not monopolized and institutionalized, but rather was diffused within the society. As normal political institutions broke down, bureaucratic ways of accomplishing things ceased to be effective, and old personal ties became increasingly important for getting things done. It is those patron-client ties that I am talking about.

The current trend is toward a re-institutionalization of the system and a reaffirmation of bureaucratic approaches to accomplishing things. In a top-down system, though, it is difficult to make fundamental progress in that. Once you have a highly faction-ridden system, it is difficult to rout it out. To the extent that it is routed out, there will be an increasing importance of bureaucratic pluralism in the politics of the People's Republic of China.

Q (Lynn White, Princeton University, New Jersey): Are the reforms that are described really consistent? Are they logically unified? They seem to be a reaction to the Cultural Revolution, but the Cultural Revolution might have two very different lessons. From the lesson of its chaos, a Chinese might think there should now be more centralization, more law and order, more economic control. From a lesson of its intolerance, though, and its lack of diversity, the exact opposite conclusions might be drawn—that there should be more pluralism, more participation, more gathering of information from all sorts of people.

Are the reforms and the modernization ambiguous? Are the legal reforms to protect non-state persons or merely to rationalize and make more predictable—as, for example, Stalin's legal reforms in the 1930s did—a state apparatus? Are the administrative streamlining and the quick turnover of personnel, presumably recruited on a somewhat consistent set of principles, going to make for less diversity? Are these reforms going to increase the scope of people to decide or oppose decisions or will it really increase participation?

A: There are inherent contradictions in the reform effort, and that is one reason I have termed it an effort and not a program. There are a lot of thrusts to what the Chinese are trying to do, some of which require a dispersion of authority while others require a concentration of authority. It is not clear how one reconciles that. The Chinese are trying to make the ideology looser, if you will, more compatible with a wide range of different kinds of initiatives. No one really knows what eventual balances should be struck. At the same time, they are seeking to articulate an ideological framework that would legitimize the whole effort.

Evaluation of China's Bureaucratic Reforms

By HONG YUNG LEE

ABSTRACT: Among the various reforms initiated by the post-Mao leadership in China, the most crucial for stability of the political leadership and continuity of the policy line is the bureaucratic reform. In the name of making the state apparatus more efficient for economic development, the central Party leaders promoted to leadership positions a new set of cadres who are "revolutionized, better educated, professionally competent, and younger." This article evaluates the results of the reforms in three important organs: the Central Committee, the central government ministries, and the provincial Party secretaryship. The article finds that although a large number of the bureaucratic technocrats has replaced veteran cadres of the civil war era, the gains are temporary, and the regime's efforts to rationalize and institutionalize the personnel management further will encounter much more serious obstacles imposed by the structural conditions of the Leninist party-state.

Hong Yung Lee is an associate professor in the Department of Political Science at Yale University and a former fellow at the Woodrow Wilson International Center for Scholars. His publications include The Politics of the Chinese Cultural Revolution *and numerous articles in professional journals. He is currently working on a book entitled* The State in Socialist China.

NOTE: The author wishes to thank Deborah Davis-Friedmann for her careful reading and valuable suggestions.

I T is well known that one of the most important political bases for the present leadership of Deng Xiaoping and Hu Yaobang is the 3 million key officials who were purged during the Cultural Revolution (CR), but reinstated to powerful positions after the fall of the Gang of Four. It is with their support that the Deng-Hu group managed to shift the regime's main goal from revolution to economic development and to ease out the de facto beneficiaries of the CR, Hua Guofeng and his supporters.

Once these former victims of the CR regained politically prominent positions, they were ready to address themselves to such crucial questions as why the CR occurred, what was wrong with the pre-CR Chinese political system, how they could prevent the recurrence of future political upheavals, and what kind of political and economic institutions China must develop. Their reflections on such questions led them to embark on sweeping structural reforms not only in the state apparatus but also in such functional fields as economic planning, agriculture, industry, and education.

In the political arena, the Deng-Hu group reversed the past trend for political power to impose its will increasingly tightly over the various sectors of the society. More specifically, the group promised to "institutionalize, regularize, and rationalize" the ruling machines as well as the personnel management of cadres who operated these apparatuses. Toward this end the regime has enacted a series of laws and regulations, has established organizational tables to define clearly the responsibilities and functions of each office, and has discouraged the concurrent holding of more than one government, Party, or military position.

Among the various structural reforms and policy innovations, most crucial for China's future is the effort to upgrade the quality of the existing cadres. This is because characteristics of the political elite, rather than institutional arrangements, will continue to have a more direct bearing on what course China will pursue in the future. Institutionalization of any political system in a short period is extremely difficult. Moreover, such crucial questions as how much democratization in politics and use of market mechanisms in economics the reforms should initiate are not yet settled. Thus whether or not China will enjoy political stability and whether or not the policy initiatives of the past few years will continue depend largely on who will be occupying positions of authority at national, local, and enterprise levels. Well aware of this point, the Deng-Hu group has been making a great effort to create a new set of cadres who are not only functionally competent but also politically loyal.

THE PROCEDURE FOR REFORM

The groundwork for the administrative reforms was laid in early 1979 when the official news media initiated criticism of the Maoist practice that emphasized exclusively political criteria for personnel management and inferred political loyalty from "class status" while rejecting anyone with "complicated social relations" or "historical problems."[1] The news media declared that the regime intended to use such objective criteria as ability, age, and cultural level, which have direct bearing on job performance.[2] Soon there were

1. *Jiefang ribao* [Liberation daily], 11 Oct. 1970.
2. *Beijing ribao* [Beijing daily], 27 Feb. 1980.

even reports that the Party would reject the prerequisite of seniority, creating an impression that the regime wanted to depoliticize cadre management.[3] Emphasis was placed on selection of cadres who were "better educated, professionally competent, and younger in age." That slogan soon met with strong opposition from the existing cadres, even from among recently rehabilitated cadres. In response to the resistance, Deng Xiaoping amended the criteria by urging that the reform made the cadre corps "revolutionized" as well as "better educated, professionally competent, and younger in age."[4]

The slogan tells little about the meaning of the word "revolutionized" or its relative weight vis-à-vis other factors. However, a careful reading of the official media indicates that as the Deng-Hu group successfully proceeds to consolidate its power base, the importance attached to being revolutionized increases. In 1982, Song Renqing, director of the Organizational Department of the Central Committee (CC), flatly declared that "those with talent but without political reliability should not be given an important responsibility."[5] All official documents recently issued to guide the Party consolidation seem to attach increasing importance to political factors, and "revolutionized" is now interpreted to mean strict observance of Party discipline and commitment to the present policy line—in brief, it is equivalent to political loyalty to the Deng-Hu group.

Close examination of the several stages of the recent reforms provides some insights into the nature of the regime. In line with the shrewd, pragmatic, but bureaucratic outlook of the Deng-Hu group, the actual process of simplifying administrative structures started, in 1982, with the ministers and vice-ministers of the central government.[6] After finishing the reorganization of the central government, the regime moved to readjust the leadership of the functional departments of the CC—such as the Organizational Department and the Propaganda Department—in the summer of 1982. With the two important central organs secured with reliable new appointees, the Deng-Hu group then moved to convene the Twelfth Party Congress in September 1982. Not surprisingly, a large number of new appointees in the central government and the Party organs entered the Twelfth Central Committee.[7]

Administrative reform at the provincial level started in the later part of 1982, after reorganization of the Central Committee, and readjustment of the leadership was completed in March 1983. As was the case with the reorganization of the central organs, provincial reform began with the top-level leadership—that is, with secretaries and provincial Party committees. The newly established provincial leadership in turn supervised the reshuffling of the leadership directly under them in such functional units as organizational, propaganda, and agri-

3. *Renmin ribao* [People's daily], 28 June 1980; ibid., 22 July 1980.

4. *Issues and Studies*, pp. 81-103, (Mar. 1981).

5. *Renmin ribao*, 1 Sept. 1982.

6. For a detailed analysis of the government reform, see Hong Yung Lee, "Deng Xiaoping's Reform of the Chinese Bureaucracy," in *The Limits of Reform in China*, ed. Ronald Morse (Denver, CO: Westview Press, 1983).

7. For a detailed analysis of the Twelfth Central Committee, see Hong Yung Lee, "China's Twelfth Central Committee: Rehabilitated Cadres and Technocrats," *Asian Survey*, 23(6):673-91 (June 1983).

cultural departments, as well as in Party committees at the municipal, district, and county levels. Having placed politically reliable as well as functionally more competent officials in the key leadership positions, the Deng-Hu group was then ready to carry out the Party rectification campaign in the following three years.

The strategy adopted by the present leadership for bureaucratic reform was extremely realistic and pragmatic. It started with the core leadership group at the central level and then moved slowly and steadily to the less important cadres at the same level, as well as proceeding down to the leadership group at the next level. A reorganized leadership group at each level supervised the reshuffling of the leadership at the next level. Supplemented by the central authority's detailed guidelines specifying age, education, and other requirements for the new leadership, this method must have ensured the maximum influence of the Deng-Hu group even at the lower levels. The documents on the forthcoming Party consolidation make it clear that the same method will be used.

This purely bureaucratic method, in sharp contrast to Mao's strategy of mobilizing masses simultaneously in every sector, did not leave much room, however, for the ordinary cadres or masses to exercise any meaningful influence on the selection of their leaders. Although the official news media frequently underscored the need to consult with the masses, using such methods as opinion polls, there is no evidence that the opinions of the masses were systematically solicited. If there were any input from the ordinary people, it must have been limited to such lower levels as factory and brigade party committees.

REDUCTION IN GOVERNMENT AND PARTY SIZE

At the beginning of the reorganization of the central government organs, the regime announced its plan to reduce the total number of organs directly under the State Council from 98 to 52; the total number of ministers, vice-ministers, heads, and deputy heads of commissions from 1000 to fewer than 300; and the number of directors and deputy directors of the bureaus from 5000 to fewer than 2500.[8] As shown in Table 1, the total number of ministers and vice-ministers—excluding heads and deputy heads of commissions, offices, and agencies—were reduced by 70 percent. The provincial secretaries were reduced by 50 percent. Thus it seems that the regime has achieved approximately its original quantitative targets.

The reorganization actually reduced the number of central government organs from 98 to 61, instead of to the expected 52. This was done by abolishing many commissions, such as the State Agricultural Commission; merging some ministries, for example, the Ministry of Power Industry with the Ministry of Water Conservancy; and at the same time establishing new ministries, such as the Ministry of Aviation Industry and the Ministry of Electronic Industry.

Reduction of personnel at the levels of functional bureaus of the central government and departments of the provincial governments appears to be equally impressive. The bureaus with staff functions were merged, and some of the support functions—such as running nursery schools for the ministry personnel's children and operating motor pools—were transferred to newly

8. *Daily Report,* 9 Mar. 1982.

TABLE 1
SCOPE OF CHANGES IN THE CENTRAL COMMITTEE (CC),
PROVINCIAL PARTY LEADERSHIP, AND CENTRAL MINISTRIES

	Before the Reforms, Total Number	Total Number	After the Reforms			
			Survivors of the Reforms		New Cadre	
			Number	(%)	Number	(%)
Members of the CC	354*	341†	151 of 354	(43)	190 of 341	(56)
Provincial Party secretaries	229	137‡	66 of 229	(29)	71 of 137	(51)
Ministers and vice-ministers	474	143§	49 of 474	(10)	94 of 143	(62)

NOTE: Not included are the heads and deputy heads of commissions.
*Eleventh CC.
†Twelfth CC.
‡Reduction of 50 percent.
§Reduction of 70 percent.

established, independent corporations that will eventually operate on the principle of profit and loss.

The reductions in personnel and government organs were not without cost to the regime, however. As a means to force retirement, the regime developed attractive pension benefits and promised to continue certain types of privileges to retirees. The result was an increase in the financial burden to the state. Moreover, the regime established an elaborate advisory system that reaches from the Central Committee down to the lower level, with each advisory group hierarchically organized with its own chair and vice-chair. Depending on the future relationship between the advisory groups and the decision-making bodies at each level, this advisory system may later cause some political problems for the regime.

In terms of personnel changes, only 43 percent of the Eleventh Central Committee members made it into the Twelfth CC—slightly higher than the portion of the Eighth CC members who bore the brunt of the Cultural Revolution but lower than the portion of the Ninth CC and Tenth CC members affected by the purges of Liu Biao and the Gang of Four. Of the incumbent provincial Party secretaries, 27 percent survived the reforms, and only 10 percent of the ministers and vice-ministers managed to retain their positions after the reforms. This high casualty rate means that despite the overall reduction in the number of positions, the Deng-Hu group could promote a large number of cadres of their choice. After the reorganization, members of the newly promoted cadres constituted a majority: 62 percent in the central government, 56 percent in the CC, and 51 percent in the provincial secretaryship. On the whole this represents changes even more sweeping than those created by the mass mobilizations in the Cultural Revolution.

If everything is equal, it is reasonable to assume that it would have been easier for the Deng-Hu group to exercise its influence in deciding who would be promoted to leading positions than in

TABLE 2
AVERAGE AGE OF THE LEADERSHIP AFTER THE REFORMS

	Survivors of the Reforms		New Cadre		Total	
	Age	(N)	Age	(N)	Age	(N)
Members of the Central Committee (CC)	70	(52)	56	(56)	63	(118)
Ministers and vice-ministers	66	(19)	59	(28)	61	(47)
Provincial secretaries	60	(13)	58	(9)	59	(22)
Directors and deputy directors of the CC organs*	68	(8)		(0)	68	(8)

*Due to the unreliability of information on the date of appointment, directors and deputy directors are counted as survivors.

deciding which incumbents would be removed. Presumably too, those who are newly promoted, owing their promotion to the reforms, would be more loyal to the Deng-Hu group than those who reached their positions before the reforms. If so, the different ratios of the newly promoted to the old guard in the central government, the CC, and the provincial secretaryship may not be accidental; rather, it may indicate the different extent to which the Deng-Hu group could exercise its predominant influence.

The need to appoint those with objective, job-related qualifications to lead the central government is generally persuasive even among those who disagree with the basic orientation of the Deng-Hu group, because the main function of the central government has been redefined as economic management rather than political leadership. However, the provincial secretaryship is a different case. Being removed from the center by one level and having had their own entrenched power structure, the provinces would not have allowed the Deng-Hu

group complete freedom in selecting new leaders.

Seats in the CC are largely honorary and prestigious but without much actual power. For this reason, the Deng-Hu group seems to have allowed a large number of senior members of cadres— with an average age of 70 years, as shown in Table 2—to remain. Perhaps, however, the Deng-Hu group did not have enough muscle to dislodge them. The latter seems to be the case with such powerful and nationally visible positions as membership in the politburo and chairs and vice-chairs of the various standing committees of the People's National Congress. However, the major problem with the veteran officials—for example, Li Xiannian and Ye Jianying— is that they do not have their own successors of young cadres, and the Deng-Hu group seems to be willing to wait until nature takes its course.

Table 2 shows significant age differences between the leftover and the newly appointed groups—from 13 years in the CC to 2 years in the provinces. Although not shown in the table, substantial age differences exist between the full members of the CC, ministers, and first secretaries on the one hand, and alternate members, vice-ministers, and secretaries on the other. The difference between the full and alternate members is 10 years; between the ministers and vice-ministers, 5 years; and between the first secretaries and secretaries, 10 years. This indicates that despite the official rejection of seniority, it is still an important factor. The reforms, however, lowered the average age of the new leadership group by 5 to 7 years, largely by bringing in a younger generation—those in their late 50s. The average age of the new leadership group is still rather high, though, and for this reason the Deng-Hu group, as we will see later, is preparing a list of successors to the present leadership.

CAREER HISTORIES OF THE NEW LEADERS

Information on the educational level of individual leaders is scarce, and for those who have been working for a long time, practical knowledge obtained through on-the-job training must be as important as formal education. Table 3 examines the career backgrounds of the new leaders. Several observations can be made.

First, because very few officials—only 12—are senior enough to have started their careers from the level of ministers, secretaries, or directors in the early 1950s, it is obvious that the first generation of Chinese revolutionaries is disappearing from the important organs that this article examines. Many of the veteran senior members of cadres are too old to hold any demanding positions and are retired to advisory positions.

Second, a large proportion—40 percent—of the present ministers and vice-ministers started their careers at the level of director and deputy director of the functional bureaus of government ministries. If one includes those who had career experience in the functional departments at the provincial level, the number of persons with long work experience in functional fields rises to 55 percent. The term most appropriate for this group is "bureaucratic technocrats."

Anyone who reached the level of heading functional bureaus or departments before the Cultural Revolution must have some technical expertise. The bureaucratic technocrat, however, should be distinguished from professionals who receive job-related training prior to taking bureaucratic positions. If one follows Gouldner's distinction between intelligentsia and intellectuals, the bureaucratic technocrats resemble the intelligentsia, whose main function is to utilize their expertise to improve and maintain, rather than to change, the existing system.[9] Nonetheless, promotion of career bureaucrats with functional competency acquired through on-the-job training, rather than through formal education, should be considered a substantial improvement, particularly compared to the practice of Mao's era.

Third, the quality of the provincial leadership appears to have improved, too. Of the new leaders, 37 percent had once served as director or deputy director of the functional departments at the same level. Their functional competency, however, is much lower than that of the central government leaders. Of the new provincial leaders, 29 percent are from the secretary positions at the lower level. Moreover, few people moved from factory management positions to become

9. Alvin Gouldner, *The Future of Intellectuals and the Rise of the New Class* (New York: Seabury Press, 1979).

TABLE 3
CAREER BACKGROUNDS OF THE NEW LEADERSHIP

Background		Ministers and Vice-ministers		Directors and Deputy Directors		Secretaries		Total	
		N	(%)	N	(%)	N	(%)	N	(%)
Government	Vice-minister	2	(2)	3	(14)	7	(7)	12	(6)
	Bureau director	35	(40)	2	(9)	3	(3)	40	(20)
Party	Provincial secretary	2	(2)	1	(5)	0		3	(1.5)
	Municipal, district, or county secretary	3	(3)	2	(9)	28	(29)	33	(16)
	Director of provincial functional organ	13	(15)	4	(18)	36	(38)	53	(26)
	Factory position	10	(12)	0		1	(1)	11	(5)
Mass organizations	Schools	3	(4)	2	(9)	2	(2)	7	(3)
	Chinese Youth League	2	(2)	6	(27)	11	(11)	19	(9)
	Labor unions	0		0		1	(1)	1	(0.5)
	Professional organizations	16	(19)	2	(9)	3	(3)	21	(10)
Military	Political committees	0		0		4	(4)	4	(2)
Total*		86	(99)	22	(100)	96	(99)	204	(99)

*Percentages do not sum to 100 due to rounding error.

TABLE 4
AREAS OF WORK EXPERIENCE OF THE NEW LEADERSHIP

Work Experience	Ministers and Vice-ministers		Secretaries		Directors		Total	
	N	(%)	N	(%)	N	(%)	N	(%)
Coercion —public security, the military	8	(9)	8	(7)	1	(5)	17	(8)
Production —industry, agriculture, finance, transportation	55	(60)	36	(32)	4	(18)	95	(42)
Ideology —propaganda, education	10	(11)	7	(6)	2	(9)	19	(8)
Political work —secretary, organization secretary-general	7	(8)	47	(42)	7	(32)	61	(27)
Mass works —Chinese Youth League, labor unions, nationalities	2	(2)	13	(12)	8	(36)	23	(10)
Other functional work —legal work, public health, diplomacy	9	(10)	1	(1)	0		10	(5)
Total	91	(100)	112	(100)	22	(100)	225	(100)

provincial secretaries, whereas 11 percent of the central government leaders followed that career pattern and 18 percent of the 86 ministers and vice-ministers have such technical titles as "engineer." More people moved from the central government positions to the provincial Party secretary positions than vice versa. This is particularly so if one uses the positions immediately preceding the reform as a basis for counting. This comparison makes it clear that the functional competency of the central government cadre is much higher than that of the provincial Party secretaries.

Fourth, as far as any sign of factional favoritism is concerned, it is worth noting that 6 out of the 20 leaders of the central Party organ had once served as leaders in the Chinese Youth League (CYL), the organization that Hu Yaobang headed before the CR. Even though the main function of the CYL is to train future Party leaders, the concentration of former CYL cadres in the central Party organs can be interpreted as part of Hu's effort to staff the organs with those personally close to him. It should be noted also that, in sharp contrast to the CR period, professional soldiers are systematically excluded from the key Party and government positions.

Table 4 shows that 60 percent of the ministers and vice-ministers are identified as having work experience in production—industry, agriculture, finance, and transportation. Although we do not have comparable figures for the pre-reform leadership, this figure appears to be quite high, indicating the regime's commitment to economic development. Among the subcategories of production, most people have experience in production rather than planning—for instance, economic or management planning—and surprisingly few people have work experience in agriculture. Moreover, it should be noted that the proportion of cadres with experience in the ideological and political fields is quite low—8 percent and 10 percent, respectively, among the central government leaders.

In contrast, a high percentage—42 percent—of provincial Party secretaries have their career backgrounds exclusively in what I call political fields—positions in such organizations as secretariats, organizational departments, offices of the secretary-general, and Party committees at the lower level. This sharp contrast between the two groups of leaders may be due to the different functions that the government and the Party are expected to perform. Or it may imply that, as noted, the Deng-Hu group's influence was checkmated by the entrenched local interests. Whichever may be the more valid reason, there is no doubt that the provincial leadership will continue to be more conservative, willing to defend the vested interests of the Party.

Conspicuous in Table 4 is the under-representation of mass organizations. Most of the persons under the category of mass works—a category comprising only 10 percent of all work experience—are former CYL officials and those with experience in nationality affairs. As far as I can determine, only one person with a career background in labor unions was promoted to provincial leadership. This contrasts sharply with the situation at the time of the Gang of Four, when many cadres of the provincial labor unions were promoted to the position of Party secretary.

On the whole, the regime so far has been quite successful in achieving its original goals. Reduction of the number of offices and personnel at the various levels is quite impressive, even though it seems that the total size of the cadres increased from 20 million to 21 million.[10] My analysis, by and large, confirms the regime's claim that the total number of provincial cadres has been reduced by 34 percent, and those cadres at the municipal and district levels, by 36 percent. Moreover, the majority of the new leadership is newly promoted, constituting more than 50 percent of the leaders at the municipal and district levels. According to one report, the educational level of the provincial leadership has been substantially raised; now 43 percent of the provincial cadre has a college-level education, in contrast to 20 percent before the reforms. For the municipal and district cadres, the proportion with a college-level education has risen from a mere 14 percent to 44 percent.[11] As noted, the level of specialized knowledge possessed by the post-reform cadres appears to be substantially higher than those of their predecessors.

The way the official media report the improvement of the cadres' level of education confirms the hypothesis that the requirements of age, educational level, and professional knowledge are more strictly observed for those who are newly promoted than for incumbents.

10. *Renmin ribao*, 22 July 1983.
11. Ibid., 1 Jan. 1984.

For instance, it is reported that 70 percent of those who are newly promoted to provincial leadership and "more than two thirds" of those who are promoted to municipal and district leadership have a college-level education.[12] If one assumes that the average age of the newly promoted is about 58, one can surmize that many of them graduated from college around the time that Mao established the People's Republic of China.

It appears that the regime has systematically used the strategy known as "first entrance, then exit."[13] That is, the old, incumbent cadres recruit their own successors and train—or watch—them for a while, and only when the new successors have proven their ability and loyalty will the old cadres retire. By this method, the Deng-Hu group hopes to ensure stability of the political leadership, continuity of the policy line, as well as the authority of the senior cadres, while at the same time reducing the average age of the entire existing leadership and raising its educational level and technical competency.

CONTINUING PROBLEMS

On balance, the present Deng-Hu group has succeeded in making the cadres in the top-level positions a bit more competent professionally and at the same time politically reliable. This success is largely due to the shrewd strategy of carrying out reforms gradually from the top down and stage by stage, a strategy designed to maximize the influence of the Deng-Hu group. In addition, the attractive retirement program has neutralized possible resistance from those who would lose the most as a result of the reforms. Moreover, instead of setting up highly inflated goals, the regime showed flexibility by making concessions to the existing cadre corps and by postponing the realization of highly ambitious goals. In this context, the Party consolidation campaign, although exclusively an internal Party affair, should be understood as part of the continuing effort to improve the quality of the cadres and to rationalize the ruling structures.[14]

Although the bureaucratic reforms are apparently successful on several counts, some problems persist. The lower the level, the stiffer the resistance that the reforms encounter. For instance, until recently 60 percent of the state-owned enterprises have finished reorganization of their leadership; but only half of the reorganized leadership meets the specifications that the central authority set up.[15] The average age of the new leaders at all levels is still high, and the levels of their cultural and functional knowledge are still unsatisfactory. For instance, the leading cadres in the organs directly under the Beijing municipality have few officials below the age of 45 and, worse still, 30 percent of them will reach retirement age by 1985.[16]

In order to deal with these problems, the Organizational Department of the CC recently instructed the cadres in personnel management at all levels to prepare an eight-year plan for further rationalization and to produce by the first half of 1984 a list of a third echelon of cadres.[17] The "third echelon," which is

12. Ibid.

13. *Hung qi* [Red flag], no. 2 (1981).

14. "The Decision of the Central Committee of the Communist Party of China on Party Consolidation," *Beijing Review*, 17 Oct. 1983, pp. 1-15.

15. *Renmin ribao*, 3 July 1983.

16. Ibid., 1 Sept. 1983.

17. Ibid., 22 July 1983.

discussed with increasing frequency in the official news media, refers to cadres slated to succeed to the leadership in the future.[18] The concept combines three sets of ideas: the ideas of the Soviet Union's *nomanklatura*—the list of individuals eligible for certain positions; the Chinese idea of consciously training successors; and the currently popular idea of competition. Those individuals designated as third echelon will receive special training and prove themselves by competing for a limited number of leadership positions.

As the Deng-Hu group consolidates its power position, the requirements of age, cultural level, and technical knowledge are more restrictive. Now the regime rejects the idea that long experience in actual work can be a substitute for formal education.[19] For the age requirement, the regime insists that all those in the third echelon should be under the age of 40.[20] Ironically, this age group belongs to what is known as the lost generation, whose education was disrupted by the CR and whose political reliability is questioned so much that they are admittedly the main target of the forthcoming Party consolidation campaign.[21]

Besides these specific problems, there are some deeply rooted structural obstacles to further improvement of the quality of the cadres. For instance, the total number of college graduates in China is estimated to be almost 5.6 million, whereas the total size of the cadres is 21 million and the number of Party members is 40 million.[22] Moreover, by making college degrees a pre-requisite to cadre positions—the positions that will continue to be the exclusive source of power, prestige, and attractive economic reward—the new criterion will have profound implications for China's social stratification. Not surprisingly, many cadres with a working-class background publicly protest that "when too many intellectuals join the Party, the Party will change its nature."[23] Tragically, it is also true that China lost the right moment to train "proletarian intellectuals," as Stalin did forcefully in the 1930s and many Eastern European countries did successfully in the 1950s.[24]

In post-Mao China, where Mao's ghost still lingers, how fair it is to use formal education as the major criterion for cadre recruitment will largely depend on what kind of educational opportunities the children with working-class backgrounds can have. The present college admission policy exclusively emphasizing academic achievements—and giving no consideration to class background—will certainly benefit the children of incumbent cadres and existing professional groups while leaving the children from the working class bitter.[25]

Another structural limit lies with a political consideration that the Deng-Hu group cannot avoid. No political faction can pursue purely objective cri-

18. Ibid., 1 Sept. 1983; ibid., 10 Sept. 1983.

19. Ibid., 22 July 1983.

20. Ibid.

21. *Beijing Review*, 17 Oct. 1983, pp. 1-15.

22. *Renmin ribao*, 22 July 1983.

23. Ibid., 4 July 1983.

24. Sheila Fitzpatrick, "Stalin and the Making of the New Elite, 1928-1929," *Slavic Review*, 38(3):378-402 (Sept. 1979); Peter C. Ludz, *The Changing Party Elite in East Germany* (Cambridge, MA: MIT Press, 1968); Thomas A. Baylis, *The Technical Intelligensia and the East German Elite* (Berkeley: University of California Press, 1974).

25. For new educational policy, see Jonathan Unger, *Education under Mao* (New York: Columbia University Press, 1982).

teria for personnel management to the extent of undermining its own power position. Similarly, the Party cannot drop certain aspects of Marxism-Leninism for the sake of economic development. This necessary political consideration imposes basic constraints on the present effort to rationalize and institutionalize the personnel management system. In some respects, even the state constitution is tailor-made to accommodate the existing distribution of political power among the top leaders and contending groups. For the same reason it is not a surprise to find no sign that the personnel management system will be democratized.

The effort to rationalize and institutionalize the personnel management system aims to make it a more effective tool of the state rather than more receptive to the interests and demands of the various social groups. Infusion of the large number of bureaucratic technocrats can make the system a bit more efficient, but not necessarily representative of the various social forces.

Furthermore, as shown by many studies on the Soviet Union and other socialist countries, the technocrats in socialist society will not replace totally the "red" politicians—officials who owe their positions to their political reliability rather than to their expertise— because red politicians play many important roles for the normal operation of the imperfect socialist system.[26] For instance, under China's present economic system, in which profit is used as the main criterion for evaluating the performance of each enterprise and scarce goods are largely allocated by the state plan, what are needed are not only technocrats but also political managers who use their political connections— guanxi in Chinese—to obtain essential materials for inputs. This type of official is needed not only for the enterprise but also for the ordinary workers, because the bonuses they receive depend largely on profit, and without raw materials production cannot continue or yield a profit.

To conclude, access to decision-making positions by the bureaucratic technocrats represents a sharp departure from past practice and thereby indicates the regime's determination to foster economic development and industrialization. Industrialization, however, does not necessarily accompany political democratization. Thus one can conclude that the political implication of the changes in the cadre corps is that the Chinese political system will be more like what political scientists call authoritarian.

26. Jerry Hough, The Soviet Prefect: The Local Party Organs in Industrial Decision-Making (Cambridge, MA: Harvard University Press, 1969).

*   *   *

QUESTIONS AND ANSWERS

Q: Can your data lend themselves to a prediction of a successor after the passing of Deng Xiaoping?

A: This specific question has been the question that many Chinese specialists have been wondering about. When Americans have asked that question of the Chinese, the Chinese would pose a counterquestion, saying, Can you predict who will be elected in your next election? Did you foresee the outcome for President Carter before the election campaign? And I think we are in the same situation. But what I can say as a social scientist is that the entire effort of the reform was geared to making the succession very peaceful. On the basis of what I have said and what I have seen, I feel that Hu Yaobang has consolidated his power base successfully, and a few days ago, Deng Xiaoping actually mentioned in specific terms that if Deng died soon, even today, the present policy line will continue as it is.

ANNALS, *AAPSS,* **476,** November 1984

An Overview of Chinese Law and Legal Education

By R. RANDLE EDWARDS

ABSTRACT: This article surveys the remarkable transformation of law and legal education in China in the past few years. Not long after the Gang of Four was toppled in 1976, a long-term legal development plan was adopted. Its steady implementation has led to widespread codification, an extension of courts, a restoration and expansion of the legal profession, an ambitious and popular legal education program, and substantial growth in formal legal education. Previously an authoritarian political tradition and a preference for mediation over litigation had retarded the development of a formal and autonomous legal system in China. Today, however, the popular demand for stability and justice, the need for legal rules and procedures to improve economic efficiency, and the desire to attract foreign technology and investment serve as powerful motivations for strengthening the legal system. The resulting need for more legal specialists has spawned more than 30 new law schools, along with a growing program of legal education exchange with the United States and other countries.

R. Randle Edwards is professor of law at Columbia University, director of the Center for Chinese Legal Studies at Columbia Law School, and chairman of the U.S. Committee on Legal Education Exchange with China. He has lectured on Chinese law to numerous organizations and has published articles in various professional journals.

C HINESE law and legal education are in the midst of the most rapid and significant changes in 50 years. In China, law was first regarded as, at best, irrelevant and, at worst, a disruption of harmony and later an obstacle to revolutionary development. Law is now, however, viewed as a principal tool for the achievement of socialist justice, social stability, and economic development. The prevailing attitude toward legal education has undergone a similar change. Cut back sharply in the 1950s and virtually abolished during the Cultural Revolution of the 1960s and 1970s, legal education is now a star in the crown of the academic estabishment, attracting the brightest students and a growing share of national budgetary allocations. The purpose of these changes is to promote China's legal, economic, political, and social modernization.

My aim in this article is to describe recent developments in legal education in the People's Republic of China within the context of the Chinese government's stated goal of four modernizations—the modernization of China's industry, agriculture, science and technology, and national defense. In describing these developments, I shall also point out contrasts between Chinese and American law school curricula and teaching methodologies.

At the same time, this article will outline the general structure and process of the Chinese legal system as well as the major legal policies and the legislation recently adopted by China's current Party and government leaders. These broad legal policies shape the curriculum of China's law schools and determine teaching and research priorities. The new legal codes and important statutes illustrate China's commitment to strengthening "socialist legality." These new codes and statutes also represent the substantive content of the legal education that will be imparted to the growing numbers of Chinese legal specialists. As they embark on careers as judges, prosecutors, attorneys, and foreign trade officials, the policies embodied in the rules they have studied in law school will determine whether China can maintain order, achieve justice, and reach the higher standards of living imbued in the Chinese concept of modernization.

HISTORICAL INFLUENCES ON CHINESE LAW: DISTANT AND RECENT

Law and legal education, like all other sectors of Chinese life, can be understood only against the somewhat shadowy background of two traditions— China's millenial Confucian heritage and the 50-year history of efforts by the Chinese Communist Party to establish control and bring about a socialist transformation of China's society and economy.

These two traditions contain similarities as well as differences with respect to law and legal education. The criminal code of the People's Republic of China has only a five-year history compared with the more than 2000 years of written imperial, Confucian criminal statutes. Yet law and legal practice under both traditions have been permeated by the influence of an authoritarian political system.

China has long been and today remains a one-party system, with political directions, legal rules, and often even discrete decisions in particular legal cases flowing out and down from the center of the dominant political force, be it the imperial family or the politburo of the Communist Party. The exercise of political power and the enactment and implementation of legal rules is not subject to influence by other centers of political or economic power. Nor is political power subject to the constraint of transcendant values and rules bestowed by a divine creator. Neither has it evolved over time through conflict and compromise between a secular human society and the dominant state political power and authority.

The founders of the Chinese Communist Party placed their faith in Marxist materialism, not in what they considered bourgeois idealism represented by its belief in natural law and constitutionalism. Law, like all other elements of the so-called social superstructure, was viewed simply as a tool with which the ruling class sustained its dictatorship over the oppressed classes. Laws and legal institutions were also seen as functional weapons to be employed to achieve intermediate goals on the path from feudal society through socialist transition to the ultimate goal of Communist society. The Chinese Communists saw law as a transitory instrument, not a set of lasting values and autonomous procedures.

Operating with such elemental Marxist assumptions about the nature and role of law, it is not surprising that when the Chinese Communist Party seized political power from the Nationalists on 1 October 1949, one of its first acts was to abolish the comprehensive Six Codes that had been laboriously developed over more than 30 years, from a beginning in 1903 under the Qing emperor to their adoption under Chiang Kai-shek in the mid-1930s. The discarded rules were not replaced by comprehensive new laws, because Mao Zedong and

the Party did not want to straitjacket the revolutionary forces. The political and social priority at that time was to suppress and eliminate enemy classes, feudal habits, and reactionary ways of thought. As Chairman Mao said,

[A] revolution is not the same as inviting people to dinner, or writing an essay, or painting a picture, or doing fancy needlework; it cannot be anything so refined, so calm and gentle, or so mild, kind, courteous, restrained and magnanimous. A revolution is an uprising, an act of violence whereby one class overthrows another.[1]

In short order most of the lawyers, judges, and law professors trained under the Nationalists were discarded, as were the Nationalist codes. The Nationalist judicial system was replaced by kangaroo courts run by the aroused peasants who enforced "revolutionary justice" over "evil" landlords. When a limited number of courts was reestablished in the early and middle 1950s, they were staffed largely by politically reliable Party members with little or no formal legal training.

Law schools were also sharply curtailed in number and in operations. In 1947 there were 37,000 law students in China; in 1949 there were 63 law schools. By 1952 most of the law schools had been closed or merged, and there were but 3800 law students throughout China. By the first Golden Age of Law in the mid-1950s, following the promulgation of a state constitution in 1954 and a short-lived experiment with the establishment of a legal profession, there were 10 law schools and 8200 students enrolled.

1. "Report of an Investigation into the Peasant Movement in Hunan (1927)," trans. in *Selected Works of Mao Tse-Tung* (London: Lawrence and Wishard, 1954), 1:27.

The promising movement toward greater legal formality and predictability, comprehensive codification, and open trials in the mid-1950s was blocked by Mao in 1957 when he pushed through an "anti-rightist" campaign that purged scores of leading law professors and Party officials who advocated codification and the estabishment of a more rational and stable socialist legality. After the dismal failure of Mao's Great Leap Forward in 1958, advocates of political and economic pragmatism and gradualism forced Mao to accept some policy compromises and to promulgate various statutes in the early 1960s. Statements issued after Mao's death in 1976 also reveal that work on drafts of criminal and civil codes continued in the early 1960s.

The hopes of those advocating an ambitious program to promulgate codes, train lawyers, and strengthen courts were completely dashed, however, when Mao unleashed the Great Proletarian Cultural Revolution in 1966. Primarily intended by Mao to discredit Party moderates who opposed his leftist commitment to "continuing revolution" and "politics over economics," the Cultural Revolution quickly got out of hand, eventually paralyzing the Party, disrupting the economy, and decimating institutions of higher education, including virtually all law schools. Law was one of the principal targets of the radical Cultural Revolution faction, which successfully exhorted mobs of youthful Red Guards to "smash the police, procuracy, and the courts."

Along with the institutional casualties were untold millions of human beings who were wrongfully and maliciously detained, tortured, and sometimes executed. Prominent among the most abused victims were high Party and government officials and their families. It is not surprising that when these officials and their supporters turned the tables and overthrew the Gang of Four after Mao's death, they sought to enact laws and establish procedures to ensure prosperity and security and to reduce to a minimum the prospects of a repetition of the horrors of the Cultural Revolution.

THE FOUR MODERNIZATIONS AND THE THREE MOTIVATIONS

Law and legal education in China are designed to promote policy aims designated by the leaders of the Chinese Communist Party. Since the reemergence of Deng Xiaoping as China's paramount leader five years ago, the overriding purpose of all policies and institutional reforms has been to assure the achievement of the four modernizations—in industry, agriculture, science and technology, and national defense. Deng and his supporters, who now command the key positions in every sector of the government, economy, and society, have set in motion a long-range reorientation of laws, personnel training and selection, and policy-enforcement procedures, all calculated to enhance stable and rapid economic growth.

In the realm of education, the political criteria for selection and promotion have been replaced by criteria of merit—determined primarily by results on a uniform national examination—for admission to hierarchically structured educational institutions. Placement in choice jobs is determined chiefly by academic achievement in first-rank institutions of higher education, although personal relations still exert some influence.

As I noted earlier, prevailing Party policy stresses the importance of law

Framingham State College
Framingham, Massachusetts

and the necessity for rapid expansion of the ranks of well-trained legal specialists. In 1978 an eight-year plan for development of law, legal institutions, and legal education was adopted. The program called for the opening of at least one law faculty in each of China's 29 provinces, the speedy reestablishment of the legal profession, the expansion of courts, and the progressive drafting and promulgation of criminal and civil codes, as well as scores of other important laws and regulations.

While equally ambitious goals for industrial growth established at the same time had to be trimmed back later, virtually every target contained in the eight-year plan for legal development has been met on schedule. Thus, as China's vice-minister of justice noted in January 1984 at the first national meeting on legal education held in China in more than 20 years, there are now 35 institutions of higher education in law in China. This represents an increase of 250 percent over the pre-Cultural Revolution high point of 10 law schools in 1957.[2] The number of law students has also climbed dramatically, from 1300 in 1978 to 12,000 in 1983, far more than the pre-Cultural Revolution peak of 8200 in 1957. The number of lawyers has reached approximately 15,000 in 1984, compared to around 2500 in 1979.[3] These figures are still minuscule compared to the United States, where 581,000 lawyers practice and 220,000 students are currently enrolled in law schools, but the number of

American lawyers and law students has stabilized, whereas the number of Chinese lawyers and law students continues to rise steadily.

The enactment of scores of laws and regulations—including a code of criminal law, codes of criminal and civil procedure, an economic contract law, a patent law, and a law on joint ventures with foreign capital—also offers dramatic testimony to the seriousness of the Chinese leadership's commitment to strengthening legality. These developments promise increased social and political stability and enhanced economic predictability, which are attractive to foreign investors as well as to Chinese citizens.

What are the principal reasons for these unprecedented developments in Chinese law and legal education? Three motivations seem to have triggered China's law reform movement and to provide continuing impetus for a lasting commitment to build a regular and predictable legal process. These motivations are as follows:

—a popular demand for legal protection against arbitrary behavior by Party or government officials or by other citizens;

—the need for clear guidelines for economic activity whether the actor be an individual, a collective, or a state-owned corporation; and

—the need for a systematic network of rules and procedures in civil, economic, and commercial law to attract and protect foreign capital and technology.

The demand for legal protection against the kind of arbitrary behavior that characterized the Cultural Revolution resulted in the first major legislative

2. "We Must Exert Ourselves to Create a New Situation in Legal Higher Education," *Fa zhi bao* [Legal system news], 9 Jan. 1984, p. 1.

3. Mark Sidel, "Legal Education and Legal Training in the People's Republic of China: A Preliminary Survey" (Manuscript, Columbia University Law School, 1984).

enactments after the fall of the Gang of Four. These were the codes of criminal law and criminal procedure. This same concern has led to the reestablishment of legal advisory offices to provide inexpensive or free counsel to defendants in criminal proceedings. Concern for regular and fair enforcement of the criminal law has also significantly influenced the pace of expansion in legal education, the nature of law school curriculum, and the content of the numerous law journals that have emerged in recent years.

The need for clear guidelines for economic activity aims to address the difficulties of the bad old days of the Cultural Revolution and even earlier, when contracts were not enforced, goods were often shoddy in quality and delivered late, and resources were not fully utilized due to the lack of precise legal rules governing rights, obligations, and other essential terms that shape relations between producers and consumers or workers and management. In short, comprehensive and detailed economic laws and rigorous enforcement by lawyers and the courts are essential to China's successful modernization. No doubt Max Weber would be well received in China today.

The third motivation, for the enactment of a systematic network of rules and procedures in civil, economic, and commercial law, is to attract and protect foreign capital and technology. China's leaders recognize that foreign technology and capital can speed up China's modernization. They have also recognized that China must establish an appropriate legal infrastructure and train sufficient personnel familiar with international and foreign economic law to attract the right foreign investors and acquire the technology necessary for modernization.

HISTORY AND BASIC CHARACTERISTICS OF CHINESE LEGAL EDUCATION

The curriculum, enrollment, job placement, and pedagogical policies of Chinese law schools represent an amalgam of European and common-law influences, as well as the strong influence of the planned nature of the Chinese economy and of the priorities established by the four modernizations program. Formal legal education in China dates only from the early part of this century. Because the private practice of law was forbidden by the imperial criminal code as a parasitic act disruptive of social harmony, there was naturally no formal education in law until the winds of social and institutional reform began to stir during the latter part of the Qing dynasty.

The law faculty of the imperial university in Beijing employed European, Japanese, and American teachers. The European influence predominated, however, for the continental civil law system was more in harmony with major elements of the indigenous Chinese legal tradition. The continental system stressed the dominant role of legislation as opposed to innovative judicial law-making, and systematic theoretical formulations of law in contrast to the American emphasis on discovering the law and developing analytical skills through rigorous examination of particular appellate decisions. Chinese legal education, like European legal education, was and remains today primarily an undergraduate academic discipline rather than a system of postgraduate professional training, as it has been in the United States for almost 100 years.

Another European characteristic of Chinese legal careers is that the jobs assigned at graduation are usually permanent. Judges begin as apprentice judges upon graduation from their undergraduate school and usually will not change or be allowed to shift to another legal career, such as prosecutor or attorney in a government-operated legal advisory office.

Compared with American legal education, Chinese law teaching remains extremely academic and theoretical, just as it was before the establishment of the People's Republic of China in 1949. This characteristic quality has been recently deplored by Liu Fuzhi, secretary-general of the Political-Legal Committee of the Central Committee of the Chinese Communist Party. In a speech before the National Seminar on Legal Education, Liu said that "higher education in law should be closely linked to practice, and we must lead our law teachers to develop our law and legal education from the vantage point of our country's current reality." He called for the "political-legal organs" to assist law schools in

establishing links with reality by regularly introducing teachers to actual conditions, providing necessary materials and case precedents, inviting law teachers to participate in relevant work conferences, helping to arrange for law students to engage in practical training, and so forth.[4]

The present reality is still some distance from Liu's aim, given that Chinese law professors have had very little direct experience in the political-legal organs or in handling legal aspects of domestic or foreign commercial relationships. As a result, many of China's foreign trade organs have adopted the expedient of running short, cram courses in foreign economic law for their contracting personnel, with foreign lawyers often invited to serve as lecturers.

Yet another feature of Chinese teaching and research that will strike the American observer as unfamiliar and somewhat puzzling is the separation of law teaching and legal research. Although teachers in Chinese law schools generally produce their own textbooks and are expected to engage in a certain amount of research work and scholarly publication, some senior legal specialists are assigned to research institutes that do very little or no teaching of law. This approach is apparently based on the model developed in the Soviet Union and followed in most socialist countries.

Chinese law teachers, like their European counterparts, rely primarily on the lecture method of teaching. Students in China do what students do everywhere—they memorize what the teacher says and attempt to repeat his or her sage words in the proper sequence at the appropriate point in the final examination. Any reasoning that takes place in an examination situation tends to be deductive from alleged first principles. This approach is in marked contrast to that employed in the American law school, where the Socratic method is used to force the student to reason inductively from complex factual situations and to analyze and synthesize independently and creatively by learning to "think like a lawyer."

Structure and curriculum

Chinese legal education has geared up to respond to domestic demands for personal security, social stability, and economic predictability and rationality and to attract foreign capital and technology through the accomplishment of three specific tasks. China intends to

4. "We Must Exert Ourselves," p. 1.

(1) upgrade the skills of tens of thousands of legal personnel, only a small fraction of whom have received any formal legal education; (2) train tens of thousands of badly needed new legal specialists; and (3) establish an extensive and sustained program of popular legal education—through the media and the schools—to increase compliance with laws and public support of socialist legality.

To accomplish these goals, China's institutions for formal higher education in law have increased in number, expanded enrollments, and instituted a wide variety of programs. In addition to undergraduate concentrations in law, there are three-year graduate programs in law, three-year programs at night schools, two- and three-year courses at correspondence schools, individual study and examination programs, television legal study courses, one-year intensive courses for senior legal personnel, shorter specialized legal study programs, and a general course in law required for high school students.

These various full-time and part-time legal study programs are directed by legal education institutions under the supervision of either the Ministry of Education or the Ministry of Justice. The Ministry of Education supervises 31 faculties of law in comprehensive universities throughout China. The Ministry of Justice supervises the newly established China University of Political Science and Law in Beijing as well as three institutes of political science and law in Shanghai, Xi'an, and Chongqing.

The China University and the three institutes under the Ministry of Justice are devoted exclusively to the training of legal personnel. Upon graduation, most students of these institutions become judges, prosecutors, or defense attorneys in government-run legal advisory offices.

A few are retained by their schools as instructors. A small number of graduates are now assigned to other government agencies, including those involved in foreign trade, as legal advisers.

One recent and important new development is the establishment of a graduate school in the China University of Political Science and Law, itself founded only in 1983. The graduate school has admitted a class of 144 students to a three-year program. Upon graduation, students will embark on careers as legal researchers or as teachers in the schools directed by the Ministry of Justice. Two more institutes of political science and law will be added to the growing network run by the Justice Ministry—one in Wuhan and the other in the Northeast. Chinese officials expect that by 1988 there will be approximately 18,000 undergraduate law students in schools under the Ministry of Justice, with 4500 graduating each year.

Another major contribution by the Ministry of Justice to the national program to increase the number of trained legal personnel is the operation of a wide array of programs designed to upgrade the skills of thousands of currently employed judges, prosecutors, public security officers, and notaries. Legal officials at provincial and higher levels are sent to a year-long retraining program at the Central Politics and Law Cadre School in Henan Province or to the In-Service Training Institute of the China University of Political Science and Law. At both of these institutions they enroll in a broad curriculum designed to bring them up to date on new legislation and to instill a commitment to enforce the law in strict compliance with the more rigorous standards of a newly strengthened socialist legal system. Legal personnel at lower levels are required to participate in similar refresher courses, offered by provincial and local governments.

Faculties of law in China's comprehensive universities play a somewhat different role from the role of the law schools under the Ministry of Justice, and they reflect both advantages and disadvantages. Graduates of faculties of law move into research in independent legal research institutes, teaching at their alma mater or at another university, or do legal work in the Chinese State Council, the Ministry of Foreign Affairs, or other government agencies. Some graduates also become defense attorneys, judges, or prosecutors, although the number of graduates of faculties of law entering these fields will be fewer than the number assigned from schools of political science and law. One of the advantages of attending a university law faculty is that the student shares in the somewhat higher prestige of university training and enjoys better prospects of assignment to an interesting and challenging legal post upon graduation. A disadvantage, at least currently, is that university law students do not have as great an opportunity to study practical legal skills as do their counterparts in the schools of political science and law.

The curriculum in both faculties of law and institutes of political science and law consists largely of required courses for the first two years of the four-year bachelor's degree program. Students in faculties of law and institutes of political science and law take essentially the same required courses, taught by the lecture method, largely from the same textbooks, which are prepared under the joint auspices of the Ministries of Education and Justice. Required courses now include jurisprudence, constitutional law, Chinese legal history, foreign legal history, civil law, civil procedure, criminal law, criminal procedure, criminal investigation, economic law, international law, private international law, forensic medicine, logic, Chinese language, basic theory of Marxism-Leninism, philosophy, Chinese Communist Party history, a foreign language, and physical education.

In the last two years students select a specialized field of legal study; that choice of specialty will determine the individual's lifetime career. Most university law faculties offer specializations in domestic Chinese law and in international law, and in recent years many faculties have added a concentration in economic law. Students in university law faculties must spend three months in a clinical program working at a court, a legal advisory office, or a prosecutor's office. The concern expressed by China's leaders that law graduates are not sufficiently exposed to the practical aspects of legal work has led to recent discussion of extending the clinical training period to six months.

POPULAR ATTITUDES TOWARD LAW: MASS LEGAL EDUCATION

China's leaders recognize that in order to make law a key instrument for achieving stability, social justice, and economic development, it will be necessary not only to train thousands of professional legal personnel but also to reverse the distrust of law and legal procedures long reflected in popular attitudes and habits. The Chinese leadership believes that citizens must know the law and regard it as both a source of support and an accessible instrument for securing their legitimate rights and resolving recurring problems.

China does not have a tradition of placing strong reliance on legal rules and procedures. Citizens and leaders alike have been guided not by law but chiefly by broad moral concepts—Confucian norms of proper behavior—that have been only partly superseded by the new Communist morality. Prevailing norms have encouraged unity and harmony and have discouraged the pursuit of personal interests in conflict with the claims of others. The Chinese have favored mediation and compromise over litigation and demands for a winner-take-all victory over one's adversaries. When a citizen is injured or disappointed because a government agent or another citizen has acted or failed to act, the customary and socially approved response has been to overlook small grievances and to seek redress for major loss or injury through community mediation or consultation among Party or government superiors.

The emphasis on compromise and nonlitigious settlement of disputes has enabled China to avoid expensive investment in legal education and in the staffing and operation of courts and other formal law enforcement agencies. At the same time, however, the absence of clear legal guidelines and regular and reliable court procedures has led to confusion about rights and obligations and to a certain popular distrust of Party and state decisions. The economy suffers when factory managers do not take their contractual obligations seriously. The entire political and legal system suffers when local Party and government leaders exercise broad discretionary powers in an arbitrary fashion, sometimes in their own personal interests.

To meet these problems, China's leaders have launched an extensive and long-term campaign of mass legal education to enhance compliance with the law and instill faith in the formal legal process. Citizens have even been encouraged to litigate when their constitutional or contractual rights are violated. To convey a sense of security to China's 800 million peasants, for example, the Chinese media have published numerous articles detailing successful lawsuits brought by peasant households against production teams or brigade leaders who resent the peasants for getting rich through their contracts to till collective soil and to retain all profits after paying the agreed rent to the collective.

Educating the general public to believe in and to rely on law—in reality a complete reversal of a deeply entrenched attitude of disregard and distrust—is certainly an ambitious project. Yet the continuing commitment of the current Chinese leadership to providing a meaningful role for law in China's economic and social life seems to be producing significant results. On a recent trip to China, I happened to notice a hotel desk clerk avidly reading a magazine. When I asked the name of the publication, she showed me the cover. It was *Democracy and Legality*, a monthly magazine published in Shanghai since 1979. I expressed surprise that she should be reading what I had assumed she would regard as a dry, highly academic legal journal. She replied that, on the contrary, she and many of her friends regularly read the magazine and claimed its popularity rested on the fact that it dealt directly with important human problems and the ways these could be resolved fairly.

This encounter and similar reports I have heard lead me to conclude that popular legal education in China is making genuine headway in disseminating information about law and legal procedures and in spreading the expectation that citizens' rights and interests will receive effective protection from an increasingly comprehensive socialist legal system.

SINO-FOREIGN LEGAL EDUCATION EXCHANGES

A recent and important development in Chinese legal education is the establishment of a substantial program of exchange with law schools and the legal profession in the United States and other countries. Beginning in 1978 and 1979, these exchanges have included the visits of a small number of foreign law students, law professors, and private attorneys to China for research, study, or teaching. Considerably larger numbers of Chinese have gone abroad for legal study, and probably more than half of the total have come to the United States.

During the first two years of Sino-American exchanges in the legal education area, most of the Chinese coming to the United States for legal study were middle-level officials from government ministries or corporations involved in China's burgeoning program of foreign trade and investment. These officials have participated in special nondegree programs in several American law schools aimed at providing a broad understanding of the U.S. legal process as well as a general grasp of important areas of American economic law that directly influence the rapidly expanding economic relations between China and the United States.

Many Chinese trade and investment officials are placed as interns in American corporations and international law firms. This experience exposes Chinese

trainees to the respective roles of law firms, banks, corporations, and government agencies in the negotiation and implementation of major international transactions. The American law firms and corporations that serve as hosts for this ongoing program gain insight into the policies and laws now guiding China's economic development and build relationships of mutual trust that are essential if long-term economic cooperation is to be established between two important economies as different as China and the United States.

An increasing number of graduate law students, legal researchers, and law teachers from China have gone abroad for study and research in the past two years. As with the trade personnel, the majority of Chinese law students, researchers, and professors have come to the United States. Most of the younger scholars are junior members of China's leading law faculties and are generally sent to the United States to concentrate on courses they will teach upon their return to China. Although a few young Chinese law teachers and a handful of younger trade personnel have enrolled in three-year J.D. degree programs in the United States, most seek the one-year LL.M. degree. Legal researchers and senior law lecturers and professors from the People's Republic generally spend six months to a year in the United States as visiting scholars. They conduct research, audit courses, visit legal institutions, and develop collegial relationships with their American counterparts.

Chinese law students and visiting scholars have received warm welcomes from a growing number of American law schools. They have received placement assistance and financial aid from a number of sources, including the Committee on Scholarly Communication with the People's Republic of China, the Fulbright program, individual law schools, United Nations agencies, and a number of foundations, including the Asia Foundation, the Ford Foundation, and the Luce Foundation.

The most ambitious program of legal education exchange between the People's Republic of China and the United States was inaugurated in 1983 with the conclusion of an understanding between the Committee on Legal Education Exchange with China (CLEEC) and the Chinese Ministries of Education and Justice and six leading Chinese law faculties and institutes of political science and law. The understanding establishes a three-year program—with the probability of a two-year extension—that is expected to enable 50 select young Chinese law teachers to earn LL.M. degrees in the United States and bring 50 senior Chinese law professors to the United States as nondegree visiting scholars. In addition, the program will sponsor U.S.-China legal conferences, assist in the development of Chinese law libraries, and arrange for American graduate students and law professors to go to China to study and conduct research on Chinese law or lecture on American law.

Already well under way, with 18 Chinese law students and professors now in the United States under CLEEC's auspices, this key legal exchange program was initiated by a major grant from the Ford Foundation. The program has also been greatly assisted by a substantial grant from the Luce Foundation to fund Chinese law library development, by a grant from the Chinn Ho Foundation to provide law books, and by support from the Asia Foundation. It is hoped that other funding agencies will join in supporting this major exchange program, as well as the separate individual exchanges that also contribute to U.S.-China mutual understanding and cooperation.

LESSONS AND OPPORTUNITIES

This examination of recent developments in Chinese law and legal education reveals that China's leaders and ordinary citizens alike have learned by painful experience about the insecurity, inhumanity, and inefficiency that can result when a large nation has no clear rules or reliable procedures to guide the people and to direct government officials. A major commitment of personnel, money, and Party prestige has been made toward the establishment of an extensive network of published rules and regular procedures. An unprecedented program of legal education has been undertaken with the goal of delivering legal services to every Chinese citizen. The search for effective legislative techniques, lawyering skills, and law-teaching methods has even been carried to that bastion of the free-enterprise system, the United States. The establishment of broad exchange relationships between Chinese and American law schools represents a rich opportunity for both sides to learn from each other and to promote the progressive establishment of laws, treaties, and cultural agreements conducive to peace, prosperity, and justice.

*   *   *

QUESTIONS AND ANSWERS

Q (Juanita Kidd Stout, National Association of Women Lawyers): In May 1983 I went to China with 32 other jurists. While there we spoke with the minister of justice and with some judges and lawyers in Beijing and four other Chinese cities. From those discussions we learned, first of all, that all lawyers are employees of the state and that there is no independent representation there as we know it in America. We learned also that most of those who are arrested plead guilty and that those who do not plead guilty are usually found guilty, and if they appealed, their convictions were usually affirmed. If the information given to us is correct, does law in China today play a significant role in establishing justice?

A: Law in China has come a long way, but as the Chinese leaders and people say, they still have a long way to go to achieve their goals. One of the goals in the area of criminal law is to increase the regularity and predictability of the system and to guarantee the rights of the accused, including the right of access to lawyers. It is true that all lawyers in legal advisory offices are on the state payroll. The concept of material incentives has not been extended to the area of legal services. The Chinese cite that absence of material incentives with pride. They say this means that poor people receive the same quality of legal service as anyone else. Who is paying does not matter; all that matters is whether those involved are committed to do justice in accordance with the law. The lawyers, the judges, the prosecutors, the accuser, and the accused all have the same aim, which is to protect the society and to achieve justice.

The high rates of pleading or being found guilty that you referred to could be arbitrarily produced. Or it could be that there is greater care in the pretrial process that the prosecution has a good case based on solid evidence before it brings formal criminal charges. The Chinese say that the American system unduly exposes people who are subsequently declared innocent to public condemnation at great expense and that such exposure is inconsiderate and unfair.

———

Q (Fred Greenwald, Norristown, Pennsylvania): Do you have any information on crime prevention? According to the statistics that I was given during a 1981 trip to China, there were far fewer cases of ordinary crime that reached the criminal courts than would be true, for example, in the United States.

A: The statistics on the amount of crime are subject to many different kinds of interpretation. One reason why there are fewer prosecutions or total convictions per capita in a certain area than there are in the United States is that China has a shortage of courts, so that many matters that in the United States would be handled by the formal criminal process in China are handled outside the courts.

There are three tiers in the criminal justice system in China. The lowest tier is a mass-enforced system: criticism, self-criticism, and criticism of others.

When an individual begins to engage in antisocial behavior, except for homicide or embezzling a million dollars, he or she will first be channeled into this system. There is not a great deal of mobility in China so the lowest tier is quite effective. There is not as much opportunity to steal cars, for example, because there are virtually no private cars and one cannot go too far. There is, however, greater mobility now than there used to be; in fact, there are many more crimes because of the increased mobility. The rising crime rate is a serious problem that the Chinese recognize in their press. The second tier of the criminal justice system is an administrative system consisting of two parts. One is police administered. The second is within all the work places, where they punish their own people through a system of warnings, demotions, fines, and so on. Thus it is primarily recidivists who enter the third tier, the formal criminal process, which is regulated by the statutes that I have discussed.

ANNALS, *AAPSS*, **476**, November 1984

China's Industry in Transition: To What?

By ANDREW G. WALDER

ABSTRACT: China's industrial reforms, while bringing major changes in the management of industry, are not particularly innovative compared to reforms in Eastern Europe. While the reforms are moderate ones, China is noteworthy for its persistence along the path of reform despite the emergence of serious problems. The problems are generic ones that have plagued previous piecemeal reforms in Eastern Europe. They are due to an unreformed price structure not designed to send signals to enterprises; to continuing shortages of industrial supplies; and to the soft budget constraint under which enterprises operate. The problems have included an uncontrolled investment drive by enterprises, price inflation of producers' goods and construction materials, shortages of materials for state-sponsored construction projects, a larger budget deficit, and indiscriminate payment of bonuses. There is still no improvement in the main measures of industrial productivity. Despite these difficulties, reform continues in all areas.

Andrew G. Walder received his B.A. from the Johns Hopkins University and his Ph.D. in sociology from the University of Michigan. Since 1981, he has been assistant professor of sociology at Columbia University, where he is also an associate of the East Asian Institute. He is the author of Chang Ch'un-ch'iao and Shanghai's January Revolution *(1978) and of a number of articles about Chinese workers, labor relations, industrial administration, and reform. He is currently completing a book about authority relations in Chinese industry.*

C HINA'S industrial enterprises are managed differently today, compared to only seven years ago. A series of reforms have affected almost every area of management practice, especially the criteria for judging enterprise success, the financing of investment, the business powers of enterprise managers, and the incentives offered workers. The reforms have coincided with truly sweeping changes in the agricultural sector that have been quite successful in raising agricultural productivity. The industrial reforms, however, despite widespread experimentation with new methods, have not been nearly so sweeping; nor have they been nearly as successful in achieving their aims. Reforms, further, have been piecemeal—even fragmented—and no single coherent reform model has yet emerged.

Observers of China have on occasion greatly overstated the magnitude of China's industrial reforms. Some have concluded that the new policy of "using economic levers, not administrative measures," represents a marked departure from "the Soviet model" and even the "dismantling of the command economy."[1] The Chinese themselves have unwittingly contributed to this misunderstanding with their repeated statements that they are moving away from the Soviet model of management. The conception of the reforms, in fact, is a good deal less innovative than these statements indicate.

CHINA'S REFORMS IN PERSPECTIVE

When Chinese economists call for a reform of their Soviet-style management

system, they are referring not to current Soviet and East European practices, but to their own 1950s vintage model that has been preserved in mummified form for over 25 years.[2] The changes introduced in China have closely paralleled changes that have been widely discussed and implemented to some degree since the 1950s in the Soviet Union and many of the Eastern European countries in its orbit. All of these countries have to some extent implemented reforms that shift to the use of economic levers, or profit and price mechanisms, in enterprise management. Even in Hungary, the country that has gone the furthest in granting to enterprises autonomy in their business operations, the reforms represent less a dismantling of central planning than a fine-tuning of it.[3] Only Yugoslavia has broken away from the Soviet central-planning mold.

China's industrial reforms exhibit changes of the same types and in the same areas as their counterparts in Eastern Europe. The East European reforms involve changes in four areas: in the organs of economic management above the enterprise, in the autonomy of enterprises in making business decisions, in the instruments of control over enterprise activities, and in the incentives offered managers and workers. In dif-

1. Robert Delfs, "Socialism's New Look," *Far Eastern Economic Review,* 28 May 1982, pp. 58-60.

2. Maoist efforts to depart from the Soviet model succeeded in weakening it without substantially changing it. The result was to intensify, not alleviate, its characteristic problems. See Andrew G. Walder, "Some Ironies of the Maoist Legacy in Industry," in *The Transition to Socialism in China,* ed. M. Selden and V. Lippit (Armonk, NY: M.E. Sharpe, 1982), pp. 215-37.

3. See Paul Hare, "China's System of Industrial Economic Planning," in *The Chinese Economic Reforms,* ed. S. Feuchtwang and A. Hussain (New York: St. Martin's Press, 1983), pp. 185-223; Hare is a specialist on the Hungarian economy who has recently paid a research visit to China.

ferent East European countries the reform programs have emphasized different areas. The more conservative reforms have stressed rearrangement of management organs, while the more liberal ones have stressed enterprise autonomy to a more significant degree. But all the reforms, conservative and liberal alike, have generally involved some changes in all these areas.[4]

In China, as in the Soviet Union, Hungary, and elsewhere, reform has involved a recasting of the lines of institutional control over enterprises. This takes three forms: the redrawing and consolidation of ministry jurisdictions, the delegation of greater control to provinces or regional planning agencies, and the formation of specialized companies or trusts that combine formerly unrelated enterprises into a single corporate planning structure. China's current reforms have involved some redrawing of ministry boundaries, but have concentrated on the formation of specialized companies that integrate the activities of closely related enterprises. This arrangement, as in Eastern Europe, is designed to reap the advantages of specialization, coordination of production operations, and sharing of technical innovation and management skills.

The Chinese reforms have also increased the formal autonomy of enterprises in business decisions. All of the East European economies have attempted to make enterprises more independent financially, responsible for their own profits and losses. In traditional

Soviet practice, enterprises were in effect budgetary arms of superior organs: they were rationed supplies, granted capital at no cost, and charged with turning out set quantities of products.[5] In all of these countries, China included, reform has brought stricter accounting practices in the financing of enterprise activities. Increasingly, enterprises are no longer given free investment and working capital in the form of grants. Capital charges and interest are gradually being worked into many enterprises' costs, and capital is increasingly lent by banks rather than granted by planning agencies. The banks are being instructed to scrutinize enterprises for credit worthiness.[6]

Autonomy, further, includes not only increased financial independence, but enterprise ability to make independent production and investment decisions as well. The number of targets given enterprises is typically decreased, enterprises are allowed to retain an increased proportion of their profits in excess of targeted amounts, and they can use these funds, within certain limits, for plant renovation, minor expansion, and welfare and housing for employees. This much is a standard feature of reform proposals.[7]

4. See David Granick, *Enterprise Guidance in Eastern Europe* (Princeton, NJ: Princeton University Press, 1978), and Athar Hussain, "Economic Reforms in Eastern Europe and Their Relevance to China," in *Chinese Economic Reforms*, ed. Feuchtwang and Hussain.

5. See Joseph Berliner, *Factory and Manager in the USSR* (Cambridge, MA: Harvard University Press, 1957), and Janos Kornai, *Overcentralization in Economic Administration: A Critical Analysis Based on Experience in Hungarian Light Industry*, trans. I. Nove, (London: Oxford University Press, 1959).

6. See Gregory Grossman, ed., *Money and Plan: Financial Aspects of East European Economic Reforms* (Berkeley: University of California Press, 1968); and Barry Naughton, "The Profit System," *China Business Review* 10(6):14-18 (Nov.-Dec. 1983).

7. See Gertrude Schroeder, "Recent Developments in Soviet Planning and Incentives," in

China has implemented these measures and has gone somewhat further. Many enterprises now have the ability to market output above their quotas and to procure supplies for this above-quota production independently. There is, therefore, as in some of the East European countries, an increased role for the market in the planned economy. But the role of the market is still distinctly supplementary—and is not really a "market" in many senses of the term, as I will explain shortly. Except for Yugoslavia and some industrial sectors in Hungary, all enterprises in the socialist countries, China included, are still given a variety of binding production targets and are still rationed supplies through a unified system of materials distribution; their labor force and wage bills are still controlled.[8] This enterprise autonomy, in fact, represents less a delegation of business powers to enterprises than simply a change in the criteria by which planning organs manage them.

Reform in China, as throughout Eastern Europe, also includes changes in the instruments of economic control over enterprises. In all of these countries the number of mandatory targets given to enterprises has been reduced, and the output target is deemphasized in assessing enterprise performance. Profit and rates of increase in profit become the index for judging enterprise performance. Planning agencies, further, rely increasingly on indirect controls over enterprise activities: accounting for capital costs as part of the costs of production, manipulation of interest rates on loans for investment funds, allowing enterprises to retain certain percentages of profits over targeted amounts, and the use of various taxes to encourage or penalize certain kinds of management behavior. China is in the midst of implementing all of these measures of control, and in fact has begun to substitute complex taxation schedules for simpler profit-retention systems.[9] This is a typical example of the substitution of indirect methods of central planning for direct ones.

In a final area of reform—work incentives—China again is moving in the same direction as the East European economies. The changes involved are larger in China's case, however, because for the 10 years before 1977 there was virtually no incentive pay in industry for either managers or workers. The Eastern European countries, in contrast, have always employed these wage mechanisms. The mere restoration of bonus pay in China—now some 18 percent of the national wage bill[10]—itself represents a major change. But China has implemented additional innovations now common in other socialist countries. Most notably, enterprises now retain larger portions of their profit to form an incentive fund to be distributed to employees in the form of bonuses. This effort to link employee pay to the overall profitability of the enterprise is reminiscent of earlier reforms in the Soviet Union and elsewhere.[11]

Soviet Economic Prospects for the Seventies, U.S. Congress, Joint Economic Committee (Washington, DC: Government Printing Office, 1973), pp. 11-38; and idem, "The Soviet Economy on a Treadmill of Reforms," in *Soviet Economy in a Time of Change,* U.S. Congress, Joint Economic Committee (Washington, DC: Government Printing Office, 1979), pp. 312-40.

8. Hussain, "Economic Reforms in Eastern Europe," pp. 99-103.

9. Naughton, "The Profit System," pp. 14-15.

10. State Statistical Bureau, *Zhongguo tongji nianjian 1981* (Hong Kong: Jingji Daobao She, 1982), p. 427.

11. See Schroeder, "Recent Developments"; and Leonard Joel Kirsch, *Soviet Wages: Changes in Structure and Administration since 1956* (Cambridge, MA: MIT Press, 1972), pp. 143-57.

China's reform efforts, in sum, represent a marked change in the way industry was managed a decade ago, but they are quite conventional when compared to Eastern European developments. China emerged from the Cultural Revolution with its Soviet-style planning system in disrepair. Since then, the old structure has been shored up, and at the same time it has begun to catch up with changes introduced elsewhere in the socialist world over the past two decades. China, to be sure, has not blindly copied any single country, but has sought to tailor its reform package to meet its own needs. The basic principles of reform, however, are identical to those followed to different degrees and in different combinations in much of Eastern Europe.

THE ORIGINS AND OBJECTIVES OF REFORM

The origins and objectives of China's industrial reforms are similar, but not identical, to those in Eastern Europe 20 years ago. The Soviet Union enjoyed spectacular economic growth rates for decades before the 1960s, largely due to two factors: the concentration of massive state investment in selected industries, especially capital goods, and a large reserve of surplus labor in the countryside and among nonworking women. By the 1960s, however, the industrial base had become more capital intensive and technologically complex. Large capital investments in industry were bringing diminishing returns. The reserves of surplus labor ran dry, making labor supply a major constraint on further industrial growth.[12] Yet another factor impelled Soviet leaders to reform: the commitment to a steady improvement in wages, housing, and the supply of consumer goods, improvements long neglected under Stalin.[13] To maintain high rates of growth without ever-increasing industrial investment, to economize on labor utilization, and to free up capital for investment in consumption and related industries, greater capital and labor efficiency was required.

China's experience, and problems, have been somewhat different. China has had high average industrial growth rates—around 10 percent annually—throughout the history of the People's Republic. Drops in these rates have occurred only in the short run, due to political disruptions of the economy, rather than any long-term trend toward increased capital intensity in industry. Moreover, there is by no means a shortage of cheap labor, or the prospect of one. Because of its still low level of industrial development and massive supplies of surplus labor, China could probably continue to rely on the traditional high-investment strategy to achieve high aggregate growth rates for decades to come.

Why, then, is reform necessary in China? One could certainly argue, and with some justification, that China's main problem for over a decade before 1978 was not the old Soviet-style planning practices themselves, but the fact that they had degenerated so badly under the impact of the Cultural Revo-

12. Arthur W. Wright, "Soviet Economic Planning and Performance," in *The Soviet Union Since Stalin,* ed. S. Cohen, A. Rabinowitch, and R. Sharlet (Bloomington: Indiana University Press, 1980), pp. 113-34.

13. Seweryn Bialer, *Stalin's Successors: Leadership, Stability, and Change in the Soviet Union* (New York: Cambridge University Press, 1980), pp. 148-58.

lution. In other words, the system was not operating at its own potential. This appears to have been the thinking behind Hua Guofeng's short-lived economic policies of 1977-78.[14]

Data on China's economic performance over the past 20 years, however, show that the problems were much too serious for a simple, administrative refurbishing. Virtually all financial measures of productivity showed serious declines in the two decades after 1957. Value added per unit of capital declined by almost 40 percent in state-owned industry. Labor productivity—value added per worker—which more than doubled in the first 15 years of the People's Republic, actually declined by 5 percent in the decade after 1965. Total factor productivity, which increased by 48 percent from 1952 to 1965, fell by 11 percent in the decade that followed.[15] China continued to have high growth rates throughout the period, but only because it continued to pour massive amounts of capital into state industry. China's problem, in other words, was not a slow decline of growth rates and an emerging labor shortage; the problem was massive industrial waste in a still-poor country.

Greater efficiency in industry was more urgently needed in China than in Eastern Europe, for a number of reasons. Transportation networks and energy production both needed heavy

outlays of new investment to prevent them from acting as bottlenecks to further economic growth. Unemployment was becoming a serious problem in urban areas, with the return to cities of rusticated youth and the growing size of age groups entering the labor force. More investment was needed in job-creating light industry. Real wages and per capita housing space both had fallen by 20 percent since the mid-1950s, and the government was committed to raising these long-neglected living standards.[16] To help raise living standards, and to make sure that workers would have something to buy with their higher wages, consumer goods production had to occupy a greater proportion of investment. China therefore turned, under quite different conditions, but with much greater urgency, to the broad path of reform taken earlier in Eastern Europe.

THE GENERIC PROBLEMS OF REFORM

The types of industrial reform carried out in China, we have already seen, share the generic features of reform efforts elsewhere in the socialist world. They have also shared the generic problems—ones that have often caused retreat from reform elsewhere. Rather than provide a detailed chronicle of the halting progress of reform—something that is at any rate available elsewhere[17]—

14. Andrew G. Walder, "The Post-Mao Industrial Reforms: Economic Administration and Enterprise Management," in *Development and Change in China*, ed. E.K.Y. Chen and S.S.K. Chin (Hong Kong: University of Hong Kong, Centre of Asian Studies, 1981), pp. 71-90.

15. Thomas G. Rawski, "Productivity, Incentive, and Reform in China's Industrial Sector" (Paper delivered at the Thirty-sixth Annual Meeting of the Association for Asian Studies, Washington, DC, 23-25 Mar. 1984), tabs. 1 and 2.

16. See Andrew G. Walder, "The Remaking of the Chinese Working Class, 1949-1981," *Modern China*, 10:3-48 (Jan. 1984).

17. See Naughton, "The Profit System"; idem, "The Decline of Central Control over Investment in Post-Mao China," in *Policy Implementation in Post-Mao China*, ed. D. M. Lampton (n.p., forthcoming); Andrew G. Walder, "Wage Reform and the Web of Factory Interests," in ibid.; and Susan L. Shirk, "Recent Chinese Labour Policies and the Transformation of Industrial Organisation in China," *China Quarterly*, 88:575-93 (Dec. 1981).

I shall treat these problems analytically, specifying some of the key defects that plague reform everywhere, and follow them with examples of the ways that each has become manifest in China.

The structure of state-set prices for industrial products and supplies is the biggest reform problem. It is widely recognized in China that the traditional pricing structure of the Soviet system sends the wrong signals to enterprise managers. Inputs for capital-goods industries have traditionally been set quite low, thus making fuel and raw materials cheap and encouraging waste. At the same time energy and raw-material industries have high costs relative to the prices for their products, and find it difficult to make a profit—and frequently operate at a planned loss. The price system, therefore, not only rigs profit earnings in favor of some and to the detriment of others, thus preventing profit from reflecting actual efficiency; it also fails to encourage efficiency in the most wasteful enterprises while failing to stimulate those whose products are in perennially short supply. In addition, so long as prices are administered, they respond slowly to changing conditions and only if and when price planners recognize the changes.

The shift to profit and other financial criteria therefore has the immediate effect simply of shifting all of the traditional management problems onto the management of prices. Since price schedules were not created for a system in which autonomous enterprises respond to price signals, a major overhaul of these irrational prices is necessary if new kinds of imbalances, and more serious ones at that, are not to occur. This is an enormous task, not only because of the sheer administrative complexity of adjusting countless prices while maintaining some overall planning balance, but, more important, because such a reform of prices is an intensely political process that requires resetting national priorities and harming the interests of ministries and provinces that might be influential enough to stall or block needed changes.

In theory, allowing prices to vary within certain limits would solve the problem of flexibility and allow prices to adjust themselves while sidestepping the political and administrative complexities of price reform. Those Western economists who urge this free-market panacea are neglecting a central fact, of which Chinese and East European economists are only too aware: the conditions that would allow floating prices to act as regulators are not even approximated in these postreform economies. Because of the general scarcity of most commodities, the monopolistic position of enterprises, and the soft budget constraint that provides a guaranteed subsidy against enterprise failure because of the social need for employment and output, there are very strong inflationary pressures embedded in the economy.[18] When inflation affects consumer prices, it has potentially explosive political consequences. When it affects raw materials and producers' goods, it adversely affects government finances and the completion of plans, as we shall see.

Because of these built-in problems, socialist economies typically resort—as China has done—to partial decontrol of only a selected class of commodity prices, while moving ahead with a slow process of revising centrally administered prices. With the partial exception only

18. Janos Kornai, *Economics of Shortage* (Amsterdam: North-Holland, 1980).

of Hungary, prices are still centrally set for all major industrial commodities in Eastern Europe. China has so far followed this pattern, allowing price negotiations for goods produced and sold after planned targets are met, but enforcing the state prices for goods produced under plan.

China, in other words, has had to face up squarely to the task of reforming its centrally administered prices, which still filter the vast majority of transactions in industry. To the great detriment of its reforms, this process has not yet begun in earnest. Price reform began with great publicity and discussion in 1978, but was subsequently halted. Initially it was to precede—as it should have—the delegation of enterprise autonomy and profit sharing, but it did not. And since that time, not much has been accomplished in this area, except for the attachment of prices to working and fixed capital, which formerly was free, the levying of financial penalties against fuel-wasting plants and those with large outstanding loans, and a reform of prices in the textile industry.[19] Current plans call for comprehensive wage and price reform in several stages, but beginning no sooner than 1985.[20]

A second generic problem of industrial reform, related to the problem of prices but independent of it, is that the so-called markets onto which nominally autonomous enterprises are being gradually thrown are not really markets. They are bounded by a number of institutional arrangements and economic conditions that distort their operation. There is still a general scarcity of commodities, and industrial materials are still rationed to enterprises within the plan. Since goods are scarce in this producers' market, it is easy to unload products. Competition is much higher among consumers—including enterprises that are trying to procure supplies—than among producers.[21]

Because the procurement of supplies is still the biggest constraint facing managers, and because capital, while no longer free, is still very cheap, the building of additional plant capacity to supply one's own needs is still a rational strategy. Enterprise demand for fixed capital under these conditions is, as Alec Nove pointed out years ago, "theoretically unlimited."[22] While the greater use of markets allows in theory for a better balance of supply and demand, greater enterprise autonomy in this kind of market tends to create new forms of imbalance and disequilibrium. In this case, Nove argues, piecemeal reform will naturally set off an "investment drive" among enterprises.

CHINA'S REFORM PROBLEMS

Such imbalances have occurred in China, and because the post-1978 leadership has implemented enterprise autonomy quite rapidly, in a piecemeal fashion, and before reforming prices, these imbalances and other unintended consequences have occurred in a big way. These problems have not only prevented the desired improvements in capital and labor productivity; they have created other economic problems

19. Rawski, "Productivity, Incentive, and Reform," pp. 10-11.

20. Naughton, "The Profit System," p. 16.

21. Hussain, "Economic Reforms in Eastern Europe," pp. 103-11.

22. Alec Nove, "Planner's Preferences, Priorities, and Reforms," in Political Economy and Soviet Socialism, Alec Nove (London: Allen & Unwin, 1979), pp. 100-111.

as well. Four of the most important problems will be mentioned here.

The first of these is uncontrolled investment spending in industry—the opposite of the stated intention of the reforms. Enterprises, precisely as Alec Nove predicted, have immediately used their increased autonomy to reinvest in expanding and refurbishing plant capacity, and in adding to their housing stock as well. This runaway spending has proven extremely difficult to control. In 1980 this extrabudgetary capital construction was scheduled to be reduced by half; instead it increased by more than half. The next year it was again scheduled to be reduced by half; it in fact declined by only 14 percent, and the decrease was offset by increases in other areas of nonbudgetary funds. The problem has continued through 1983.

This uncontrolled capital spending was a major factor in the sharp increase in the national budget deficit in 1980-81, and it has made the reduction of the deficit since then more difficult. Just as important, this overinvestment has sabotaged the central government's efforts to redirect investment into the crucial energy and transportation sectors. The center has sought to bring the deficit under control by reducing its own budgetary investments in industry, and this has had the effect of reducing investment in precisely those sectors where it needs to be concentrated.[23]

A second problem is closely related to the first: inflation in the costs of construction materials. With this increased extrabudgetary investment, competition for scarce cement, steel, glass, and other products has led to escalating construction costs. The costs of construction

have gone up 9 percent since 1978. This serves to aggravate the budget deficit, because enterprises are buying supplies for construction at higher prices, which increases the costs to the central budget and lowers the profit remitted. Largely because of this, the total losses of industrial enterprises have remained constant at ¥4 billion per year since 1978. Where in 1978 half these losses were in inefficient small steel and fertilizer plants that have since been closed, today the losses are in formerly profitable enterprises hit by rising costs.

A third problem is the diversion of construction materials from key projects designated by the central government. Because above-quota production can be marketed independently, and because these prices are higher than state-set ones, enterprises are diverting large quantities of producers' goods onto what Naughton aptly calls "quasi-markets" that are beyond the control of central planners. Since mid-1983, the central government has taken a series of measures to restrict this diversion of materials outside the plan. Diversion not only increases costs and cuts state income, but the shortages of materials for state construction projects prevents the completion of planned projects: only 47 of 80 large construction projects to be completed in 1982 were actually finished.[24]

A fourth problem is not closely related to the first three, but it has the same causes: uncontrolled spending on incentive pay that is distributed with little regard to performance. Because of the incoherent incentives embodied in enterprise autonomy under current conditions, managers have just as much incentive to hoard bonus funds as capi-

23. Naughton, "Decline of Central Control," is the source for the preceding two paragraphs.

24. Naughton, "The Profit System," p. 16, is the source for the preceding two paragraphs.

tal investment and materials, and they have weak incentives to tie their payment closely to worker performance. Because profit often reflects the price structure rather than actual efficiency, retained bonus funds poorly reflect enterprise performance. For these reasons, all of the highly publicized changes in incentive practices—the restoration of bonuses, the marked rise in wage levels, and the creation of bonus funds linked to profit—have had little apparent effect on labor productivity. Instead there has been what one Chinese economist has called a "hemorrhaging of state funds into the pockets of workers." This lack of success has led to plans to restructure completely a wage and incentive system that the head of the state labor bureau, in apparent despair, has recently called "rotten to the core."[25]

THE BOTTOM LINE

In stressing the very real problems facing industrial reform in China, I do not intend to leave the impression that it has not had its successes. China has been able to redirect investment into consumer-goods production, and the supply of virtually all major consumer commodities has greatly increased since 1977. As much new housing has been built in the past six years as in the entire history of the People's Republic. The real wages of state employees in the past six years have increased 20 percent. The opening of trade and credit links with foreign countries has brought the economy badly needed capital and foreign exchange. And whatever the fiscal problems in industry, growth has continued at its historically high rates.

But the bottom line for assessing industrial reform is whether or not it is actually improving capital productivity, thereby releasing funds for investment in neglected key sectors and for continued improvements in the standard of living. By this criterion, reform has not yet had any visible effect. Total factor productivity, according to Rawski's recent calculations, has shown no significant improvement since 1977 and remains well below the levels of the mid-1950s. Despite the fact that profit sharing is intended to focus the efforts of managers on improving financial performance, there has been no significant improvement in profit per *yuan* of output, in profits and tax receipts per unit of total capital, or in output per *yuan* of working capital.[26] High growth rates continue, but only because more labor and capital are poured into production, as was the case before reform.

Whatever progress there has been in industry, therefore, has not been due to enterprise reforms. Such redirecting of investment resources as has occurred, Naughton has shown, has not been due to the utilization of price mechanisms, but to the development of direct mechanisms—like bank loans—to redistribute funds where central planners want them.[27] If funds for increases in urban living standards, furthermore, are not coming from increased enterprise efficiency, they must be paid for by direct state budgetary subsidies. These subsidies, as a result, have ballooned since 1978, growing from the equivalent of some 80 percent of the wage bill for state employees to over 100 percent currently. The subsidies now comprise a stag-

25. Andrew G. Walder, "Rice Bowl Reforms," *China Business Review* 10(6):18-21 (Nov.-Dec. 1983); and idem, "Wage Reform."

26. Rawski, "Productivity, Incentive, and Reform," tabs. 2 and 4.

27. Naughton, "Decline of Central Control."

gering 20 percent of China's national income and will continue to increase under current conditions.[28] For the improvement in living standards of the past six years to continue, the industrial reforms must begin to improve the cost efficiency of enterprise operations. The alternative is to raise prices for urban consumer goods, something that has created considerable dissatisfaction among East European citizens.

CONCLUSION: WHITHER CHINA'S INDUSTRY?

The flood of reform proposals and experiments in Chinese industry over the past six years has sometimes given observers the impression that the reforms are far more sweeping in nature than they really are. We have seen that China's reform efforts in industry follow the logic of reform in Eastern Europe and in fact are so far a good deal less radical than reforms in Hungarian industry. Given the imbalances that have already emerged from relatively limited price decontrol and enterprise autonomy, it would make very little sense for China to move further in the Hungarian direction, eliminating compulsory targets and state prices in selected key industries and product lines. The task of coordinating China's immense industrial economy is infinitely more complex than that of province-sized Hungary, where a few large enterprises dominate most key industrial sectors.

China is still noteworthy, however, for the evident vitality of its reforming impulse. Despite the setbacks and problems of recent years, China's leaders show no apparent signs of abandoning

28. Nicholas R. Lardy, "Subsidies," *China Business Review,* 10(6):21-24 (Nov.-Dec. 1983).

reform. In many Eastern European countries, the USSR most notably, the first signs of a loss of central control of the economy—of the kind China has experienced in a big way—has led to a rapid rollback of reforms and a retreat into administrative tinkering. The response of China's leaders to their setbacks has so far been to consolidate for a brief period and then push forward with modified reform practices on all fronts.

It is precisely this activist reformism that makes it difficult to predict the eventual contours of China's industrial economy. Reform and experimentation continue in all of the areas enumerated at the outset of this article: in the organs of economic management, in enterprise autonomy, in the instruments of control over enterprises, and in work incentives. Given the problems that reform has engendered, I would expect China's mix of reform features to stress increasingly effective centralized fiscal controls—both direct and indirect—over enterprises and an effort to reshape enterprise autonomy in the state's favor. The weakness of central control is a major legacy of the Cultural Revolution that still needs to be addressed, and it is evidently responsible for exacerbating many of the problems experienced so far. Especially if these changes are accompanied by the continued formation of trusts and specialized companies, China's package of reforms in industry will look much more like the Soviet model of reform than the Hungarian.

While China may begin to travel with greater determination down a road to industrial reform that the Soviet Union has traveled very hesitantly, its more radical innovations, which lie outside the sphere of industrial management, include things that the USSR would likely never permit. The dismantling of collective agriculture in favor of semi-private, household production, the legalization of petty trade, the establishment of special economic zones for direct foreign investment, and the resurgence of a private, individual services and handicraft sector in cities are all quite radical by Soviet standards, and taken together they are quite liberal by the standards of Eastern Europe—except Yugoslavia—as well. China appears to be heading, without a fully articulated overall conception, toward moderate reform in industry, set in an economy that shares many of the features of the Soviet Union's during its New Economic Policy of the 1920s.[29] At present, this direction appears to constitute, despite the conventional nature of the industrial reforms, the distinctive Chinese-style modernization that national leaders have been promising since 1978.

29. Alec Nove likened the emerging Chinese economic system to the Soviet New Economic Policy in his talk, "China's Economic Reforms in Soviet Perspective" (East Asian Institute, Columbia University, 19 Apr. 1984).

ANNALS, *AAPSS*, **476**, November 1984

The New Course in Chinese Agriculture

By VIVIENNE SHUE

ABSTRACT: China's current reform program in agriculture is enormously ambitious in intent and highly significant for all aspects of future economic and political development. It represents a rejection of past policies of large-scale labor mobilization and communal self-reliance in favor of commercialization and individual incentives for peasants. Diversification of the rural economy, decentralization of farm management, production specialization, crop selection in accord with comparative advantage, expansion of free markets, release of labor from the land, and a shift toward household-based, rather than collective, cultivation have all been important elements of the new line. The resultant explosion of pent-up rural entrepreneurship, fueled also by marked state procurement price rises, produced dramatically positive effects on overall productivity, peasant incomes, and standards of living. These led to widespread introduction of even more radical reforms. The recent agricultural boom will be difficult to sustain, however, without worsening China's already serious budget and finance crisis. Today's leadership coalition also faces intrabureaucratic opposition from cadres at all levels who are threatened by the reorganizations, and widespread popular unease about new patterns of social inequality that may accompany greater reliance on market relations. Decentralized management, a wider role for the market, and the vigor of new commercial combines also appear to be hampering the ability of central planners to regulate the economy. Such factors are capable of producing their own political backlash. The new course is, therefore, still a risky gamble in search of a workable balance between plan and market, growth and equality, national priorities and local demands.

Vivienne Shue is associate professor of government at Cornell University. She is a member both of the editorial board of Modern China *and of the China and Inner Asia Council of the Association for Asian Studies. She has conducted fieldwork and interviews on rural local government in Hebei, Sichuan, and other provinces. Her publications include* Peasant China in Transition *(1980) and numerous articles and papers on the political economy of the contemporary Chinese countryside.*

O NCE again China's leaders are taking a tremendous gamble on a boldly iconoclastic program of sweeping reforms in agriculture. Time and again since 1949, disappointment with lagging agricultural performance has provided the impetus for staggering economic reform efforts and spellbinding social experiments in China's countryside. Land to the tiller, collectivization, the formation of people's communes, and nationwide emulation of the Dazhai (Tachai) model were each inspired by the hope of transcending China's inherited patterns of low-technology production, inefficient labor utilization, and crop yields as undependable as the weather. These earlier reform programs often became entangled in elite power struggles and policy disputes, sometimes with profoundly disrupting consequences for the Chinese people. So, many peasants and rural cadres, understandably cautious, may now wince as new rounds of radical structural reorganizations are announced and promoted by today's leaders in Beijing.

Yet those earlier dramatic agricultural reform campaigns were by no means all for nought. Over the past 30 years, Chinese agriculture has performed the not-so-small miracle of keeping pace with skyrocketing population increases. This is a record that must be the envy of many Third World countries where the agonizing malnutrition, hunger, and deprivation so visible in the cities is exceeded only by the hidden misery of those who still try to live on the land. Nevertheless, the breakthrough pursued by China's planners time and again has eluded them. Under socialism, Chinese agriculture has developed enough to support twice the population of 1949. But it has not yet yielded the surpluses

needed for a take-off to rapid and sustained industrialization.

Thus the Deng Xiaoping coalition of the 1980s, promising the people modernization and a better life for their children, had to come to grips with China's twentieth-century developmental bottleneck, agriculture. These veterans of the Cultural Revolution quickly concluded that tinkering with modifications of the Maoist structural legacy in the countryside would not do the trick. So, once again Beijing is caught up in the effort to chart a whole new course for rural development.

CRITIQUE OF LEFTISM

Much of what is happening in the countryside today is best understood as an explicit rejection of, and a search for alternatives to, the goals and methods of the immediate past.

In Mao's final years, today's reformers insist, rural policy planning and implementation were far too rigid and restrictive. Even the most natural and innocent profit-making activities were liable to be branded as capitalist and reactionary. The hardest working and most dedicated peasants had no more to show for their efforts at harvest time than the least skilled and laziest workers, because virtually all differential incentive schemes were sacrificed to the pursuit of universal social welfare and egalitarianism in income distribution. Even in China's most fertile and productive areas, farmers and cadres were hamstrung by central policies that demanded single-minded attention to grain production and neglect of cash crops, fishery, forestry, animal husbandry, and handicrafts. Yet, since state grain procurement prices were deliberately kept low, even peasants in well-endowed areas could never become prosperous. And those who lived where farming conditions were more hardscrabble were denied the income-earning sidelines that made it possible to get by and eat meat more than a half-dozen times a year.

China's current leaders, intent on demonstrating the bankruptcy of past policies, support these arguments with statistics showing that from 1955 to 1977 average per capita peasant income increased by only 1 percent a year while gross value of agricultural production was growing by approximately 4 percent.[1] And if such figures for the average are accurate, there must have been many areas where real peasant incomes were actually stagnant and declining.

As for China's distinctive commune-brigade-team structure of rural administration and production organization, the contemporary critique is just as harsh. Communes are blamed for being at once too big and too small. They were too big because of their tendency always to organize peasant labor in large groups to work on large fields or construction projects. This was done in the simplistic belief that "if it's bigger, it must be more socialist." Furthermore, in communes peasants and rural cadres were under constant pressure to raise the unit of account, that is, to increase the number of hamlets and villages that pooled their labor and thus shared together in a harvest. Raising the unit of

account was a way of smoothing out inequities among the better-off and worse-off hamlets in an area. But like the deployment of large labor groups, it was prone to free-rider problems that undermined incentives for better laborers or better-off hamlets to participate wholeheartedly.

Communes were too small and confining, however, because they practiced a brand of self-reliance not only in agricultural production for local subsistence, but also in the development of their own small, labor-intensive, low-technology factories that turned out producers' goods like farm tools, cement, and fertilizer for local use. Pursuing self-reliance, communes were apt to hoard resources to set up what were in fact redundant workshops and enterprises to serve tiny local markets with low quality products. Instead, they should have forged the sensible horizontal subcontracting and commercial linkages with other communes and counties that would have allowed them to reap the simple benefits of specialization and comparative advantage. As cell-like units of territorial administration whose cadres only gazed upward for signals from superiors and who never looked sideways for opportunities to deal with their neighbors, communes actually stood in the way of the development of natural rural markets and modern enterprises to serve peasant needs. So the argument goes.

Such criticisms are, to be sure, one sided and overdrawn. My present purpose, however, is not to weigh the truth, but merely to outline the current indictment of past policies. Armed with this general understanding of the chief causes of continuing agricultural stagnation, the Deng Xiaoping coalition set

1. Robert F. Dernberger, "The Chinese Search for the Path of Self-Sustained Growth in the 1980's: An Assessment," in *China under the Four Modernizations: Selected Papers Submitted to the Joint Economic Committee, Congress of the United States* (Washington, DC: Government Printing Office, 1982), pt. 1, pp. 42, 48-49; see also, "The Rise in Peasant Livelihood," *Zhongguo nongmin bao,* 29 Sept. 1983.

out to do two things: to give peasants tangible incentives to produce and to give them markets in which to trade.

MAJOR REFORMS

Beginning in 1978, a series of propaganda campaigns and reforms unfolded and began taking effect in the countryside. First, there was a new emphasis on diversification in the rural economy. Staple grain production was to remain the highest priority, but peasants and rural cadres were urged to pay more attention to vegetable and cash-crop cultivation, to fish ponds and other aquatic products, to fruit orchards and forestry, to pig and poultry raising, and to other income-earning sidelines. Time and resources devoted to such subsidiary production were no longer portrayed as petty capitalist deviations, but as the kind of healthy socialist entrepreneurship necessary to generate more capital for investment in agriculture, to serve legitimate consumer demands, and to raise the standard of living in the countryside. The peasant family's right to cultivate a private plot and to use it however they wished, free to choose how to dispose of its product, was reaffirmed. Preparations were made for the reinstatement and expansion of rural fairs or free markets where peasants could sell their privately produced eggs, fruits, garlic and onions, tobacco, chili peppers, and so on at prices still regulated but higher than official state procurement prices.

The always didactic Chinese press had many an investigative field day after 1978, reporting on communes, brigades, or teams that had a comparative advantage in, say, cotton, sugarcane, or fruit and that, due to what was called the ultra-left extremist obsession with grain in the early 1970s, ripped out their valuable plants and sowed rice or wheat instead, only to reap inferior grain yields and a harvest of peasant bitterness and alienation. The outraged public posturings and the ventilation of official anger over such incidents drove home the point to cadres in rural areas with a comparative advantage in cash-crop production that they should return without fear to their specialty cultivation. Communes specializing in such products and selling their quotas to the state were no longer to encounter interference or penalties from state supply officials when they in turn sought to purchase grain for their own consumption.

A simultaneous campaign stressing the importance of production-team autonomy highlighted central determination to keep those commune and county cadres, who were heavily implicated in past leftist errors, out of day-to-day production management affairs. The lowest-level production-team leaders were to be given more leeway in determining just how best to allocate land, labor, and other inputs to meet their quotas and start new undertakings. Central leaders were betting that, in the liberalizing atmosphere, shrewd peasant team leaders all over China would find ways to overfulfill state-set quotas while still conserving resources for investment in new diversified or specialized production ventures to boost team income.

To back up these atmospheric changes, a series of substantial, phased commodity procurement price rises was put into effect throughout the country. In 1979 prices for 18 categories of agricultural products were raised. Further upward adjustments came in 1980, especially for cash crops. Increases ranged from 20 to

50 percent for different commodities, so the actual impact on incomes certainly varied greatly by area. Economists estimate the combined effect to have been a 25-to-35 percent improvement in prices paid to farmers, however, generating an immediate windfall in incomes distributed through the collective to peasants.[2] This long overdue series of price adjustments raised spirits in the countryside and gave impetus to the rest of the rural reform program.

Next, national attention was shifted to the successes claimed for a variety of new peasant remuneration systems being experimentally implemented in selected units around the country. Grouped together under the umbrella term "the responsibility system," these schemes ranged from the adoption of simple task rates for work done within the collective and over-quota bonus payments for certain jobs to across-the-board division of team land to be contracted out to individual households for cultivation.[3] What all variations of the responsibility system shared was the goal of tying individual income more directly to individual effort and skill.

In the old, more collectivist arrangement, every peasant worked on collective land for work points. At harvest time, the team's net income was divided by the total of all work points earned by all members, to derive a real value per work point. Then each household received a basic grain ration plus compensation—mostly in kind—according to the number of work points earned by all household members. In this manner, people were paid according to their work, and if their earnings were insufficient to support them, they could borrow—overdraw work-point values—from the collective. Work points were not, therefore, a fixed wage; they represented an entitlement to a certain share of the collective harvest.

Thus the compensated real value of an individual's work depended heavily on the success of the collective as a whole, which in turn depended heavily on the labor of others. And this was what the post-Mao leadership found wrong with the older arrangement; it encouraged malingering, it discouraged initiative and hard work, and it contributed to unacceptable levels of disguised underemployment in agriculture. Systems that would allow the individual more direct responsibility for actual income earned through work performed were first advocated as a supplement; later, they were quickly allowed to replace the old collective harvest-sharing model that had been one of the hallmarks of Chinese socialism.

First promoted for use in poor, backward, and mountainous areas where collective agriculture was admittedly faltering, the responsibility system, in a bewildering variety of forms, now has swept the whole country. In some areas it was embraced ahead of schedule by eager peasants who threw official timetables to the wind, and in other areas it

2. Dernberger, "The Chinese Search," p. 45; Nicholas R. Lardy, *Agricultural Prices in China*, World Bank Staff Working Paper no. 606 (Washington, DC: International Bank for Reconstruction and Development, 1983), p. 8; Frederic M. Surls and Francis C. Tuan, "China's Agriculture in the Eighties," in *China under the Four Modernizations*, pt. 1, pp. 428-29; and Dai Yuanchen, "Different Prices for Farm Products," *Beijing Review*, 22 Aug. 1983, pp. 21-24.

3. On the variety of types of responsibility systems see Tang Tsou, Marc Blecher, and Mitch Meisner, "The Responsibility System in Agriculture: Its Implementation in Xiyang and Dazhai," *Modern China* 8(1) (Jan. 1982); and

David Zweig, "Opposition to Change in Rural China: The System of Responsibility and People's Communes," *Asian Survey* 23(7) (July 1983).

was virtually forced on reluctant communities by cadres responding to signals from above.[4]

By the end of May 1983, some form of responsibility system was reportedly in use in 98.3 percent of all rural production teams in China.[5] Two forms of contracting with households now seem to be most popular. One resembles a sharecropping agreement, with the team in the role of landlord. The land, owned by the team, is divided out to households who agree to farm it and turn over a certain quota of certain crops to the team. They are paid in work points for their quota deliveries, but may keep or sell on the free market anything they produce over quota. The team meets its collective tax and sales obligations to the state, deducts some more for community welfare expenditures and investment, and distributes the remainder among the households. As part of the initial contract, the team promises to supply, at agreed prices, fertilizer and other needed inputs to the farming households. This system retains a certain role for the collective in production planning and management and maintains something of the collective harvest-sharing principle.

The second type of household contract system is a more radical departure, resembling a rental arrangement, but virtually eliminating the role of the team or collective. Land, tools, and other means of production are distributed to households that agree to make fixed payments of taxes and fixed deliveries of

commodities for sale directly to the state. Households may also be required to make fixed contributions toward community health and welfare facilities or toward the maintenance of collectively operated irrigation works, for example, but these contributions are sometimes waived. In this system there are no work points or collective harvest to distribute. Households keep for their own use all that remains after they meet their contractual obligations. If the harvest fails, they are responsible for their own losses.

With the direct incentives for hard work and carefully planned resource use entailed in these contract systems, the expectation is that peasant households will practice highly tailored and refined divisions of family labor. In large families, labor-intensive, garden-style cultivation may be practiced on the small grain and vegetable plots, while still freeing up time for some family members to work on livestock, special cash crops, handicrafts, sideline food processing, and retail marketing. Tens of millions of Chinese peasants, now freed from the necessity of earning work points by putting in time on collective lands, are taking up new part-time and full-time occupations in specialized production, market brokering, subcontracting, transport, and other services. Virtually tied to the land in the past, they now move freely between village and town, pursuing their special trades and nailing down business deals with state trading agencies, with collective units, and with other self-employed peasant households.

New rural prosperity

The effects of these reforms on agricultural productivity and rural living standards have been more rapid and

4. See William H. Hinton, "A Trip to Fengyang County: Investigating China's New Family Contract System," *Monthly Review* 35(6) (Nov. 1983), esp. p. 2.

5. Wang Dacheng, "Take the Road to Common Prosperity," *Beijing Review* 26 Sept. 1983, p. 4.

more dramatic than anticipated. With some exceptions, Chinese weather conditions have not been bad in the last few years, and output of major crops has increased across the board. Although total area sown to grain has actually declined in favor of other crops, grain production is moderately higher. Sidelines and cash-crop production have improved far more decisively: cotton increased 66 percent between 1978 and 1982; edible oils, 126 percent; and pork, beef, and mutton, 58 percent.[6] In terms of share of gross value of agricultural output over those years, animal husbandry rose from 13.2 percent to 15.5 percent, cash crops went from 14.6 to 16 percent, and forestry and fishery shares also climbed, while the value of output share of staple grain crops fell from about 68 to 63 percent.[7]

Average per capita peasant incomes rose from ¥134 to ¥270, while per capita rural consumption indicators for grain, cooking oil, meat, and synthetic fabrics and purchases of bicycles, wristwatches, sewing machines, radios, and other consumer goods registered sharp improvements. Peasants' personal savings deposits were markedly up over the period. Farm families, sensing improved prospects for the coming years, have been putting their savings into new housing at such a rate that protected forests are now endangered by the pressing demand for lumber, and bitter disputes over the availability of land for new house sites have sprung up all across the country.[8] Construction proj-

ects everywhere one looks and rural roads clogged with farmers, their animals, and all manner of vehicles getting goods to market are often the dominant visual impressions of foreign travelers returning from China today.

Some rural households with ample labor power and other resources and with access to good commercial and marketing opportunities are pulling well ahead of the average for recent years. In 1978 only 2.4 percent of rural households enjoyed per capita incomes over ¥300, but recent reports indicate that over one-third of all households now fall into that income range.[9] Such fortunate households are also now able to make private purchases of trucks and major pieces of farm equipment that will further improve their capacity for self-enrichment.[10] Examples of entrepreneurial peasant households that have taken advantage of the reforms to make dramatic improvements in personal income are featured continually in the Chinese press to encourage those still not persuaded that being the first to get rich will actually be regarded as socially acceptable and even a glorious contribution to socialist modernization.[11]

Agriculture has performed far better under the first wave of reforms than has industry, where, because of more complex institutional arrangements, the

---

6. "Output of Major Agricultural Products," *Zhongguo nongmin bao*, 29 Sept. 1983.

7. "Rates of Increase and Shares of Gross Value of Agricultural Output," *Zhongguo nongmin bao*, 29 Sept. 1983.

8. See, for example, "Properly Manage the Use of Land in Villages and Townships to Build

Houses," *Renmin ribao*, 19 Apr. 1982; Sun Xupei, "The Widespread Practice of Construction of Residences in Funan," *Renmin ribao*, 2 July 1982; and "Rectification of the Party's Workstyle Will Lead to Success in Improving Civilian Lifestyle," *Fujian ribao*, 14 Jan. 1982, trans. in *China Report*, JPRS 80380, 23 Mar. 1982, pp. 53-54.

9. Wang, "Take the Road."

10. "Peasants Buy Trucks," *Beijing Review* 4 Apr. 1983, p. 7.

11. On continuing peasant uncertainties, see "Change in Peasants' Mentality," *Beijing Review* 10 Jan. 1983, pp. 6-7.

impact of similar reform programs has been dulled. Therefore, the leadership's initial projections of higher state budget allocations for investment in agriculture have not had to be met. Individual peasant households and collectives have been investing and raising output so successfully while also using farm inputs so much more efficiently that state finance authorities have been able to realize some savings by holding state allocations to agricultural investment to about half the intended levels.

Such quick successes have led, in turn, to new waves of reform proposals and even more radical departures in rural economic organization and management. The people's commune itself, long heralded as the proudest of the new socialist creations of the Chinese people, is now targeted for virtual disestablishment nationwide by the end of 1984.[12] The old commune was consciously designed to fuse governmental/administrative functions and authority with economic decision-making authority over existing structures of residence and social intercourse, so as to create one comprehensive rural unit.

The decommunization reform under way at present calls for the effective separation of governmental and economic decision-making authority. While the term "commune" may be retained, newly established township governments are going to be handling civil administration while economic activity will be reorganized into a host of new private, collective, and state-run companies, corporations, and combines that will carry on business relations with one another through contracts, not through the old hierarchical command relationships associated with a planned economy.[13]

The intent here is to loosen the grip of unpredictable politics and unimaginative bureaucracy on rural economic organization so as to allow for the expansion of commerce more in accord with the particular natural contours of the local human and economic environment. The new flow of business is expected to cut across old administrative boundaries to establish mutually beneficial linkages and to realize economies, efficiencies, and demonstration effects that habitually eluded the previously more fully planned and locally self-reliant system.

Great numbers of such companies, corporations, and combines have already mushroomed into existence all over China. Some of them sell shares and pay dividends to collectives and even to individuals. Some are vertically integrated enterprises coordinating all elements of production, processing, and marketing of a single product such as dried fruit or frozen chickens. Some are horizontally integrated, coordinating all the agricultural, industrial, and commerical activity of a single township or county. Some consist of only a few households or individuals pooling resources and selling goods to wholesalers or selling services to other companies or individual consumers. Some deal over long distances and trade directly with both state and cooperative agencies, and even with foreign corporations. All of them are supposed to handle their

12. See "Complete the Work of Establishing Township Governments by the End of Next Year," *Renmin ribao*, 23 Nov. 1983; and "With Measured Pace and Leadership Press the Reform Separating Government and Collective in the Countryside," *Renmin ribao*, 7 Nov. 1983.

13. For more detail on the coming decommunization, see Vivienne Shue, "The Fate of the Commune," *Modern China* 10(3):259-83 (July 1984).

business through voluntarily negotiated contractual agreements. And it is in this that they differ from the state-run commercial organs of the past that worked to meet state-set quotas with inputs allocated mainly through the state supply system.

An associated development is the emergence in the countryside of what are called specialized households.[14] These are farm households whose members stop laboring on the collective's land entirely and devote all their efforts to some form of specialized production or service such as mink raising or machine repair. While many such households go it alone, others in similar lines of work tend to form themselves into small companies that undertake to guarantee quality and supply and can better command contracts from major purchasers. Some of them even hire laborers for wages to supplement the family's work. These specialized households now stand at 13 percent of all rural households in the country,[15] and they represent a new mechanism for freeing surplus rural laborers from the land and integrating them into the urban-based economy through commerce.

14. Specialized households are very prominent in Chinese reports now; for just a few interesting discussions see Jin Qi, " 'Specialized' Peasant Households," *Beijing Review* 6 Sept. 1982, p. 3; Kang Jiusheng, "Functions and Tendencies in the Development of Specialized and Keypoint Households in the Rural Economy," *Zhongguo jingji wenti*, 20 May 1983, pp. 58-61; "A New Thing That Merits Great Attention...," *Shanxi ribao*, 21 Aug. 1982, reprinted in *China Report*, JPRS 81834, 28 Sept. 1982, pp. 87-89; Lu Shoujia, "How Will the Rural Areas Develop with 'Double Contract System' in Effect?," *Renmin ribao*, 9 Mar. 1982; "Service Type Specialized Households Very Welcome in Qinghu Commune," *Zhongguo nongmin bao*, 14 June 1983.

15. Zhang Zhongyi, "China's Economy Achievements in 1983," *Beijing Review* 20 Feb. 1984, pp. 14-20.

These second-wave reforms—decommunization, the new economic combines, and specialized households—are very much in the midst of unfolding at present. It is still difficult to tell how widespread they are or how lasting they are likely to be. They are creatures of the new prosperity in the countryside. They are also clearer expressions of the present leadership's vision of the future for the Chinese countryside. They are part of the trend toward rapid commercialization of agriculture. These new economic forms regulate their business by means of contracts that in part reflect market relations. And they provide avenues for untied surplus rural labor to be integrated into the larger economy. Their current, still tentative, existence probably depends on sustaining the rural economic boom of the last few years. Sustaining that growth may prove much more difficult than getting it under way.

PROBLEMS, DILEMMAS, AND DOUBTS

All this good news of recent growth and change in Chinese agriculture has not come to us unalloyed by reservations and doubts. With so much at stake, and with so many changes occurring all at once, it is no surprise to find China's leading coalition now enveloped in a swirl of economic-structural issues, political-bureaucratic struggles, and social-ideological concerns that bid fair to remain unresolved for some time. In a short discussion such as this, it is not possible to do justice to all these areas of uncertainty. But a sense of the breadth and depth of the present dilemmas over agriculture can perhaps be conveyed by looking briefly at four general questions now under vigorous debate within China and among those in the West most conversant with Chinese affairs:

1. Is the current trajectory of agricultural growth sustainable?

2. What are the perceived and the actual effects of the reforms on the pursuit of equity and equality under socialism in China?

3. What are the likely sources and dimensions of bureaucratic backlash to the reforms?

4. How will the Party's leadership resolve its own internal divisions and ambivalences over the benefits of market socialism versus the need for a comprehensive state plan and strong central direction in an economy as diverse and a polity as fractious as that of China?

Sustaining growth

Without question, the reforms outlined previously, especially the procurement price rises and the widespread adoption of the responsibility system, have induced an impressive spurt of growth in agriculture. Latent entrepreneurial energies, buried savings, and idle labor have all been mobilized at once to invigorate the rural economy. But this spurt may rather quickly run its course if some of the economic distortions it has engendered are not soon brought under control.

Because of the central planners' commitment to subsidize food prices for urban consumers, the rapid leap upward in prices paid to peasants has put an inordinate strain on the central budget. Chronic central-budget deficits over the last few years have been more than a minor annoyance, and they have been very much the result of the exploding costs of subsidizing urban consumption. The equivalent of 25 percent of national-budget revenues has recently

been going to such subsidies,[16] suggesting that there is deep anxiety among Chinese leaders about the political-economic losses that could come with urban unrest.

As noted earlier, direct state investment in agriculture has been lowered in recent years, easing this budget strain somewhat. But given the emerging pattern of farm family expenditure of recent windfall profits, that decrease must be little consolation for central finance authorities. Peasant consumption is up sharply and family savings are being poured heavily into new private housing, because property rights in housing have always been guaranteed to China's peasants and because family housing is the only major item of private inheritance for succeeding generations. Peasant investment in housing is, of course, competitive with investment in agricultural production; to sustain the current rate of growth, direct state allocations to agricultural investment may therefore have to be raised once again. Furthermore, insofar as certain forms of the responsibility system are undermining the social salience and the economic strength of the collectives, team-, brigade-, and commune-supported capital-construction projects such as irrigation works may lapse or fall into disrepair, creating further pressure on central revenues to take up the slack.

In view of these likelihoods, central authorities may soon face some hard choices between effectively raising taxes on farm incomes or passing some of the costs of higher farm prices onto urban consumers in the form of higher food prices—with the inflationary pressures that would entail. For reasons like these, Western economists following Chinese

16. Lardy, *Agricultural Prices in China*, p. ii.

affairs are looking for a retightening of controls in the rural sector before long.[17]

Equity and equality

For 25 years the undisputed major social cleavage in China has been between urban dwellers and rural dwellers. By any measure, peasants as a group have had a lower standard of living, greater income insecurity, inferior education and welfare services, and far less opportunity for upward mobility than their privileged urban compatriots. Thus, insofar as the current reforms have improved the welfare and life chances of peasants vis-à-vis workers and state employees, they have made a long overdue contribution to social equity in China. Few who are acquainted with the realities of grinding poverty in the Chinese countryside find it possible to quarrel with the impact of Deng Xiaoping's reforms on these grounds. But from the point of view of newly emerging patterns of intra-village and interregional inequality, the matter is much more in doubt and is the subject of heated dispute both in China and in the West.

As some agricultural regions with fertile lands, favorable climatic conditions, well-developed irrigation systems, or a comparative advantage in cash-crop cultivation are permitted to specialize and build on their strengths, they will realize profits for reinvestment that will soon put them far ahead of more poorly endowed regions. China has always had its regional disparities, of course, but current policies threaten to widen them significantly, while credible mechanisms for interregional redistributions are not yet in place. Sensitivity and uneasiness over these issues are already very much in evidence among Chinese officials. The ethos of developmental equity has a long, if not unblemished, history in China, and the representatives of underprivileged rural districts can be expected to draw heavily on that moral heritage in the infighting for special investments and subsidies over the coming years.

With the adoption of the rental type—that is, the so-called full responsibility systems—and the emergence of specialized households, the issue of intra-village inequality and faltering provision of collectively financed social services has become even more urgent, and the media have made a concerted effort to blunt criticisms of the reforms and reassure the Chinese people on this score. Statistics are released to show that China's very poorest peasants are absolutely better off under the reforms even as it is admitted that the gap between the richest and poorest peasants is widening.[18]

But in a boom period such as we have just seen, it is not surprising that nearly everyone will be doing better. The concern is for the longer term, for the economic downturns and slumps. It has been the team and brigade collectives that have provided the safety net for the poorest. The collective guaranteed a job and minimum subsistence. Now in many areas collectives are selling even their tractors and other equipment to individual households.[19] Formerly collective

---

17. See, for example, Nicholas R. Lardy, "Agricultural Reform and the Rural Economy" (Paper delivered at the Annual Meeting of the Association for Asian Studies, Washington, DC, 23 Mar. 1984).

18. Jin Qi, "The Income Gap," *Beijing Review* 21 June 1982, pp. 3-4; Wang, "Take the Road."

19. Keith Griffin, "Epilogue: Rural China in 1983" (manuscript, Oxford University, n.d.) presents some interesting data gathered in Sichuan on sales of team assets to households.

irrigation works can now be managed as companies—for profit and on a pay-as-you-go basis.[20] The collective's functions are diminishing. Contracts and market relations are spreading, and with market values goes the expectation that there will be winners and losers in the game.

Not every peasant household can become specialized. Not every family will be blessed with male children. Not everyone can escape serious illness. Without a strong and authoritative collective organization, who will enforce the village welfare contributions in bad harvest years? Among Chinese peasants, frustrated by long years of stagnation and waste, support for the new policies is clearly very broad; but we do not yet know how deep it is. We will have a better idea when they are tested by harder times. Even now there is plenty of evidence of concern and conflict over the weakening of communal norms of distribution. When we read a crime report in the Chinese press about a mob of unprovoked rural vandals and pilferers breaking into a pear orchard, recently contracted out to one household, and stealing the fruit and breaking down the new wall around it, we would be justified, I believe, in suspecting that many of those in the mob were fraternal team members who had put in their share of back-breaking labor in that orchard in past years and who were there to protest its privatization and to reassert their rights to the harvest.[21]

Bureaucratic backlash?

Throughout the lower-level bureaucracy there are officials who have long been deeply committed to the progressive and egalitarian social policies of the past. Consciousness of their misgivings about the potential consequences of some of today's reforms and calculated attempts to short-circuit their objections are often clearly visible just below the surface of public discussions of these issues in China now. As household-based economic activity flourishes at the expense of collective organization, some segments of the rural population are going to feel the effects more than others. Women who used to labor on the collective, for example, will now spend nearly all their time working in the family context where they are directly subject to patriarchal authority. They may find some of their personal freedoms curtailed once again in their relative isolation in conservative, male-dominated households.[22] The labor of children for the household now can net sums that a few years ago were unimaginable; children—and especially the girls—may be dropping out of school much sooner to go to work.[23]

The rural primary school system itself may soon be much changed, with poorer communities losing their better teachers to towns and villages able to offer higher salaries and more amenities.

20. On irrigation see, for example, Lin Ben and Yan Zhenyu, "Solution to the Problem of Farmland Irrigation Difficulties," *Fujian ribao*, 18 Mar. 1982, trans. in *China Report*, JPRS 81009, 9 June 1982, pp. 15-17.

21. An incident that raises some of these questions was reported in "Anhui Province Arrests Looters of Fruit Farm," *Daily Report: People's Republic of China*, 4 Dec. 1979, pp. 01-02.

22. Margery Wolf, *Revolution Postponed*, (n.p., forthcoming) makes this argument most persuasively.

23. Yi Mu, "Attention Should be Paid to Rural Students Who Unlawfully Quit Schools," *Shanxi ribao*, 26 Oct. 1982, trans. in *China Report*, JPRS 82440, 10 Dec. 1982, p. 123; a helpful account of the effects of the agricultural reforms on rural education can be found in Deborah Davis-Friedmann, "Provision of Essential Services in Rural China," in *Rural Public Services*, ed. Richard Landsdale (Boulder, CO: Westview Press, 1984).

Poorer peasants also may be finding that previously collectively operated clinics where they could be treated at very low cost are now being run as companies and raising fees for services. Health care for some may therefore be declining.[24] If such tendencies are not contained, if they are aggravated and become contentious, they will provide grist for the mill of those within the bureaucracy who are skeptical or resentful of the current line.

Some of the reforms are actually directly threatening to rural cadres themselves, of course. As the functions of the collective diminish, there is less for team, brigade, and even commune cadres to do. In many villages these people were glad to shed their arduous and relatively unremunerative leadership roles for the chance to get back to family farming and marketing. In other villages, however, cadres resent the loss of prestige, the small perquisites of office, and the relative job security of the past. This group of local notables may just be waiting for present policies to run into difficulty, when they will find a constituency for reassertion of the old forms.

For commune and county cadres, the situation is complicated by an ongoing campaign for upgrading the quality of rural administrative personnel. The center is pushing for younger people with higher quality, more specialized technical training.[25] There are now

responsibility systems for cadres, too, that tie their incomes to success in meeting contracted targets and that carry pay penalties for failure. Salaries are no longer so secure; previously fixed promotion routes look doubtful in all the ongoing reorganizations. Many state and Party cadres, who are in effect becoming executives and employees of the newly forming companies and corporations, are having to adjust even to the possibility of lay-offs and firings. While many low-level bureaucrats may welcome these challenges, reports out of China today make no secret of the fact that many others are worried by it all, dragging their feet and sometimes even sabotaging reforms that threaten the securities of the old system.[26]

The dilemmas seem especially poignant for those rural cadres who have made Party work their specialty. With decommunization and the deliberate separation of politics from economic management, what profile the Party can expect to have in the countryside is far from clear. Party membership used to be one of the essentials for talented young people mapping out a career in China. For many today, the future looks brighter in independent entrepreneurship. Vigorous media assertions to the contrary notwithstanding, rural Party workers are already struggling with a growing sense of their own irrelevance.

Yet the center still needs committed people in the countryside. All the new contracts will have to be monitored and enforced. Labor flowing from countryside to cities and towns will have to be

24. Davis-Friedmann, "Provision of Essential Services in Rural China"; see also William C. Hsiao, "Transformation of Health Care in China," *New England Journal of Medicine,* 5 Apr. 1984, pp. 932-36.

25. See, for example, "Jining Prefecture Assigns Agricultural Technicians to Commune Leading Posts," *China Report,* JPRS 82782, 1 Feb. 1983, pp. 102-3; "Jiangsu Villages in the Midst of Decommunization, Basic Level Cadres Heading toward 'Four Transformations,' " *Zhongguo nongmin bao,* 28 June 1983.

26. See, for example, Wang Jiafu et al., "On Several Problems of Understanding in the Course of Executing the Economic Contract Law," *Renmin ribao,* 27 Aug. 1982; "Liaoning Popularizes 'Double Contracting System'," *China Report,* JPRS 92983, 16 Feb. 1983, pp. 94-96.

regulated. The increased scope for black markets and other illegal economic activity will have to be controlled. People committed to keeping a socialist orientation in development must remain on the job, or the viability of central planning and the legitimacy of the entire system will be in doubt. Right now these indications of cadre dissatisfaction and bureaucratic backlash are but a minor leitmotiv in what is otherwise an idyll of praise over the new reforms. Latent bureaucratic discord, however, like latent concern for communal equality, may swell into outright opposition and resistance if the reforms do not continue to deliver economic growth or if they appear to be going too far too fast.

Weighing plan and market

Just how far and how fast all these reforms should go is certainly not a matter of complete agreement among Chinese leaders today. Published discussions of the need to reconcile state plan and market forces in such a way that they reinforce, and do not compete with, each other most often consist of platitudinous abstractions, suggesting just how difficult it is, in current Chinese conditions, to reach real consensus about concrete aspects of the work of remolding the economy.

The expansion of the role of incentive schemes and of market relations was initially inspired by the desire to promote production and growth in agriculture so that the state could capture greater resources for national investment. Those in leading circles who strongly favor market solutions now argue that they be even more broadly applied to boost popular confidence in the current line and release even more entrepreneurial enthusiasm. But those in the leadership who remember that the ultimate goal was supposed to be to enhance the ability of the state to plan and coordinate rapid development are uncomfortable when bureaucratic controls are loosened. They worry that the state will not be able to claim a sufficient share of the new prosperity to maintain its leading role in the economy.

Their concerns do not appear to be premature. Many of the new economic combines are, after all, direct competitors to elements of the state-run economy; their operations may expand the economic pie, but they can also take business and other resources away from state organs. The new companies and combines have usually also been given very favorable effective rates of taxation, allowing them to accumulate impressive sums of capital in a short time. And once in possession of such resources, they do not readily give them up. The decentralization of economic decision-making authority that has come with expansion of market relations is already causing enormous difficulty for central planners trying to cut back the overall rate of capital construction in the country.

Runaway spending on new projects not in the state plan but undertaken by localities and other low-level units has reached amazing proportions. Excessive decentralization in finance led to reports in 1983 that extra, or over-plan, investment had reached almost 40 percent of the year's total budgeted investment figure.[27] Local units with money to spend were obviously ignoring central finance directives. A related phenomenon is the failure of general state revenue to increase in accord with overall economic growth. In 1982 revenue amounted to

27. "Quarterly Chronicle and Documentation," *China Quarterly*, no. 96, p. 764 (Dec. 1983); see also "About Extrabudgetary Investment," *Beijing Review*, 26 Sept. 1983, pp. 26-27.

only 25.5 percent of national income, the lowest proportion ever recorded.[28] Tax breaks and special revenue sharing arrangements that have accompanied the reforms are taking a heavy toll on the center's resources for leading the economy and commanding desired responses from the localities.

A struggle for power between the central government and local authorities is one of the major continuing themes of modern, as well as ancient, Chinese political history. The impact of the present reforms is to put more power and discretion in the hands of local officials and the managers of less bureaucratically tied new business entities. This in turn triggers anxiety on the part of patriots and Party regulars for whom socialism must mean guidance of the economy by a strong and centralized apparatus. These latter groups could make common cause with those forces in China that still favor the more radical social policies of the past; and together they might push for a rollback of the market reforms.

In this sense too, then, the Deng Xiaoping coaliton is taking an enormous political gamble. For if they are able (1) to maintain rapid agricultural growth while (2) containing the intrabureaucratic backlash to the reforms and (3) keeping the distortions in the norms of social equality within tolerable

28. "Quarterly Chronicle," p. 765.

bounds, then they will probably have enough public support to take the time they need to institutionalize the mechanisms for a workable blending of plan and market throughout the economy. But if, on the other hand, growth in agriculture starts to fall off and/or intrabureaucratic and popular dissatisfactions are seen to rise, then central leaders will want to rein in the reforms quickly. But the more they have allowed working capital and decision-making authority to come to rest in the localities and in the new economic combines, the more difficult it will be for the central apparatus to reassert its dominant leadership and control. I do not mean to imply that the state center would actually be unable to reassert control; only that the longer the commercializing, market-oriented reforms are in place and taking hold, and the more power seems to settle downward within the system, the bloodier and more politically costly that battle to reassert central controls will have to be.

China's new course in agriculture is, therefore, complex and very risky. Its early successes have been impressive, but prospects for continued high rates of growth are open to question, and potential detractors and opponents of the reforms can be found at all points in the polity. As seems so often to be the case in Chinese affairs, the stakes for the Chinese people are very high, and the future still very much in doubt.

*   *   *

QUESTIONS AND ANSWERS

Q (Lynn White, Princeton University, New Jersey): Many problems—government deficits, rural inequality, maybe party legitimacy, and others—can at least be delayed if the responsibility system continues to bring a good economic response. Has anybody studied when the marginal returns from the responsibility system will decline?

A: I think the responsibility system developed much more quickly than it was originally intended to develop by the center in China, and the response on the part of the cadres in the countryside has been one of playing catch-up with that mass over-response. Nicholas Lardy is intensely studying the future prospects for all these agricultural reforms, and it was to his work that I referred when I said that some economists were looking at this phenomenon and predicting retightening of controls in the future, but they are predicting it with the same inexactitude that I was. The areas that are possible constraints on the pattern of growth under the new reforms have been pinpointed, but the growth pattern is still risky to predict.

Q (Robert Serry, Mission of the Netherlands to the United Nations): Could the reforms in Chinese agriculture be generalized to the Soviet Union?

A (Walder): In a talk at Columbia University, Alec Nove mentioned that the Soviet Union is considering some decentralizing reforms. In fact, the Soviet reforms are vaguely similar to the ones used in China, although apparently the Soviets are not studying the Chinese reforms as a model. One of the points Nove made is that household-based agriculture simply cannot be implemented in the Soviet Union, because Soviet agriculture is so widely mechanized—those combines cannot just be pulled apart. Decentralization in the Soviet Union would be a breakdown into much larger units than in China. The resistance to linking output to reward on the household level is less ideological than technical.

Population Movement, Labor Force Absorption, and Urbanization in China

By SIDNEY GOLDSTEIN *and* ALICE GOLDSTEIN

ABSTRACT: Concern in China with problems of rural-urban population distribution, rates of urban growth, and relations between employment opportunities and rural and urban development have resulted in a firmly articulated policy regarding population movement. Permanent movement from rural to urban places and from smaller to larger urban places is strictly controlled. Yet the pressures of a large surplus labor force and the introduction of the new economic responsibility system have led to a substantial increase in population mobility, most of it temporary. Such circulation has become a major mechanism to allow rural areas to cope with their surplus labor and to raise rural standards of living. It has also allowed urban places to gain the skilled service workers and unskilled construction workers that are in short supply without putting undue pressure on urban facilities.

Sidney Goldstein, Ph.D., is George Hazard Crooker University Professor and professor of sociology at Brown University, as well as director of Brown's Population Studies and Training Center. He has undertaken research and published widely on migration and urbanization, with a particular focus on Southeast Asia, and, more recently, on China.

Alice Goldstein, M.A., is senior researcher at the Population Studies and Training Center, Brown University. She, too, has been involved in extensive research on population issues, and she has collaborated on the Southeast Asia and China projects.

NOTE: The research reported in this article was carried out by the authors in China, March-May 1983, under an Award for Advanced Study and Research from the Committee on Scholarly Communication with the People's Republic of China (CSC-PRC) of the National Academy of Sciences. The analysis is based primarily on discussions and interviews with officials, policymakers, and scholars and on observations during visits to various urban and rural locations. The authors are grateful to the CSC-PRC and to the Hewlett and American Express Foundations for funding and for the logistic support provided by the Population Research Center of the Chinese Academy of Social Sciences, which acted as sponsor for the investigators in China.

MIGRATION represents a major mechanism by which populations adjust to demographic pressures and by which equilibrium is achieved in the labor market. Its importance in population redistribution and its relation to development—and to urbanization in particular—has been long recognized and extensively studied, even when the data have been seriously restricted for such purposes. Moreover, researchers and policymakers are increasingly coming to recognize the importance and pervasiveness, both historically and currently, of short-term, temporary movement—circulation—as one response in the wide variety of adjustments populations make to changing conditions. As yet, however, no clear, consistent definition has emerged by which to delineate circulation, and research on motivations for such movement has only begun to document the decision-making process.[1] Nonetheless, it is clear that the possibilities of household labor reallocation and employment opportunities are factors in determining both the extent of population stability and, among those who move, the choice of circulation versus more permanent migration.

The question then arises as to how circulation and migration complement each other in the complex process of modernization and national development and what role each plays in the changing labor force needs of urban and rural places. Research in Africa, Southeast Asia, and Melanesia suggests short-term movement has come to play an important role in the development process in these regions, not only from the point of view of the individual or the household, but also from a national perspective.[2] Circulation helps to adjust labor supply and demand on a regional or even national basis without the social dislocation that large-scale permanent migration may entail and without placing the added strains on cities that would be created by the influx of a large group of migrants. It may also allow for the provision of services through the informal sector that are in short supply otherwise. Concurrently, the flow of funds and ideas that circulation engenders may become a critical component of rural modernization.

In recent years a large number of countries have identified migration and spatial distribution as a severe problem.[3] Given the concerns with the problems of big cities and with rural-urban migration, temporary movement together with rural development may well provide governments with the basis for alternative distribution policies. Circulation may become a major mechanism by which some or many of the undesirable effects of permanent migration on the mover and on conditions at origin and destination can be avoided or at least reduced. We know little about these relations, largely because of the limited research done on temporary movement. As a result, planners and

1. Murray Chapman and R. Mansell Prothero, "Themes on Circulation in the Third World," East-West Population Institute, Working Paper no. 26 (Honolulu, HI: East-West Center, 1982).

2. Ibid.

3. In 1981, 75 of 126 less-developed countries considered their distribution of population to be inappropriate and to require substantial modification, and 45 other countries considered it to be only partially appropriate; only 6 less-developed countries regarded their population distribution as acceptable. United Nations, Department of International Economic and Social Affairs, *World Population Trends and Policies: 1981 Monitoring Report*, vol. 2, *Population Policies*, United Nations, Population Studies no. 79 (New York: United Nations, 1982), tab. 49.

policymakers have been slow to recognize the role circulation may have in the national development process, especially in the redistribution of the labor force.

In this respect, the situation in China may be of particular interest because of that nation's centrally planned economy and carefully articulated and controlled migration policy. To some extent, Chinese planners have recognized the value of temporary mobility as an alternative to permanent migration and have provided for it in the more formal planning process. To an even greater extent, they have recognized the need to develop alternative nonagricultural job opportunities in rural areas and small towns as a way to absorb surplus rural labor.

The concerted efforts of the Chinese government to control population growth through its one-child family policy has, understandably, received worldwide attention. Less well known outside China is the considerable attention given by Chinese government officials at all levels to problems related to the rural-urban distribution of the population, to the rates of urban growth, and to the relations between employment opportunities and rural and urban development. These concerns have led to the emergence of a clearly and firmly articulated policy regarding population movement and the distribution of population between rural and urban places and among urban places of different size.

China's efforts in these areas, like those in fertility control, are of critical significance for the future development and modernization of the nation. Moreover, the efforts to control population distribution and to achieve orderly urban growth merit continuing monitoring and evaluation for the lessons they may provide for other developing countries. To the extent that many developing countries have rated problems of population distribution even higher than those of population growth,[4] China's experiences will be of particular interest for the insights they may provide on how to avoid many of the negative consequences of too rapid urban growth at the same time that the benefits of urbanization for the overall development process and for the absorption of surplus rural labor can be realized.

Of the approximately 1 billion people enumerated in China's third census, just over 206 million were living in its 236 cities and 2664 other urban places.[5] With only 1 out of every 5 persons living in cities, China has a comparatively low level of urbanization. But because of the very large numbers involved, China has more people living in urban places than constitute the total populations of all but three other countries in the world— the United States, the Soviet Union, and India. The Chinese situation is particularly challenging and interesting because, concurrently, almost 800 million persons still live in rural areas and are largely engaged in agricultural activities.

4. United Nations, Department of International Economic and Social Affairs, *World Population Trends and Policies: 1979 Monitoring Report*, vol. 2, *Population Policies,* United Nations, Population Studies no. 70 (New York: United Nations, 1980).

5. According to the State Council, a city is defined as a place that contains a population of at least 100,000 or, if it has a smaller population, as the location of the provincial leadership organs. Other places are defined as urban (1) if they contain 3000 or more people, of whom at least 70 percent are engaged in nonagricultural activities; or (2) if they have populations of 2500-3000 and at least 85 percent are nonagricultural. Li Chengrui, "On the Results of the Chinese Census," *Population and Development Review,* 9:331 (June 1983).

Therefore, as the Chinese themselves recognize, the concerted efforts now in process to modernize and develop the country must sooner or later involve the absorption of several hundred million more rural persons into nonagricultural activities and possibly into urban places.

As in other countries, considerable motivation exists among the rural population to move into cities. As is true worldwide, differentials in quality of life remain great between urban and rural places, even after concerted efforts to reduce them. Better housing, sanitation facilities, and educational opportunities; more varied entertainment; and availability of consumer goods all provide convincing stimuli for a shift from village to city.

In China a second factor also operates: the difference in ownership systems that characterize urban and rural places. In cities, most job opportunities exist in state-owned enterprises, in contrast to collective ownership in rural areas. In cities, therefore, the state is responsible for providing jobs to all able-bodied residents. Such employment has been particularly attractive because it carries job security, stable and higher income, free medical care, retirement pensions, housing subsidies, and other fringe benefits for the workers and their families. Such lifelong security—the iron rice bowl—has acted as a powerful attraction for peasants whose current income depends in large part on natural forces and on decisions made by the collective leadership about distribution of income, and for whom old-age security, other than support from children, has been far from institutionalized.[6]

6. Deborah Davis-Friedmann, *Long Lives: Chinese Elderly and the Communist Revolution* (Cambridge, MA: Harvard University Press, 1983), pp. 18-19.

Although some of these factors will undoubtedly change with the institutionalization of the responsibility system, to be described more fully later on, the attraction of urban places for peasants is likely to remain strong. Because of this and because of the vast size of the rural population reservoir, China potentially faces in exacerbated form many of the serious problems associated with urban growth and rural development confronted by other less developed countries. The Chinese situation is much more critical because of the much larger population involved and because of the rapidity with which change is occurring in China. Even a 10 percent shift from rural to urban would involve 80 million persons and lead to about a 40 percent increase in the urban population. On the other hand, the Chinese have already given considerable attention to the problems of both population growth and population distribution and, over the course of several decades, have experimented with various efforts to control urban growth—especially the growth of big cities—and to absorb surplus labor in rural areas and smaller urban places.

There is, of course, also a third difference. The nature of the political situation in China is such that once a given policy is adopted, it can be implemented more rapidly and thoroughly than in most other developing countries.

China is thus concurrently embarked on several policies designed to deal with its demographic problems: the one-child family policy, strict control of urban growth, and regulation of population movement. It has also introduced a new agricultural responsibility system, designed to increase agricultural productivity, absorb surplus rural labor, and raise the quality of life in rural areas.

Each policy is designed directly or indirectly to affect one or more aspects of the population system. Yet, because all are interrelated, each policy has a potential impact on how people react to the other efforts to control population growth and distribution. This article will focus on the impact of the responsibility system on population movement and the problem of surplus labor.

THE INDIVIDUAL RESPONSIBILITY SYSTEM

Despite the high hopes for agricultural production following introduction of the people's communes in 1958, China's agricultural output in the next two decades failed to gain the desired momentum. The increase in the agricultural output value of only 84 percent, coupled with a population that grew from 646.5 million to almost 1 billion, meant that per capita gains in crop production in the next two decades were minimal at best. The Chinese government recognized the urgent need for change and in 1979, consonant with the general effort toward modernization, adopted a new agricultural policy.[7]

This policy has a number of key components, including

—the restoration and enlargement of private plots for peasants;

—the encouragement of household sideline occupations and rural trade fairs;

—an increase in the purchase prices of major agricultural and sideline products;

—import of 10 million tons of grain annually in order to lighten the burden on peasants;

—a shift from stressing grain production to a more diversified economy, thereby enlarging the avenues open for income generation; and

—the establishment of a flexible production responsibility system, capable of being tailored to local conditions.

A 1983 estimate indicates that as many as 93 percent of rural production teams in China had introduced the responsibility system.[8]

As a result of these changes, agricultural output value is reported to have risen substantially over the following three years, at an annual average of 7.5 percent compared to an average of 3.2 percent in the preceding 26 years, 1953-1978.[9] The nation tallied an increase in grain, cotton, and oil-bearing crops, and a substantial rise (about two-thirds) in peasant per capita income, with almost half of the total average annual income—that is, ¥107 of ¥223 (US$1 = ¥2.4)—derived from private plots and household sideline occupations. Moreover, rural-urban differentials are beginning to narrow, as indicated by changes in the relative income for peasants and city workers. Between 1978 and 1982, the average net income of peasants is reported to have risen by 93 percent; in contrast, that of workers rose by only 58 percent. Reflecting these changes, the disparity between the two groups was reduced by 21 percent, with a parallel reduction in the 1978 disparities in expenditure between the urban and rural population.[10] A key factor in the great

7. Lu Baifu, "The Way for Agriculture," *Beijing Review*, 24 Jan. 1983, pp. 14-17, 21.

8. "New Achievements in Rural Economy," *Beijing Review*, 5 Sept. 1983, pp. 6-7.
9. Wang Dacheng, "Take the Road to Common Prosperity," *Beijing Review*, 26 Sept. 1983, p. 4.
10. "Peasants Closing the Gap," *China Daily*, 9 May 1983.

progress made in agricultural production is seen to be the responsibility system per se.

The responsibility system is based on contracts involving three parties: the state, the collective, and the peasant household. At the highest level, the state works out the rural production plan, assigning types of crops and volume to various regions and allocating quotas to the collectives. The collective, in turn, through its production brigades, contracts out tracts of land to peasant households who agree to grow given quantities of the specified crops. The collectives are also responsible for distributing work animals and large and medium-sized farm tools to peasant households. At the lowest level the peasant household is required to deliver its quota to the collective and, through it, to the state. The collective retains a share of the earnings from the sale of the crops for its own use. The balance of agricultural production is owned by the peasant households and is subject to an agricultural tax at the household level.

Within this broad, general framework, variations exist in the application of the responsibility system in different communes, as the following examples illustrate. In an agricultural complex located on the outskirts of Beijing, the responsibility system operates in two ways. One method involves giving an annual quota for production to a group of peasants—not individual households. The group must fill its quota by growing and selling products and giving *yuan* to the complex; the complex, in turn, gives work points, which have monetary value at the end of the year. If the quota is overfulfilled, 30-50 percent of the surplus cash is divided among group members; the rest goes to the complex.

The second method involves the signing of a contract between the complex and the contracting unit. The complex has 1400 contracting units, of which 400 are individual households and 1000 are groups of households that have agreed to work together. The contract stipulates that 20 percent of the income generated is given to the general complex, that the unit pay a state tax, and that it pay a 5 percent management fee to the subcomplex. The remaining income is divided among unit members. Peasants can decide for themselves which system to follow.

At all times, ownership of the land remains with the complex, which also decides exactly what is to be grown. The economy thereby remains planned. Moreover, the products are sold to the complex, which in turn sells them to the state at prices fixed by the state; they are not sold on the free market. Peasants are also allocated individual plots, however, with all members of a specific brigade given an equal amount of land—for example, in one brigade 300 persons divide one hectare equally. The amount of land allocated to a single household thus depends on the number of persons in that household. Peasants are free to sell whatever they produce on these plots at free markets.

A somewhat different approach is illustrated by the Lijia brigade, part of a Shandong commune located outside the city of Weifang. The brigade's 170 agricultural workers are divided into eight groups; it is these groups that sign contracts with the brigade. The amount of land assigned to a group depends on the number of its workers. If the group exceeds its production quota, the excess products—grains as well as vegetables— must be sold to the brigade. The excess is bought at a price that is higher than the contract price, but none of it may be sold on the free market. Nor does the brigade provide its members with private plots. The group divides its income on the basis of work done, taking into account the amount as well as the productivity of the land cultivated by its individual members. This system is used by some brigades in the commune; others sign contracts with individual households.

The agricultural responsibility system clearly permits variation in interpretation by individual communes. For the peasant household it allows flexibility in organizing productivity and especially a high degree of self-management. Work assignments are no longer randomly determined by arbitrary orders. Yet the responsibility system conforms to the socialist principle of distribution, namely, that those who work more also receive more income. Within the limits imposed by the agreement with the collective, the peasant has the right to use the land to maximum advantage, although he has no right to sell, lease, or transfer the land. At all times, the land is owned collectively, as are the large farm machines and irrigation systems. Public ownership of the basic means of production—land, machines, and water—it is argued, ensures maintenance of the socialist system of agriculture.

The responsibility system is thus seen as a key element in China's efforts to modernize while meeting the needs of its largely rural population. At the same time, the kinds of activities encouraged under the new system have had considerable, and sometimes unforeseen, impact on several of the nation's other policies, including efforts to increase food production, to control population growth, and to limit movement into cities.

According to reports in the Chinese press, in some locales where peasants are enjoying greater returns from commodity production, some see little benefit from being committed to agriculture.[11] They have therefore begun returning their contracted lands to the commune. Most of the peasants adopting this attitude are from households specializing in industrial and sideline production or involved in commune- and brigade-operated enterprises. Evidently, part of the problem stems from what are considered burdensome taxes and other expenses imposed on the peasants by some communes. By engaging exclusively in industrial production and sideline activities, such taxes may be avoided. In other locales, peasants who preferred farming and were especially successful farmers enlarged contract areas and began specializing in the production of particular crops, usually not grains, to their greater advantage. Such crops may not always be the ones most needed by the nation as a whole.

Introduction of the responsibility system also led, in many places, to reactions that had significantly negative implications for the success of family-planning programs in rural areas. As families realized that their incomes would be affected by productivity, many evidently concluded that larger families would be an economic asset. More children, it was thought, would provide more labor that could be used either to exceed agricultural production quotas or to earn income in nonfarm activities. Such conclusions were reached after calculating the relative monetary advantages of having more than one child against the added costs incurred through

11. "Readjusting Rural Contracted Farmland," *Beijing Review,* 24 Oct. 1983, p. 6.

both childbearing expenses and the loss of benefits given to one-child families.[12] Still others evidently concluded that the added income and grain generated from the responsibility system was more than sufficient to allow enjoyment of a higher standard of living for the family as a whole while also allowing adherence to more traditional values concerning family size and sex preference.

The potential threat of such attitudes and behavior to the success of the one-child family policy was recognized early by officials. A concerted effort has therefore been undertaken, both through education and through more concrete measures, to prevent the responsibility system from indirectly undermining the family-planning program.

In many areas of China, peasants are now called upon to sign two contracts. In these, two kinds of production are taken into account: agricultural production and human production. Under the contract relating to production of children, a couple agrees that if they have more than one child—in rare instances, more than two children—the benefits reaped from their economic contract will be curtailed. This may take the form of

—loss of extra land for private plots that is given as a bonus to the one-child family;

—assignment of responsibility for growing a less lucrative product, for example, grain instead of fruits and vegetables;

—an increase in the quota of production that must be delivered to the state, for example, from 400 to 600 jin per mu;

—assignment to less productive land;

—loss of job preference in one of the commune's workshops or factories; and

—an actual monetary penalty to be paid to the state.

Overall, therefore, two responsibilities are simultaneously stressed, one with respect to production of products and the other with respect to the production of children. It is clear, however, that efforts to control fertility in this way have not met with universal success; it was reported that it is still difficult for peasants in remoter areas to understand and appreciate the policy. In other areas, especially in the more fertile and productive provinces, such as Guangdong, many peasants are willing to pay the penalties for having more than one child. Again, the importance of an intensive education program is stressed, as is the importance of the development of nonagricultural activities that, it is hoped, will stimulate stronger linkages between rural and urban places, including increasing adoption of urban values by rural residents.

One manifestation of the growing links between village and urban place has been an increase in the geographic mobility of peasants. Here again, the responsibility system is having an impact on China's policies for urban growth and migration.

12. An important element in the success of China's one-child family policy is an elaborate system of incentives and disincentives. Although the specifics of implementation may vary from one province and local area to another, one-child families are clearly given preferred treatment with respect to education, child-care services, medical care, job placement, housing space in urban places and land allocation in rural areas, and family allowances. The policy also calls for reliance upon necessary and feasible restrictive measures, which may take the form of negative applications of these incentives.

POLICIES FOR URBAN GROWTH
AND MIGRATION

China's strategy for future urban development grows out of the belief that the rapid growth of big cities has given rise to many problems related to housing, employment, and infrastructure, and that the number of big cities and the size of their population need correction. China also recognizes that the needs of its rural masses—numbering 800 million—must be met. Urbanization, it is therefore argued, must be harmonious with the development of industry and agriculture; this, in turn, requires that city development be tied to agricultural production and that heavy industry must serve light industry and/or agriculture. The need to develop all three concurrently lies behind the basic urban policy of (1) strictly limiting the size of big cities; (2) properly developing medium-sized cities; and (3) encouraging the growth of small cities and market and agricultural towns.

Whereas big and medium-sized cities are seen as the location of heavy and light industry, small cities and towns are viewed as the potential location for handicraft and workshop activities, with labor supplied largely from the rural surplus. Such places, it is argued, require less investment while they also serve as catalysts for changing rural into urban populations. What is perhaps most interesting about the stress on the development of small places as the proper course of urbanization is the magnitude of the transformation that it would involve. Although planners recognize that any one town can absorb only a limited number of people, they point out that the large number of such places allows the aggregate effect to be great. For example, if each of the nation's 2100 county seats increased its population to

50,000 persons, 39 million people would be absorbed over the current 61 million county town residents. And if each of the 54,000 commune seats increased to an average of only 5000 persons, some 270 million would be resident in these centers.

Paralleling China's urban policy and closely tied to it is its policy on migration. Above all, migration must fit the needs of the planned economy, and any movement that is allowed, especially to urban places, must be compatible with economic development. Since urban growth is to be carefully controlled, migration to urban places must also be carefully controlled. A set of specific principles has been developed to meet these goals:

1. Rural-to-urban population movement must be strictly controlled. This applies especially to movement to Beijing, Shanghai, and Tianjin.

2. Movement from town to city, from small to big city, from rural places to suburbs must be properly limited.

3. Movement between places of similar size does not need control.

4. Movement from large to medium or from medium to small urban places, or from urban to rural places should be encouraged.

The basic mechanism by which such movement is controlled and defined is the household register system. Each individual in China has an official place of residence, the record of which is maintained at the brigade level in rural areas and at the neighborhood level in urban places by the Public Security Bureau. To effect a permanent change in residence, permission must be granted by the appropriate authorities in the places of origin and/or destination. Peasants can generally obtain an urban household register in only one of three ways:

1. Enrollment in a university carries with it urban household registration, which is then retained.

2. If cities expand and take over farmland, peasants displaced in the process may become entitled to urban household registration. The same may be true if factories or the railroad takes over the land, even though the city itself does not expand.

3. Permanent employment in an urban place leads to urban registration, but in such cases family members of the employee must generally retain their rural household register, even if they in fact live in the city.

Altogether, the number of peasants who are issued urban household registration is relatively small. In Shandong Province, for example, rural-to-urban migration constituted 24 percent of all migration in 1982. The balance comprised persons who already held urban household registration. Of the 24 percent, half were students enrolled in universities; almost all the others were workers employed by factories. Only a very small proportion consisted of family members of workers and cadres who were being reunited in the cities.

The net result of these combined policies is seen not only as a way to avoid big-city growth while still providing urban job opportunities and spreading urbanism as a way of life, but also as the best way to integrate the city more fully with the countryside. Serving as a key link between urban and rural would be the small cities and towns, which have both urban and rural characteristics.

How is such development of small cities to occur? Local industry and small workshops operated by communes and brigades are seen as providing the operative mechanism. In some areas, such as Suqian County in Jiangsu Province, peasants are actually given governmental help in making the transition from agricultural to nonagricultural activities. Such help takes various forms, including financial assistance, provision of raw materials, and technical training. Peasants may obtain permits allowing them to become specialists in such service activities as tailoring, carpentry, and blacksmithing, and even to hire up to three apprentices. Others may be given permission to open shops or operate small factories, or to purchase tractors, carts, or boats for transportation. Technically qualified peasants may be allowed to operate nurseries, bookshops, or clinics and are offered technical guidance to enhance the quality of their activities.

That these economic activities constitute a drastic break with earlier restrictions is recognized by the state. Accordingly, reports indicate, the government is providing legal protection and adequate publicity to the new policy as a way of ensuring that peasants are not deterred from engaging in such activities out of fear of being stigmatized by fellow peasants by being out-of-line.[13]

As such brigade and individual enterprises increase and involve more of the rural population, the resulting concentration of nonagricultural activity is expected to provide the basis for the development of small towns, with a concomitant growth in transport, communication, and service sectors. Some of the workers would then be allowed to trans-

13. Jing Wei, "Responsibility System Revives Jiangsu Countryside" *Beijing Review,* 28 Nov. 1983, pp. 17-22.

fer their household registration to the towns, while others continued to commute from villages. Moreover, it is anticipated that as service and industrial activities develop, financial resources for development of the infrastructure will be generated.[14] Thus, use of local land, local labor force, and local natural resources will combine to provide the basis for absorbing surplus rural labor and creating small towns.

The linkages to larger urban places are reinforced by these developments. One such link is created through the tie-in of small, rural factories with large, urban plants. The small workshops produce component parts for the larger factories, thereby obviating the need for more urban construction and for the movement of workers into cities. Production of commodities for the urban market also helps relieve the pressures resulting from the inability of urban industry to meet market demand.

Such interaction between urban and rural industries and the involvement of urban experts as advisers to the newly developing rural industrial and commercial activities provide further opportunities for urban ideas and know-how to spread to rural areas. Most important, given the government's strong determination to control big-city growth,

14. Funding for such development is seen as coming primarily from the commune or brigade savings that are being generated by the responsibility system. Local government may also provide some capital. Further aid would come from urban-based factories and unions that might contract with communes to make various components for their products and would thereby provide raw materials, equipment, and possibly even land. The state ministries, such as the railroad, may also assist by providing land. Once a town is sufficiently developed, the state then expects to step in and provide some of the needed infrastructure.

is the contribution rural industry has made to the creation of urban facilities in rural locations, already stimulating the transformation of some commune seats into small towns. The location of small factories and commercial establishments in such places, coupled with the use of commune income to improve school, medical, recreational, and business facilities as well as roads and other infrastructures allows peasants to enjoy more of the amenities of urban life and thereby helps both to improve the quality of rural life and to reduce the desire to move to cities.

While narrowing the preexisting gap between rural and urban places, rural industrialization is not without its problems. Environmental pollution from industrial waste is already troublesome, calling for concerted remedial efforts to prevent serious damage to agriculture and fish production. Energy shortages present another serious challenge; lack of sufficient energy has impinged on the speed of rural development and has added production costs in those places where energy supplies have had to be transported great distances. A third immediate concern focuses on lack of adequate planning with respect to the choice of products to be produced. It seems ironic that, in a highly planned economy, many decisions are evidently made in terms of locally perceived market conditions. As a result, reports suggest, too much duplication of effort occurs, with many small factories producing the same product, leading either to underutilization of factories or to production of surplus products. Recognition of the need for better planning and even for consolidation may serve to correct this situation in the future.

Despite these problems, rural industrialization is proceeding at a rapid pace and is being welcomed at all levels. As a brigade leader in Jiangsu Province pointed out,

To live better, you must run industry and sideline occupations in a big way while doing a good job at farming. How can one count on farming alone for a better life when our village has only an average of 0.05 hectare of farmland for each person?[15]

Indeed, China's policymakers and planners believe that, if these policies can be successfully carried out, in the process, everyone wins: big-city growth is controlled, urbanism is enhanced, rural labor surplus is absorbed, and economic and social links between rural and urban areas are strengthened.

THE PROBLEM OF
SURPLUS LABOR

Because the responsibility system encourages greater efficiency in the use of manpower and peasants can themselves decide on manpower allocation, a large number of peasants are no longer required for farming and are regarded by officials as surplus labor. As many as 200 million peasants may be displaced by the year 2000. In addition, approximately 20 million rural youths are also entering the labor force annually. Absorption of this huge number of persons into productive rural employment is a major challenge that is being met in a variety of ways, several of them related to the responsibility system.

One response, at the household level, has been the proliferation of peasant sideline activity. This may involve raising pigs, ducks, or geese, or the growing of fruits or vegetables on private plots.

15. Jing Wei, "Industry Thriving in Jiangsu Countryside," *Beijing Review,* 12 Dec. 1983, pp. 20-23.

These items can then be sold either to the state or in the free markets. Such sideline production has led to a larger volume and better quality of marketable agricultural products. Peasants may also engage in producing small handicraft items, such as baskets or small wooden bowls, which they can easily sell themselves. Others may engage in cottage industry, under contract to brigade- or commune-run workshops.

The most lucrative endeavors, however, are hauling for construction companies. Most villagers—men and women— who engage in such efforts use two-wheel carts that are manually pulled. No onus is attached to such work since it reportedly generates among the highest incomes in the entire village. Some of these individual endeavors have been so successful that as many as 20 peasants in one brigade had already been able to save enough money since the introduction of the responsibility system to buy small trucks. The trucks cost about ¥6000 but generate earnings of as much as ¥10,000 a year when used for construction hauling.

At the commune and brigade level, the response has taken the form of a very substantial growth of rural industry: food processing, production of farm-related products such as fertilizer and small farm machinery, construction supplies such as cement and bricks, and other small industrial products or components. Such development is a key component of the new economic policy and is closely related to the responsibility system. It has resulted in the absorption of an increasing proportion of the rural labor force. In May 1983 it was estimated that China had 1.3 million commune- and brigade-run enterprises, which employed a total of 30 million workers.[16] These account for more than 10 percent of China's total industrial output value. The experience of some communes will perhaps best illustrate how the system works to effect change and the amount of variation that exists in how it is applied in different settings.

One example is provided by a brigade on the outskirts of the city of Luoyang. The major agricultural activities focus on growing winter wheat, corn, and tobacco, with the fields divided among the households on a per capita basis. The vegetable fields are cultivated by small teams. Of the 1200 villagers, 500 are members of the labor force; but over the last few years some 120 were surplus labor, and 20 young people enter the work force each year.

In order to absorb this surplus, the brigade has developed a number of sideline industries, including a workshop making construction components and a brick-making workshop. These workshops operate under contracts from a factory in the city that also provides the raw materials to the brigade. In addition, the brigade raises fish in three large fish ponds and recently opened a bakery to make cookies and cakes. It buys its raw materials from state stores and sells directly to shops in the city. Indicative of how highly motivated the workers are to develop these new enterprises further, the bakery employees had taken Sunday to go into the city to learn about hygiene and quality control. The brigade head reported that they plan to enlarge the present factories to continue to absorb surplus workers. The enterprises were seen as particularly appropriate since they required relatively low skill levels

and thereby matched the quite limited qualifications of the labor force.

On a much larger scale than the activities of this Luoyang brigade are the projects of an agriculture, industry, and commerce complex—formerly a commune—outside Beijing. The complex includes 28,000 persons in the labor force, of whom 19,000 are engaged in agriculture and 9000 in nonagricultural work. The complex produces 10 percent of the agricultural products, especially vegetables, needed by Beijing's population, yet two-thirds of its gross output value results from nonagricultural products and services. Among the nonagricultural activities are 16 factories producing such varied items as farm tools, conveyor belts, furniture, cement, water drums, and tractor carts. These factories are run by the complex itself; the 20 subcomplexes have additional factories providing still more diversity.

It is evident that the responsibility system has worked well here. Not only has the quality of agricultural produce improved; peasant income has also risen. In 1978, before the responsibility system was introduced, the average per capita income was ¥229. By 1982 it had risen to ¥500. The complex also reported that it had no problem of surplus labor. Young people were able to engage in farming while waiting for jobs in factories. It was pointed out that since the introduction of the responsibility system, young people did not mind engaging in agriculture since they could use their training to increase output and therefore to increase their income; in the past, added skills could not be used to great individual advantage.

Not only has the reorganization of commune activities directly benefited its members; by generating greater income for the complex itself, a variety of social

16. "New Firms to Help Rural Collective Enterprises," *China Daily*, 23 May 1983.

services are now provided. Hospital care is provided free, nursery and kindergarten fees have been cut in half, a retirement system has been instituted, and a home for the childless aged has been constructed. The complex has built a cultural center, housing a library and several recreation rooms, and films are routinely shown. A number of urban amenities have thus been introduced as part of the complex's goal of raising the quality of life for its members. By so doing, it is argued, the desire to move into the city itself is attenuated.

Even in those communes where nonagricultural work was introduced long before institution of the responsibility system, workshop activity has proliferated in recent years. A brigade in Shandong Province introduced nonagricultural activities as early as the mid-1960s; it has since built restaurants and hotels and also has organized transportation and construction teams. The rapid change in the character of the brigade is evidenced in the statistics on its labor force. In 1960 the nonagricultural workers constituted only 20 percent of the total labor force. That figure increased to 35 percent by 1970, and to 60 percent by 1980. By 1983 three-fourths of the labor force was engaged in nonagricultural activity, and only one-quarter of the brigade's total income was derived from agriculture; the rest came from industrial output and sideline activities.

The decision of who goes into agriculture and who enters nonagricultural work is made among the brigade members. Individual preferences are taken into account, as well as the training and likely future development of individuals. For example, young people with more education may be trained for skilled work, and may even be sent elsewhere for specialized training. Those with

greater physical strength may be assigned to work in agriculture; middle-aged peasants with rich farming experience are likely to stay in agriculture. As agriculture becomes more scientific and mechanized in the future, it is expected that the greater need for skilled labor will provide growing opportunities to those who would like to remain in rural areas but also wish to use their education to greater advantage.

In response to the changing balance between agricultural and nonagricultural work, some rural households may, in cooperation with others in their brigade, withdraw from crop raising altogether and devote their energies entirely to industrial enterprises. But specialization may also occur in agricultural production. In several brigades in Wuxi County, for example, such agricultural activities as the raising of rice seedlings were contracted out to households with special expertise. The labor thereby saved was, in turn, utilized for industrial or sideline production under the responsibility system. These changes were seen as ensuring a more balanced and integrated development of industry, agriculture, and local sideline production.[17] More commonly, one or several household members will participate in rural-based industry while others within the same household will continue to engage in farming—referred to popularly as "half-industry, half-agriculture households."

The foregoing examples of the operation of the responsibility system suggest that these efforts are clearly serving several purposes. They are raising rural income, providing jobs for a large proportion of the surplus labor force, and they are forging links between rural

17. "Farm Production a Matter of Balance," *China Daily,* 23 May 1983.

areas and the cities. If these changing conditions thereby reduce the desire for rural-to-urban migration and make small towns and villages desirable places in which to live, then the new policy will have succeeded in one of its major goals. But until such programs are sufficiently widespread and well established, a strict migration policy remains in place throughout China. At the same time, however, the volume of temporary mobility in China is consistently reported as having increased rapidly in recent years as a result of the responsibility system and in part in response to China's policy of restricting permanent movement to its cities and towns.

TEMPORARY POPULATION MOVEMENT

The temporary movement of surplus rural labor into urban places emanates largely from the sideline activities encouraged by the responsibility system. At least four different forms of temporary mobility can be identified.

1. One prominent way in which the individual responsibility system has fostered movement is manifested in the free markets that are proliferating in cities. Among peasants living in the suburban districts surrounding the inner city, from which travel to the market is relatively easy and fast, daily circulation is perhaps the most common form of mobility. In the early hours of the day scores of individuals can be seen walking, bicycling, and pushing or pulling carts en route to markets. The largest number bring agricultural products that they have grown and/or gathered themselves. Some bring handicraft products that they have produced; and still others may be serving as middlemen, bringing goods that they have purchased from other peasants in their commune. Most, it was reported, are able to dispose of their products in a single day either through retail sales or a combination of such sales and sales of the remaining products to state markets. Some will be able to make use of storage facilities for unsold products in the marketplace itself or in the homes of friends or relatives to avoid carrying the products back to the suburban communes.

For those coming from rural—as opposed to suburban—areas, for whom the travel time is longer, the circulation process may be extended over several days. Some individuals actually fly from one province to another in order to take advantage of markets where their products are much rarer and therefore more in demand and likely to sell at higher prices. Evidently restrictions on such long-distance mobility have been gradually relaxed and recent announcements suggest that such movement may even be encouraged as part of the flexibility associated with the responsibility system.

2. Still another way in which the individual responsibility system fosters migration involves the commune or the brigade per se. A growing number of communes and brigades are operating shops in the city for either agricultural or industrial products produced by the commune. In such instances the commune evidently receives permission from the city to operate the enterprise and is expected to pay an appropriate tax to the city. Members of the commune or brigade are assigned to live and work in the city for a specified period. There is often a regular turnover in personnel who continue to be considered rural residents even while living in the city, based both on the locus of their household register and because they receive their grain ration through the

commune. Usually such migrants are not accompanied by family members.

In Handan, an industrial and mining center in Hebei Province, for example, more than 10,000 peasants living in the various communes surrounding the city now work in hotels, cinemas, restaurants, and other enterprises sponsored by their communes and brigades.[18] An additional 10,000 peasants are reported as operating private enterprises, such as snack stands and shoe repair services. As a result, only 60 percent of the rural labor force continue to farm the land, and 20 percent of the communes' aggregate income of ¥130 million comes from the service industries they operate.

3. Communes and brigades also contribute to mobility between rural and urban areas through the initiation of contracts with unions engaged in construction. Under such arrangements, the commune provides a specific number of construction laborers. Usually these are young and male. They may shift from city to city, as old contracts are completed and new ones initiated. In some instances work assignments in a particular city may continue over several years, as, for example, in construction activities at major universities. The number of such construction workers in China is considerable. In Guangzhou alone, it was estimated that as many as 30,000 to 40,000 individuals were living in the city under such contract arrangements.

Even more may be doing so in such places as Shenzhen, Foshan, and other urban places that are undergoing expansion. Indicating that reliance upon peasants as construction workers in cities is likely to increase is a recent statement by Xiao Tong, vice-minister of urban and rural construction and environmental protection. He reported that construction of new buildings in satellite towns and in industrial and mining areas will be undertaken mostly by rural collective teams on a contract basis.[19]

4. A fourth form of mobility exists that probably represents the most drastic adjustment of the system to changing conditions in rural areas. Despite the absorption of large proportions of the surplus rural labor in nonagricultural activities in rural areas, in commune-operated shops in the cities, or through commune contracts with unions for temporary workers, many peasants are evidently without work. On their own, they have decided to engage in service or sales work in other rural or urban places. Some are domestics or engaged in child care; some sell their services as carpenters or mattress makers, for example. Still others may become itinerant merchants. While away from their official village of residence, they live with relatives, friends, employers, and sometimes even in small hotels. Most frequently, they seem to engage in the kinds of activities that allow them to obtain housing, jobs, or grain and oil rations without having to obtain a household register in their new location. A domestic, for example, can live with her employer and draw upon her employer's grain and oil rations, while holding a job clearly not assigned by the government. A carpenter can do the same, taking advantage of the housing and food provided as part of the return for his services as he moves about from one assignment to another.

Unfortunately, no body of statistics is readily available to document the volume and characteristics of these various

18. "New Jobs from Shrinking Farmland," *China Daily*, 2 Mar. 1983.

19. "Peasant Builders to Take on Bigger Role," *China Daily*, 10 Mar. 1983.

types of temporary movement. This difficulty reflects the nature of the registration system. Although a permanent, legal transfer of household registration is carefully controlled and documented, temporary movement is not. Temporary residents can easily obtain temporary registration from the Public Security Station if they are living with relatives or friends. Residence in a hotel or in union facilities requires no temporary registration at all. Temporary residents involved in free markets are registered with the Industrial and Commercial Bureau. The net result is a complex system of registration that does not lend itself to centralized statistics or at least to their ready availability.

This deficiency is recognized, not only by researchers, but also by city planners. They perceive the growing importance of temporary movement to cities and the demand it is creating for and on hotels, restaurants, recreation facilities and parks, transportation, and sanitary and health facilities. City planners are frustrated at not being able to ascertain the volume and character of such movement so as to take better account of it in planning. An estimate for Chengdu City, for example, suggests that as many as 50,000 persons may be temporarily residing in the city, exclusive of daily commuters. This is probably a minimal figure since it is based only on records kept in neighborhoods and hotels. It also does not indicate the length of stay, the amount of turnover, or the purpose of the sojourn.

Another estimate suggests that as many as 1 million persons are entering or leaving the inner city daily as commuters. These consist of factory workers and staff, junior and senior school students, and peasants. Still another survey, conducted by the Labor Force Department of Chengdu, shows that 40,000 peasants commute daily to temporary work in the city, other than the free market. Of these, 10,000 are approved by the municipal government for temporary construction or porterage work with unions. The other 30,000 are not officially approved and are engaged primarily as private workers in such jobs as carpenters, domestic servants, and nurses.

This evidence of heavy temporary migration is also indicated by a case study of a nearby commune in which 10 percent of the 10,000-person labor force has jobs in the city. Of the 1000, about 600 are in construction work contracted by the commune; 100 serve as porters; and 300 are engaged privately.

If anything, these data suggest that the overall estimate of 40,000 peasant temporary migrants for the city may be too low. Although only estimates, these data nonetheless support the conclusion that mobility in its various forms and especially temporary movement play a key role in the demographic and economic dynamics in China.

Clearly, temporary migration has become a major mechanism by which rural areas cope with their surplus labor and with the challenges introduced by the responsibility system for raising the quality of rural life. From the point of view of the rural area, such migration allows the surplus labor to engage in productive activity and not become a liability to the brigade or the commune. By going to the city or to another rural area to earn income, the individual is able to contribute to the support of agricultural development through remittances used by the brigade for purchase of machinery, fertilizer, and other items. At the same time, since such individuals usually go to the city only if they know they can find employment, they are not seen as putting pressure on urban facilities, but rather as providing a desirable function. All these temporary urban dwellers, as well as the rural labor force engaged in nonagricultural work, are thus considered to be contributing to the modernization of the countryside, forging links between the countryside and the city, and integrating farming, industry, and service activities.

"LEAVE THE LAND BUT NOT THE VILLAGE"

As much of the foregoing discussion has made clear, one of the functions of the responsibility system is to provide the mechanism whereby surplus rural labor can turn to nonagricultural activities while still largely maintaining a rural base. This is being achieved by encouragement of a more diversified economy, including the development of forestry, animal husbandry, sideline occupations, and fisheries; establishment of joint enterprises combining agriculture, industry, and commerce; and establishment of service trades and cultural and educational facilities in rural areas and commune seats. Closely tied to these changes, the responsibility system has also stimulated considerable temporary movement, some over great distances, from rural to urban places. This circulation has provided still another mechanism for absorbing surplus labor, for transferring capital from urban to rural places, and for satisfying the desires of many peasants to participate in urban life.

Such temporary movement and the expected job opportunities to be provided by rural-based industry and sideline activities in small towns should serve to prevent the surplus rural labor force from flooding into the large cities on a permanent basis. Such development is thus regarded as a way of avoiding the experiences of other developing countries, which have been characterized as having led to the mass movement of population into big cities and to the transfer of rural poverty to urban places. In contrast, the Chinese argue that their new agricultural policy and the responsibility system provide the best approach to raising the income level of the rural population, to creating more job opportunities for the anticipated massive increase in surplus rural labor, and to fostering the eventual concentration of commodity production and specialized activities in selected rural areas that have the potential of becoming small urban centers.

The success of all such efforts in the longer run depends on the success of the family-planning program, for unless the large number of young people now entering the work force—about 20 million annually—is reduced substantially, the ability of the economy to absorb the surplus labor created by modernization and by mechanization of agriculture will be seriously threatened. The one-child family policy is designed in part to meet this threat. Even if the policy is successful, about 10 million people will be added to the population each year until the year 2000.

Yet, in spite of greater rural income resulting from the responsibility system and in spite of controls on urban growth, the attractions of the cities remain strong, especially in areas other than those surrounding such major centers as Guangzhou, Shanghai, Chengdu, and Beijing, where opportunities have flourished and where many rural residents report themselves as happy to stay in rural areas. In more remote and poorer areas, the turnabout in attitude has not taken place and is not likely to do so until the standards of living are raised substantially and the urban-rural differentials reduced much more. The complexity of the linkages between fertility, migration, and urban growth is perhaps best illustrated by the story told of a family-planning worker who asked a peasant couple, "If you could have anything you want in return for having only one child, what would it be?" The response came quickly: "If you guarantee we can change our registration to the city, we'll have only one child."

*   *   *

QUESTIONS AND ANSWERS

Q (Dario Scuka, Library of Congress, Washington, D.C.): What is the impact of the loss of farmland as urbanization expands and small towns are created? And what is the source of capital formation for this new infrastructure in the absence of a credit economy?

A (S. Goldstein): The loss of farmland is a serious problem that the Chinese are concerned about. As you may know, in the case of big cities in particular, they have adopted a procedure to try to control farmland loss. The procedure is to incorporate a number of the rural counties into a municipality in order to ensure that the city proper has enough farmland surrounding it to provide it with its daily needs for produce and to ensure that factories, housing, and the like do not take over too much rural farmland. I am not aware of the particular devices that the small towns themselves are using. I suspect it is not a problem that Chinese officials have yet faced because they simply do not yet see the small towns as taking over that much farmland. In part they envision a large number of the individuals whose economic activities are in those places to continue to live in the rural locations.

With respect to the capital, while there are some loans that will be available, it is assumed that to a great extent most of the capital will in fact be generated by the rural population, by the communes. Through a process of remittances and sales, the commune will then have the surplus income to develop the infrastructure of the small towns themselves; loans will be available from larger governmental units only where such assistance is essential.

———

Q (Joan Gregg, New York City Technical College): It is my impression that, since the Chinese are very attached to their children, an only child has more of an option to remain with his or her family than does a child with siblings. Where a family has more than one child, all the children except for one will be sent to other places. Do you think that if each family is only going to have one child that the government will take this into account in redistributing the population, that is to say, that the government will take more care to keep that one child within the district where the parents live? Or do you think that the government will continue to shift populations, irrespective of the parents' being bereft of all children?

A (S. Goldstein): I do not see how the government can introduce that policy because the idea, if it works, is for most of these families in fact to have only one child. In theory there should not be many families with two, three, or four children. Adoption of the policy you advocate would mean that every child would be allowed to stay at home or in the same location. That would make it very, very difficult to carry out the other kinds of economic planning that require that, once individuals receive certain kinds of education, the state then has the right to assign them to jobs in other locations. So to my knowledge, subject to correction, there is no plan to give priority of the kind you suggest. However, this may change 10 or 20 years from now when these children are entering the labor force and when parents are aging.

COMMENT (Cho): If China wants to accomplish the stabilizing of its population at 1.2 billion by the end of the century, something like 85-95 percent of the couples would have to have one child. Therefore, if a non-relocation policy is introduced 90 percent of the people would be confined to their localities; such confinement would not be practical.

———

Q (James Schulz, Brandeis University, Waltham, Massachusetts, and Gerontological Society of America): The migration question, the one-child family policy, and the inability to prevent or the need to allow the one child to move away from the parents raise a general question: how will parents be supported in their old age?

A (Cho): My understanding is that China is a socialist country, and therefore elderly people are taken care of. I am referring to the system of five guarantees for all households, through the collectives, of food, housing, clothing, medical care, and funeral arrangements. The impact of the new responsibility system on the system of five guarantees has yet to be assessed. The elderly are taken care of at a certain subsistence level; they will not be spending their retirement in luxury. The one-child policy is implemented in the context of the government's provision of subsistence-level care for the elderly. The situation, of course, is different in countries like Korea and Taiwan, where I would say that at this point a good majority of the elderly are dependent upon their children. I think that dependence on children would be much less in China as it is a socialist regime.

COMMENT (S. Goldstein): This is not my area of expertise, but I think in the urban labor force, individuals are entitled to pensions when they retire. The pensions amount, if I remember correctly, to something like 75 percent of their wages. The pensions are one of the attractions of urban places. In the rural areas there is no such pension system, as far as I know. It is up to either the children or the commune to take care of older individuals. Such care is actually a provision of the Chinese constitution, so that if children do not care for their parents, they could literally be punished.

COMMENT (Philip Olson, University of Missouri, Kansas City): According to information I received when I was in China in the fall of 1983, there are now a number of communes that have introduced a pension system. Those communes are mostly in the metropolitan areas, not in the outlying rural areas, but there is now a pension system in the more well-to-do communes.

———

Q: Do you have the impression that the control over temporary migration is completely in the hands of individual urban authorities? Do you know what the central government is doing about that, if anything?

A (S. Goldstein): One of my biggest surprises when I was working in China was the amount of local variation. I went there expecting homogeneity in policy across the country. While there is a certain abstract homogeneity, when it comes to implementation there is tremendous variation. In virtually every community where we conducted research, policy was implemented slightly differently. Depending on how much pressure the communities were under, some worked under the law of averages, some on a person-by-person basis, while all of them tried to adhere to the general formulation.

My general impression is that at the moment temporary migration itself is not very extensively controlled because leaders are trying to feel their way. They realize they have to allow a considerable amount of temporary migration if the responsibility system and the different ways of handling the problems of surplus labor are to be at all successful.

Nationally, because they have not collected much data on temporary migration, they really do not know how much of it is occurring. One of the purposes of my next trip to China is to provide training in how to do research on this topic, because they finally have decided that they have to learn something about it if they are going to have a policy on it.

At the moment I do not think temporary migration is a serious problem and I do not think the national authorities are very much worried about it. To some extent I think they see it as a form of experimentation. In talking to a few government officials I was told that China hopes, as the population pressure decreases and as economic conditions improve, to be able to relax some of its current restrictions on permanent migration. The Chinese see temporary migration as a way of experimenting to see what would happen if permanent migration were less restricted. If temporary migration works, they might let it continue. If not, they may impose stricter controls on it. In theory they have a way of controlling it; in practice they do not seem to do so to a great extent.

Population Dynamics and Policy
in the People's Republic of China

By LEE-JAY CHO

ABSTRACT: This article reviews recent changes in population policy and demographic trends in the People's Republic of China. Recently available estimates of birth and death rates for the last several decades are examined in the context of political events and disruptions in China. China heralds the world's most comprehensive and perhaps most effective birth control program, aimed at stabilizing the Chinese population at 1.2 billion by the turn of the century, and has made remarkable progress in controlling population growth during the last decade. The dramatic fertility decline in recent years is analyzed and compared with the trends in Japan, Korea, and Taiwan. The extent of China's fertility decline is found to be unequaled anywhere in the world. A potential conflict between promotion of agricultural production by individual families through the new responsibility system and the birth control policy is also discussed.

Lee-Jay Cho is director of the East-West Population Institute and chairman of directors at the East-West Center and adjunct professor of sociology at the University of Hawaii. He has served the governments of Malaya, Indonesia, and Korea as a demographic adviser and has been a member of the U.S. National Academy of Sciences Committee on Population and Demography. His publications include Population Growth of Indonesia *and* Differential Current Fertility in the United States.

NOTE: The author is grateful to Professors Ronald Freedman and Philip Hauser, Chi-hsien Tuan, and Hoil Choi for their valuable suggestions and comments on this article, and to Robin Loomis, Janis Togashi, and Sandra Ward for their assistance. This research is supported in part by funds from the Hewlett Foundation.

ALTHOUGH China's population constitutes almost one-quarter of the world's total, until recently little was known about it. From the outside, it was difficult to assess either the size of the population or growth trends. Moreover, because of political upheavals, including the Cultural Revolution, it was difficult to conduct population research within China.

In the last few years we have witnessed dramatic changes in the collection of Chinese population information. In light of such statements as Deng Xiaoping's on the "deplorable absence of annual series of statistical data, and the need for real social science research," [1] the changes are understandable. A census was conducted in 1982, the first since 1964; it was followed several months later by the National Fertility Survey, covering one in a thousand households. Furthermore, the Chinese government restructured its administrative organizations to allow for development of better population policies and programs. In consequence, demand for population data and their scientific analysis has increased greatly.

The 1982 census counted a population of 1.008 billion in mainland China. This is almost double the 1949 figure of 542 million. There appear to have been three major waves of population growth during the last 30 years. Between 1950 and 1959 the average annual absolute number of births was around 20 million, and from 1962 to 1970 the annual figure was 26 million. With the massive implementation of planned birth programs in 1971, average annual births showed a moderate decline to about 20 million

and were further reduced to 18 million during the years 1976-81. The annual average growth rate slowed from 2.6 percent in 1970 to 1.5 percent in 1982; this decline is especially dramatic when translated into absolute numbers. [2]

Since 1949, when the People's Republic of China (PRC) categorically denied the existence of any population problems, China has shifted its position on population policy; it has now emerged as the nation with the world's most comprehensive and perhaps most effective birth contol program. Its leadership is committed to stabilizing the population growth rate in the shortest possible time. There appears to be a consensus among outside observers that the PRC has made remarkable progress in reducing its population growth rate during the last decade. [3] This conclusion is confirmed by the results of the 1982 census and the National Fertility Survey. [4]

2. *Quanguo qian fen zhiyi renkou shengyulü zhouyang diaucha fenxi* [China 1982 National Fertility Survey] (Beijing: State Family Planning Commission, 1983).

3. Pi-chao Chen, *Rural Health and Birth Planning in China* (Research Triangle Park, NC: International Fertility Research Program, 1981); Ansley J. Coale, "Population Trends, Population Policy, and Population Studies in China," *Population and Development Review*, 7(1):85-97 (Mar. 1981); John S. Aird, "Population Studies and Population Policy in China," *Population and Development Review*, 8(2):267-98 (June 1982); Tuan Chi-hsien, "China's Population in Perspective," in *China among the Nations of the Pacific*, ed. Harrison Brown (Boulder, CO: Westview Press, 1982), pp. 69-83.

4. The sampling ratio for the survey was one one-thousandth and the sampling unit was a street committee in the urban areas and a production brigade in the rural areas. The survey, which interviewed 310,485 units—there were only 23 refusals—employed the address list of the 1982 census to conduct face-to-face interviews on basic household questions and birth histories of women of childbearing ages.

1. Deng Xiaoping, *Selected Writings* (Beijing: People's Publishing, 1983), p. 167.

REVIEW OF PRC
POPULATION POLICY

It is useful to look at China's birth control policy for two broad periods, 1956-70 and 1971-83. In the mid-1950s the PRC was officially committed to a policy promoting birth control, but only after the Cultural Revolution ended in 1976 did a fundamental change take place in the leadership's perception and hence in birth control policy and its implementation. At that point the issue of overpopulation began to assume significance for modernization and development policy. In the absence of clear, long-range guidelines, birth control policy between 1956 and 1970 shifted between leftist and rightist lines, reflecting the continuing political and ideological struggles over the issue of population control. But the last decade has witnessed the emergence of a stronger policy and a more unified and gradually intensifying fertility control campaign. These developments were discernible in 1976, especially after Chairman Mao's death and fall of the Gang of Four.

The early period

Chairman Mao's famous statement in 1949—that people are the most precious of all things—was to become the principal premise of all subsequent statements on the population question in China.[5] Mao simply rejected the notion that population posed any problem in the Malthusian sense; and to the extent it was recognized that China had

a problem, Mao sought the solution in the ideology of revolution plus production. Mao's uncritical reliance on Marx and, perhaps, his ignorance of fundamental demographic laws inhibited the planners and policymakers in Beijing in the early years of the Communist regime from realistically raising the issues of population growth and birth control.[6]

The PRC embarked on its First Five-Year Plan in 1953. The government was alarmed by the result of the 1953 census, which revealed that the population was growing at a rate of well over 2 percent per annum. Consequently, it quietly began to take measures to promote birth planning and relaxed restrictions on induced abortion. By 1956, birth control as a national policy seems to have been firmly established. It became clear that in the controversy over an official position on birth control the view of such moderates as Zhou Enlai had prevailed.[7] In 1957 Mao made his well-known anti-natalistic statement that the human race in its procreation had been in a state of total anarchy and had failed to exercise control.

China's first active birth control campaign in the 1950s turned out to be short lived, however. Mao's Great Leap Forward, first heralded in late 1957, essentially relied on a large-scale rural labor force to achieve capital construction. Again the leftist view of accepting China's population as an asset rather than a liability gained prominence during 1958.

The failure of the Great Leap Forward and subsequent natural disasters in China created one of the country's

5. See, for example, Chen Pi-chao, "The Politics of Population in Communist China: A Case Study of Birth Control Policy" (Ph.D. diss., Princeton University, 1966); Tien H. Yuan, *China's Population Struggle: Demographic Decision of the People's Republic of China* (Columbus: Ohio State University Press, 1973).

6. Liu Zheng et al., *China's Population: Problems and Prospects* (Beijing: New World Press, 1981).

7. Chen, "Politics of Population in Communist China."

worst economic crises, and between 1958 and 1962 the birth control campaign, for all practical purposes, came to a standstill.

As part of the government's effort to recover from the economic disaster, in the early 1960s China resumed its campaign to promote birth control. Restrictions on induced abortion and surgical sterilization were lifted, and the production and supply of contraceptives were increased.

The Birth Planning Office of the State Council was established in 1964. Corresponding functions in the provincial and autonomous regions provided a basis for the organization and large-scale implementation of birth control policy. However, this second birth control effort, which appeared to have some impact, was abandoned also, in 1966, this time because of the Cultural Revolution. Although the campaign was not officially called off, there was virtually no progress in birth planning in China over the next four years.

As political order was gradually restored in the late 1960s, the birth control policy was slowly resumed. After two decades of vacillation and hesitation, China accepted its demographic realities in 1970 and finally cleared the way for what has come to be regarded as the world's most effective population policy and program.

Birth control policy since 1971

As Chairman Mao gradually withdrew from the active political scene, Zhou Enlai and his moderate supporters began in the early 1970s to push steadily toward modernization. Since then, China's birth control policy and program have been more consistent and vigorous. The objectives of the policy have become clearer and more specific. The program has been diversified and strengthened. There is clearly a new commitment on the part of China's leadership to economic modernization and development, which can be seen as part of the government's decision to redirect national priorities after the ravages of the Cultural Revolution. That commitment has emerged despite the cost of some modification in the Communist ideology.

After Chairman Mao's death in 1976 and the subsequent fall of the Gang of Four, the modernization of agriculture, defense, industry, and science and technology—called the four modernizations—became China's task of highest priority. That leadership regarded the solution of the population problem as an essential part of the modernization effort is reflected in the 1978 and 1982 PRC constitutions. Chairman Hu Yaobang stated in his report to the Twelfth Party Congress: "In the economic and social development of our nation, the population problem is the most important problem. The implementation of the family planning program is one of the basic national policies."[8]

The great emphasis placed on family planning has been translated into a massive communication campaign directed at the Chinese people. From remote villages to large cities, family planning messages are ubiquitous—on large billboards, on television, and in scholarly journals.

Over the past decade there has been a shift in the rationale for family planning. At one time emphasis was on the

8. Xu Dixin, "On the Relationship between Population Growth and Economic Development," in *Renkou yenjiu* [Population research], People's University of China, Institute of Population, no. 2 (Beijing: China Publications Center, 1983).

welfare of mothers and children. Now it is on improving the standard of living for the masses, providing employment for the rapidly increasing labor force, raising per capita gross national product, increasing per capita arable land and productivity, and improving housing and sanitary conditions.

It is to be emphasized that the PRC distinguishes its efforts to reduce the population growth rate from any form of Malthusianism. Justification of the birth control policy is officially regarded as being consistent with Marxist principles. This view has been stated by Xu Dixin:

"Our objective in the implementation of the family planning program is to bring about an appropriate relationship between population growth and socialist economic development; and also under the socialist system, we must plan human reproduction just as we plan material production." [9]

Significant changes have occurred in the Chinese population control program. Since the 1970s the government has actively promoted three reproductive norms as the basic guidelines for family planning. These norms are implicit in the campaign slogan Late, Sparse, and Few, which refers to the timing of marriage, spacing of births, and number of children, respectively. In the cities men are urged to delay marriage until age 28 and women, until 25; in rural areas the suggested ages are 25 and 23, respectively. Although the first child may be planned immediately after marriage, couples are encouraged to increase the interval between births to four or more years. Before 1978, the party slogan was One Is Not Small, Two Just Right But Three Too Many, referring to the number of children in a fam-

ily. In 1978 this was changed to One Is Best, Two the Maximum. [10]

When the growth implications of even these target numbers were understood, in 1979 the Chinese government launched its drastic and ambitious policy of the one-child family. [11] The stated goal of the one-child policy is to stabilize China's population size at 1.2 billion by the year 2000. The objective presents a great challenge. As Vice-Premier and head of the State Family Commission Chen Muhua remarked in 1979, "Only if 95 percent of the couples of reproductive age in urban areas and 90 percent in rural villages give birth to only one child will the total population of our country be controlled at 1.2 billion by the end of this century." [12]

Since 1980 the one-child family policy has been given impetus by various economic incentives and disincentives. Provincial authorities have considerable discretion in implementing the policy, and some of them are already offering—and withholding—such economic rewards as free education, free medical care, extra food rations, monthly bonuses, and preferential job assignments. [13] But apparently there is still no consensus on how the one-child policy should be implemented.

9. Ibid., p. 5.

10. Yang Deqing, ed., Renkouxue gailun [General discussion of population theory] (Beijing: Hebei People's Publishing, 1982), p. 148.

11. Chen Muhua, "Birth Planning in China," in Research on the Population in China: Proceedings of a Workshop, ed. Robert J. Lapham and Rodolfo A. Bulatao (Washington, DC: National Academy Press, 1981).

12. Ibid.

13. Fifth Shanxi Provincial People's Congress, 29 June 1982; Wang Pingshan in Nanfang ribao [Southern daily], 15 May 1983; see translations in "On Province-level Fertility Policy in China," Population and Development Review, 9(3):553-61 (Sept. 1983).

The post-Mao leadership has made a special effort to institutionalize pragmatic approaches in carrying out its modernization. One such approach was the introduction in 1979 of what is called the responsibility system, designed to increase agricultural production. Under this system Chinese farmers are obligated to turn in a certain portion of their production to the government but are allowed to keep for themselves anything above that quota. In effect this is a micro-level capitalistic incentive system. There may be a conflict between the responsibility system and the government's efforts to reduce fertility.[14] Because of the low level of agricultural technology, the productive value of children may increase if the system gives farmers an incentive to produce larger crops. Already there appear to be signs of an upturn in fertility in the rural areas.

Coercion or persuasion?

Since 1949 the Chinese political system has enabled the party and the government to penetrate deeply into Chinese society, right down to the residential districts and villages. The regime has been highly successful in imposing social discipline while mobilizing the population for national purposes. According to Chen Pi-chao and Tuan Chi-hsien,[15] among others, the success of population control policies among China's predominantly rural population is largely due to the government's capacity to mobilize, educate, and motivate the masses through its organizational network. China's birth control program is unique, combining a mass-oriented national campaign with the most intimate and personal approach. Thus it is difficult to distinguish persuasion from coercion in the Chinese population program.

The responsibility system

As already mentioned, the responsibility system, introduced to increase agricultural production, may have demographic consequences. There appear to be two possibly conflicting sources of incentives and benefits pertaining to childbearing, especially in rural areas.

On the one hand, the family planning policy may be translated into material and other benefits that the government can provide to individual families for having only one child or two at the most. This approach will work when all rural families constitute a collective production system in which each family is given equal average compensation for its labor; but under these circumstances there must be strict monitoring of fertility behavior, with strong punitive sanctions for obvious departure from the prescribed norm. This has likely been the case in rural China.

On the other hand, under the responsibility system there is a strong incentive for individual families to work harder to increase their own incomes beyond the average based on the membership of the collective unit. Chinese farms are not yet modernized and mechanized, and it may be years before adequate labor-saving technology is introduced to raise agricultural productivity. Hence individual families require working bodies to generate the desired extra production and to

14. "On Province-level Fertility Policy in China."

15. Pi-chao Chen, *Population and Health Policy in the People's Republic of China,* Smithsonian Institution, Interdisciplinary Communications Program, Occasional Monograph Series, no. 9 (Washington, DC: Smithsonian Institution, 1976); idem, *Rural Health and Birth Planning in China;* Tuan, "China's Population in Perspective."

earn extra income by engaging in agricultural production marginal to the principal collective work. Although a large collective can purchase and employ labor-saving technology and equipment, individual families cannot. Thus value may be put on having larger families in anticipation of earning greater income later.

Furthermore, there is a cultural bias favoring male offspring and large families. Especially in the rural areas these two preferences are likely to reinforce each other to raise fertility or at least to make it difficult to reduce fertility further. What seems to be emerging in rural China is a conflict between individual family economic production and fertility control.

As the responsibility system and decentralization of decision making become successful in increasing agricultural production and thus raising rural farm income in China, whether or not the functions of the collectives will continue as in the past is an important question. Farmers operating outside the collective farms in the communes may end up earning more and consequently may become reluctant participants in collective agricultural production. Because of the smaller income from the collective, the collective's functions may not be perceived as in the past, when it was the principal source of individual livelihood. Consequently, implementation of the birth control program through the collectives may weaken the program and result in less compliance by farmers with the government's one-child policy.

What will be done to resolve this conflict? The Chinese government can be expected to strengthen the family planning program further in some ways so that higher fertility for individual fami-

lies would be more costly both economically and otherwise.

There is another demographic implication of the responsibility system. Fairly significant inequalities in income and revenues exist in China today. Although the incomes presented in Table 1 are based on incomplete data, they nonetheless provide compelling evidence of income inequality.

Personal income levels appear to differ substantially between cities and rural areas. Shanghai shows the highest personal income. According to official income data, there are significant variations in the levels of income among different provinces. Anhui Province had an income level in 1979 equivalent to $48 U.S. while Beijing suburban communes had $238. Due to the difficulty of obtaining accurate data on personal and household income in China and due also to definitional problems, the data shown in Table 1 may not accurately indicate the differences in the quality of life that are associated with differential income in the market economy countries. Nonetheless, income differences in China are remarkable and are likely to have interesting demographic implications.

In some ways economic inequality is an ideological contradiction that needs to be overcome in a socialist system. If one accepts that per capita output is higher in cities than in rural areas, then urbanization is a positive force for economic growth and modernization. It has often been suggested that a period of inequality is inevitable in the early stages of modernization. The introduction of the responsibility system, designed to encourage production incentives and decentralization of decision making, has led to a rapid increase in farm production and has helped to absorb the under-

TABLE 1
PERSONAL AND OFFICIAL INCOME IN CHINA, 1979

Location	Yuan	Dollar Equivalent
*Personal income**		
Shanghai City	2783	1800
Beijing City	1546	1000
Tianjin	1546	1000
Official income†		
Beijing suburban communes	368	238
Shanghai suburban communes	260	168
Suburban commune national average	300	194
Hubei Province	200	129
Shenyang Municipality, Liaoning Province	147	95
Zhejiang Province	120	77
Heilongjiang Province	110	71
Henan Province	109	70
Shanxi Province	104	67
Liaoning	100	65
Tibet Autonomous Region	100	66
Jiangsu Province	95	63
Sichuan Province	80	52
Guangdong Province	78	50
Anhui Province	75	48
Qinghai Province		
Low estimate	70	45
High estimate	150	97
Gansu Province		
Low estimate	70	45
High estimate	162	105
Xinjiang		
Low estimate	66	43
High estimate	107	69
National average	102	66

SOURCE: Clifton Pannell, "Urbanization and Economic Development in Mainland China" (Paper delivered at the Conference on Urban Growth and Economic Development in the Pacific Region, Institute of Economics, Academia Sinica, Taipei, 9-11 Jan. 1984), p. 24.
*Annual per capital income from sideline production.
†Annual per capita income that is derived from collective labor. Excludes income earned from household sideline production, which was reported as ¥53.0 ($38.60) per household in 1979.

employed in both rural and urban areas. In cities the service sectors have increased and small-scale family enterprises have sprung up. Consequently, there is likely to be increased movement of people from rural to urban places. Thus an increase in per capita agricultural output would contribute to a higher level of urbanization throughout China.

POPULATION CHANGE
AND DYNAMICS

Because of a recent dramatic decline in the population growth rate, the third and most recent wave of population growth was substantially smaller than the second and largest wave, which produced an average annual increment of some 26 million. The major part of population growth in the last 30 years has been due to the change in the birth and death rates.

Figure 1 shows the birth rate in terms of the total fertility rate (TFR)—defined as the number of births a woman would have during her childbearing age, given the current birth rate—from 1940 to 1981 and the crude death rate from 1950 to 1982. These trends are interesting in light of their major fluctuations.

The death rate showed a rapid decline from 1950 to 1957; then for the next several years, during the period of political upheaval known as the Great Leap Forward, it more than doubled. Since 1962 it has gradually diminished, leveling off at 6.6 in 1982. The death rate presented here is based on death registration statistics and is subject to some underregistration; when adjusted, the level would change somewhat but the trend would remain the same. The decline in China's death rate over the last 20 years is fairly typical of Asian developing countries. Similar declines have been observed in South Korea, Taiwan, and Malaysia.

Between 1957 and 1962 there was a dramatic dip in the birth rate, coinciding with the Great Leap Forward. Major disruptions took place at this time when, for example, 70 million young people, mostly men, were pulled out of their villages to work in steel mills, mines, and large-scale capital construction projects. The resulting separation of families must have contributed to the drop in fertility. Moreover, soon after the movement began, there was a major crop failure, which led to some starvation.

In 1961 the TFR reached its lowest level—3.3 births per woman—but by 1963 it had risen to an all-time high of 7.5. This is an interesting phenomenon because it demonstrates that birth rates can be reduced to unusually low levels and then immediately bounce back when conditions change. By 1962 the Great Leap Forward had, for all practical purposes, come to a standstill.

From 1964 to 1968 there was another prominent dip in the birth rate, the lowest level occurring in 1967. This dip coincided with the height of the Cultural Revolution, during which there was great social and political upheaval in China, particularly in the urban areas. The correlation of the disruption with a drop in urban fertility can be seen clearly in Figure 1.

In addition to the two major fluctuations in the birth rate, we find minor zigzags prior to 1955. The first drop, occurring between 1945 and 1950, coincides with the Civil War; the next, around 1950, coincides with the collectivization of farm communities in China.

Changes in the birth rate appear to coincide with political events and disruptions. Whether this correlation is spurious or whether there is a genuinely causal relationship between the two phenomena is a difficult empirical question to answer in the absence of adequate data. The ways in which political events in China might cause fertility change should certainly be investigated.

The fertility rate consistently and dramatically declined after 1970 until around 1980, when it increased to a minor extent in both rural and urban areas. The slight increase in the TFR in 1981 may be due partly to a marriage boom resulting from the new marriage law of 1980, which reduced the minimum marriage ages from 23 to 20 for women and from 25 to 22 for men. People who would have postponed their marriages are now marrying and having children. Even if individual fertility remained low, the marriage boom would contribute to an increase in the number of births. The rise in TFR may also be due to the new responsibility system.

The dramatic fertility reduction in the last decade is largely attributable to a strong birth control policy. China's birth rate reduction has not been equaled elsewhere in the world. There is, of course, the case of Japan's rapid fertility transition, during which the birth rate declined from 34 to 17 births per thousand in the 12 years beginning in 1955. The Japanese birth rate soared to its highest level shortly after World War II, but abortion and birth control were easily accepted by the largely well-educated, urban population of Japan. In China, however, most people reside in villages, have a relatively low level of education, and therefore are less receptive to fertility control.

We are able to attribute the decline in the Chinese birth rate since 1964 to three kinds of changes: (1) in the age structure; (2) in age at marriage and in marital structure, which is the proportion of married women to the total population by age group; and (3) in the fertility level of married women.

Table 2 presents results of the analysis of change in the crude birth rate for China over the years 1964, 1972, and 1981. Between 1964 and 1981 the birth rate declined by almost half—49 percent—from 42.2 to 20.6. Of this decline, about 17 percent was due to the increased age at marriage, which led to postponement of childbearing. More than two-thirds of the fertility decline was due to a reduction in marital fertility; that is, married women were practicing contraception and so were having fewer children. An official study conducted in China in 1983 found that, among the 170 million women of childbearing age,

70 percent were practicing birth control. Of that group, 50 percent were using intrauterine devices (IUDs), 35 percent— male or female—had accepted sterilization, 8 percent were using pills, and a negligible proportion was using condoms.[16]

In contrast, the changing age structure of the population produced more women of childbearing age and hence tended to increase fertility, but it was responsible for only about 14 percent of the change in the crude birth rate. In other words, 86 percent of the factors affecting the birth rate worked to lower it, whereas 14 percent worked to increase it. The strong birth control program, together with the policy to raise the age at marriage, effectively operated to reduce the birth rate to the lower level.

In the nine years between 1972 and 1981 the crude birth rate declined by 40 percent, from 34.5 to 20.6. What is interesting in China's fertility trends is the tendency for fertility levels to decline to a low point and then to rise somewhat. Political events, disruptions, and policy action may bring about a lowering of the birth rate, but unless people at large accept the low level as the norm, the birth rate will rise again to whatever level is consonant with popular norms.

The trend of the rural fertility decline shown in Figure 1 corresponds roughly to the trend for the total population because 80 percent of the Chinese population still lives in rural areas. During the 17-year period from 1964 to 1981, the rural birth rate declined by nearly

16. Japanese Organization for International Cooperation in Family Planning, *World and Population*, JOICFP pub. no. 9 (Tokyo: JOICFP, 1983).

TABLE 2
PERCENTAGE OF CHANGE IN CHINA'S CRUDE BIRTH RATE DUE TO SPECIFIED FACTORS: 1964, 1972, 1981

Period and Factor	15-19	20-24	25-29	30-34	35-39	40-44	45-49	Ages 15-49 †	
1964-81*									
Age structure	-4.0	-1.5	-14.2	-2.7	1.5	0.6	0.0	14.4	(-20.3)
Marital structure	12.9	9.8	0.6	0.1	0.0	0.0	0.0	16.6	(23.4)
Marital fertility	1.8	10.8	18.7	32.3	22.2	10.0	1.0	69.0	(96.8)
Total	10.6	19.1	5.1	29.6	23.8	10.7	1.0	100.0	(100.0)
				CBR declined 48.7 percent, from 40.2 to 20.6					
1972-81*									
Age structure	-1.4	-0.9	-8.8	-1.5	0.8	0.3	0.0	9.3	(-11.5)
Marital structure	7.5	14.2	2.0	0.1	0.0	0.0	0.0	19.3	(23.8)
Marital fertility	-0.5	1.9	19.8	34.7	22.0	9.1	0.8	71.3	(87.7)
Total	5.5	15.2	13.0	33.3	22.8	9.4	0.8	100.0	(100.0)
				CBR declined 40.3 percent, from 34.5 to 20.6					
1964-72									
Age structure	-8.9	-3.1	-30.0	-7.2	4.3	1.8	0.0	23.1	(-43.1)
Marital structure	22.9	-5.0	-3.0	-0.1	0.0	0.0	0.0	7.9	(14.8)
Marital fertility	9.3	37.0	18.7	27.8	21.9	12.0	1.6	68.9	(128.3)
Total	23.3	28.9	-14.3	20.5	26.3	13.8	1.5	100.0	(100.0)
				CBR declined 14.2 percent, from 40.2 to 34.5					

SOURCE: *Quanguo qian fen zhiyi renkou shengyulü zhouyang diaucha fenxi* [China 1982 National Fertility Survey] (Beijing: State Family Planning Commission, 1983), pp. 49-50.

*Due to the unavailability of age and marital distributions for 1981, 1981 rates were used with the 1982 age and marital distributions.

†Figures in parentheses are the sum of the actual percentages in each row. Due to rounding error the sum of the total percentages may not equal 100.0.

half, from 42.7 to 21.7, as shown in Table 3. A decrease in the fertility of married women was the cause of 56 percent of the reduction, and a rise in age at marriage accounted for about one-third of the reduction. Much of the fertility decline in rural areas occurred during the 1970s. For the most recent nine-year period, from 1972 to 1981, rural fertility declined by 43 percent, from 37.9 to 21.7. Of this decline, 70 percent was due to a reduction in marital fertility and about 27 percent was due to changes in marital status.

In urban areas the birth rate declined by 54 percent between 1964 and 1981. About three-quarters of the decline was due to a reduction in marital fertility and only a small proportion was due to changing age at marriage. Prior to 1964, rising age at marriage had already contributed to a substantial reduction of fertility in urban areas. Reduced marital fertility and increased age at marriage, combined with the changing age structure, had a fairly substantial effect on the urban fertility trend, an effect divided almost equally between the 1960s and the 1970s. During the period 1964-72 the birth rate declined by 34 percent, from 28.6 to 18.9, and during the period 1972-81 it declined by 30 percent, from 18.9 to 13.3. The impact of the Cultural Revolution (1966-76) on fertility appears to have been greater in urban than in rural areas.

Comparison with Taiwan and Korea

It is instructive to compare the fertility decline in mainland China with that in Taiwan and in the Republic of Korea during comparable periods. As shown in Table 4, the crude birth rate in Taiwan declined by 40 percent, from 38.7 to 23.3, between 1960 and 1980. This decline occurred while mainland China's birth rate was declining by about 50 percent in the comparable but slightly shorter period of 17 years from 1964 to 1981. If one looks at only the 10-year period from 1970 to 1980, the birth rate in Taiwan fell by only 14 percent, whereas from 1960 to 1970 there had been a hefty decline of 30 percent. During the 1960s about 60 percent of the drop was due to lower marital fertility and about 25 percent was due to higher age at marriage. Thus although Taiwan experienced a rapid fertility decline in the 1960s, mainland China's decline was much more dramatic.

In Korea the birth rate declined by 49 percent over the 20-year period from 1960 to 1980 (Table 4). This decline was somewhat similar to mainland China's during roughly the same period. Almost two-thirds of the Korean decline was attributable to a reduction in marital fertility, and one-third was due to rising age at marriage. During the 1960s the Korean birth rate declined about 31 percent; half of the decline was due to reduction in marital fertility, about 36 percent was due to change in age at marriage, and 14 percent was due to changing age structure. In the 1970s the decline in the birth rate was less dramatic, only 18 percent. A further reduction in the marital fertility rate was responsible for about 62 percent of the decline, the changing age structure for about 21 percent, and rising age at marriage for only 17 percent. It is apparent that mainland China's fertility transition was more dramatic than either Korea's or Taiwan's, especially during the last 10-year period.

The birth-rate levels for the three populations are now roughly the same—

FIGURE 1
TOTAL FERTILITY RATES (TFR) AND CRUDE DEATH RATE (CDR) FOR CHINA, 1940-82

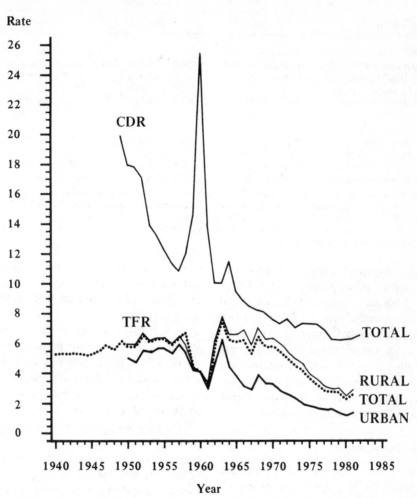

SOURCE: State Family Planning Commission, *Quanguo qian fen zhiyi renkou shengyulü zhouyang diaucha fenxi* [China 1982 National Fertility Survey] (Beijing: State Family Planning Commission, 1983), pp. 152-54.

NOTE: Rates are plotted on the same scale, but total fertility rates are rates per woman and crude death rates are rates per thousand.

21 for mainland China, 22 for Korea, and 23 for Taiwan. In the course of two decades, the three populations reached roughly similar, low levels of fertility. However, the manner in which the levels were reached was different in each case.

China, Taiwan, and Korea share a Chinese cultural background. To achieve their lower birth rates Taiwan and Korea have employed voluntary family-planning programs with strong government support. But rapid economic and

TABLE 3

PERCENTAGE OF CHANGE IN CHINA'S URBAN AND RURAL BIRTH RATES DUE TO SPECIFIED FACTORS: 1964, 1972, 1981

Area and Factor	Period		
	1964-81*	1972-81*	1964-72
Urban			
Birth rate decline	53.6 (28.6 to 13.3)	29.6 (18.9 to 13.3)	34.1 (28.6 to 18.9)
Due to age structure	21.9 (−39.1)	22.0 (−61.5)	13.2 (−18.0)
Due to marital structure	4.9 (8.8)	10.1 (−28.1)	28.3 (38.5)
Due to marital fertility	73.1 (130.3)	67.9 (189.5)	58.4 (79.4)
Rural			
Birth rate decline	49.2 (42.7 to 21.7)	42.7 (37.9 to 21.7)	11.3 (42.7 to 37.9)
Due to age structure	10.9 (−13.9)	3.1 (−3.3)	25.8 (−53.1)
Due to marital structure	33.2 (42.5)	26.8 (28.6)	40.7 (83.9)
Due to marital fertility	55.9 (71.5)	70.1 (74.7)	33.6 (69.2)

SOURCE: *Quanguo qian fen zhiyi renkou shengyulu zhouyang diaucha fenxi*, pp. 49-50.

NOTE: Figures in parentheses are actual percentages.

*Due to the unavailability of age and marital distributions for 1981, 1981 rates were used with the 1982 age and marital distributions.

social development and rapid urbanization were taking place in both Korea and Taiwan, whereas in China social and economic development and urbanization proceeded more slowly. It is amazing, therefore, that the Chinese population policy and program have been so effective in bringing down the birth rate—mostly through acceptance of contraception and abortion.[17]

Differential fertility

In the PRC differences in rural-urban residence, income, and educational attainment appear to be significantly correlated with differential fertility. A small fertility survey, for example, conducted in late 1981 in the Beijing metropolitan area, which includes a large rural community, revealed substantial urban-rural

17. The populations of China and Korea sanction abortion; Taiwan does not, but has not enforced its code against abortion.

differences in fertility within the metropolitan area.[18] The average number of children ever born to women of age 41 in the rural community was 3.8, compared with 2.3 for the city area in 1981. Women with a university education had borne 1.7 children; those with a high school education, 2.0; and those with no formal education, 4.1. Among women 35 years old, those with at least a high school education had borne an average of 1.5 children, in contrast to 2.6 children for women with only an elementary education and 3.0 for women with no formal education. Women 41 years of age with a high family income had borne

18. The 1981 Beijing Fertility Survey was conducted by the Beijing Family Planning Commission and the Population Institute of the People's University of China; 8229 women were interviewed. Beijing Family Planning Commission and Institute of Population Theory Research of the People's University of China, "Dynamics of Women's Marriage and Fertility," in *Renkou yanjiu*, People's University of China, Institute of Population, no. 1 (Beijing: China Publications Center, 1983).

TABLE 4
PERCENTAGE OF CHANGE IN THE CRUDE BIRTH RATES DUE TO
SPECIFIED FACTORS: TAIWAN AND KOREA, 1960, 1970, 1980

Population and Factor	Period		
	1960-80	1970-80	1960-70
Taiwan			
Birth rate decline	39.8 (38.7 to 23.3)	14.0 (27.1 to 23.3)	30.0 (38.7 to 27.1)
Due to age structure	21.7 (−38.3)	39.0 (−178.3)	13.4 (13.4)
Due to marital structure	28.2 (49.8)	24.9 (113.9)	25.1 (25.1)
Due to marital fertility	50.1 (88.6)	36.0 (164.4)	61.5 (61.5)
Korea			
Birth rate decline	48.7 (43.1 to 22.1)	25.3 (29.6 to 22.1)	31.3 (43.1 to 29.6)
Due to age structure	6.4 (−7.3)	21.4 (−37.4)	14.7 (14.7)
Due to marital structure	31.5 (36.1)	16.5 (28.9)	36.0 (36.0)
Due to marital fertility	62.1 (71.2)	62.1 (108.6)	49.3 (49.3)

SOURCES: Republic of China (Taiwan), *1970 Taiwan Demographic Fact Book* (Taipei: Ministry of the Interior, 1971), pp. 4-5, 16-17, 20-21; idem, *1981 Taiwan-Fukien Demographic Fact Book* (Taipei: Ministry of the Interior, 1982), pp. 958-61; Lee-Jay Cho, Fred Arnold, and T. H. Kwon, *The Determinants of Fertility in the Republic of Korea* (Washington, DC: National Academy Press, 1982), pp. 38, 77; Republic of Korea, *1960 Population and Housing Census of Korea* (Seoul: Economic Planning Board, 1963), 1:76, 99; idem, *1970 Population and Housing Census Report* (Seoul: Economic Planning Board, 1972), 1:22-23, 115; idem, *1980 Korea Advance Report on Population and Housing Census* (Seoul: Economic Planning Board, 1981), p. 36; United Nations, Department of International Economic and Social Affairs, *Demographic Yearbook 1980* (New York: United Nations, 1982), pp. 192-93.

NOTE: Percentages in parentheses are actual percentage changes.

2.8 children on the average, whereas women in the middle-income category had borne 3.5 children and women in the low-income category had borne 4.3 children. Women 35 years of age in the high-income category had borne 1.9 children, but those with low income had borne 3.0.

Current policy and
future implications of
the age structure

The objective of the Chinese birth control policy is to reduce the total fertility rate to 1.5 until the year 2000. In Figure 2, which shows how China hopes to optimize levels of fertility and achieve desired levels of population size, $\overset{\circ}{\beta}(t)$ refers to the total fertility rate and $N(t)$ refers to the size of the population. The total fertility rate starts in 1978 at 2.2, descends to 1.5 around 1990, and continues at that level until 2025, then rises again by the year 2040 to 2.1, the replacement level. The total population reaches 1.2 billion in the beginning of the twenty-first century, and in the next century it declines to below 1 billion. According to this model the dependency index—the population under age 18 and over age 65 divided by the population 18-64 years old—will be less than 1 and the aging index—the mean age of the population divided by the life expectancy at birth—will be less than 0.7.[19] This is an unusually ambitious target.

19. Song Jian, Tuan Chi-hsien, and Yu Jing-yuan, *Population Control in China: Theory and Applications* (New York: Praeger Publishers, forthcoming), chap. 8.

FIGURE 2

OPTIMIZATION OF FERTILITY AND ITS CORRESPONDING POPULATION: CHINA

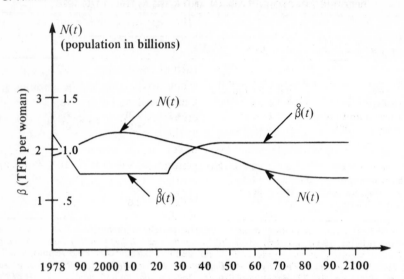

SOURCE: Song Jian, Tuan Chi-hsien, and Yu Jing-yuan, *Population Control in China: Theory and Applications* (New York: Praeger Publishers, Forthcoming).

NOTES: The dependency index is defined here as population under 18 and over 65 years of age divided by population 18-64 years of age. The aging index is mean age of the population divided by life expectancy at birth. This projection is based on the following conditions and assumptions: $1.5 \leqslant \overset{\circ}{\beta}(t) \leqslant 2.14$; maximum population $\leqslant 1.2$ billion; dependency index $\leqslant 1$; aging index $\leqslant 0.7$.

Owing to its dramatic fertility reduction, China has become the most rapidly aging nation among the less-developed countries in the world.[20] Indexes of population aging include changes in the proportion of persons 65 years of age and over, the median age of the population, the aged-dependency ratio—the number of persons 65 years old and over for each 100 persons of ages 15 through 64—and the aging index when this index is defined as the ratio of persons 65 and over to persons under 15. Also important are measurements of the extension

20. Philip M. Hauser, *Aging of Population and Labor Force for the World, More Developed and Less Developed Areas and Their Regions: Population Aging 1970-2025; Labor Force Aging 1970-2000*, Population Research Institute, Research Paper Series, no. 15 (Tokyo: Nihon University, 1983).

of life, such as life expectancy at birth and at various other ages, and the proportion of persons 75 years of age and over to those of ages 65 and over.

In 1980, 5.9 percent of China's population was age 65 and over. By the year 2025, according to United Nations projections, the proportion of persons 65 and over will have risen to 13.3 percent. In contrast, the proportion of persons 65 and over in all less-developed countries (LDCs) in 1980 was only 3.9 percent, and by 2025 that proportion will have increased to only 7.8 percent. In the 1980s the median age of China's population is estimated to be 24.4 years, as contrasted with 19.9 years in all the LDCs. By the year 2025 the median age of China's population, according to United Nations projections, will have reached 37.7 years, compared with 29.5 years for the LDCs as a whole. In 1980 in China there were 9.5 persons 65 years of age and over for each 100 persons of working age, defined as 15 through 64. This aged-dependency ratio was 7.0 for all LDCs combined. By the year 2025 the aged-dependency ratio in China will be 19.6, as contrasted with 11.8 for the LDCs in the aggregate.[21]

The tremendous increase in the older population in China is also indicated by the aging index. In 1980 there were 18.1 persons 65 and over for each 100 persons under 15. In the LDCs combined, the aging index was only 9.8, little more than half that in China. By the year 2025, China's aging index could reach 69.5, in sharp contrast to the 29.8 projected for all LDCs.[22] If present aging trends continue, the social and economic order in China will be significantly changed by the year 2025.

Expectation of life at birth in China in 1980 was 67.3 years, as compared with 55.1 years for all LDCs. By the year 2025, life expectancy at birth in China is expected to be 74.6 years, whereas in the LDCs in the aggregate it is expected to be 69.9 years. In 1980, of all the persons 65 years of age and over in China, 29.7 percent were 75 years old or older. For all the LDCs this proportion was 27.4 percent.[23]

Rapid aging of the population presents serious economic and social problems, problems that the United States and Japan are already beginning to face. Adequate solutions will cost the productive part of the economy and society greatly. The proposed change in fertility in China would be more drastic than that of the United States and Japan.

Therefore the impact of aging will be much greater. The Chinese leadership's response to this kind of concern is that "the serious aging problem will not appear within this century . . . and will not be so serious even 20 years after the turn of the century."[24] The implication seems to be that in the coming years China will make drastic efforts to increase its economic development, even at the cost of paying partly for it in the next century by turning over to the next generation heavier economic and social burdens. Once China reaches a respectable level of development in the next several decades, it may be able to handle the problem of aging.

CONCLUSION

Further tabulations of the 1982 census and proposed further analysis of the 1982 National Fertility Survey will provide bases for fascinating studies of population dynamics as they relate to recent development in China. For example, the history of marriage and fertility and some aspects of the history of mortality can be related to political, social, and economic history as well as to demographic data from other sources. As we have seen, the depths and heights of political and economic swings in China are accompanied by unusually large demographic swings. The data to be made available in the near future will make it possible to perform analyses for China's provinces and smaller areas. A systematic study of the variations in the demographic history of major areas and social groups within China can also be done. There are numerous other topics that can further our understanding of the underlying factors in population and social change taking place in China.

21. Ibid.
22. Ibid.
23. Ibid.
24. Xu Dixin, "On the Relationship between Population Growth and Economic Development."

Birth Planning and Fertility Transition

By PI-CHAO CHEN

ABSTRACT: In 1971 the government of the People's Republic of China launched the third birth control campaign. The goals were to raise the age at marriage, lengthen the birth interval, and limit the number of births per family to two in the cities and three in the countryside. A birth-quota and pregnancy-authorization system was instituted. The campaign was greatly facilitated by the nationwide network of free community-based contraceptive and abortion services and generous incentives. By the early 1980s the contraceptive prevalence rate rose to 70 percent, and the total fertility rate fell to about 2.5 children per woman of reproductive age. The year 1979 saw the introduction of the one-child campaign. By 1982 first births accounted for 47 percent of total births, and 42 percent of the one-child families had pledged to have no more children. The successful implementation of the one-child campaign will, however, lead to a rapid aging of the population. The percentage of the population older than 64 years of age will increase rapidly, from 5 percent in 1982 to 7.3-7.7 percent in 2000 and to 23-27 percent in 2050. With such a high aged-dependency ratio, caring for the aged will entail heavy fiscal outlay in the twenty-first century.

Pi-chao Chen is a professor of political science at Wayne State University, Detroit, Michigan. His studies of China's population problems and birth planning span many years and include fieldwork in rural China.

IN 1982 China took its third census. The census counted a total of 1.008 billion persons, about a fifth of the world's population. It also revealed that in 1981 the crude birth rate was 20.91 per 1000 population and the crude death rate was 6.36 per 1000; therefore the natural-increase rate was 14.55 per 1000, or a net increase of 14 million persons.[1]

Two months after the census, a sample survey of fertility was taken. Since it sampled roughly one one-thousandth of the total population, the survey has come to be known as the one one-thousandth fertility survey. The survey confirmed that the 1970s witnessed a contraceptive revolution and a drastic fertility decline. In 1982 contraceptive use among married women of reproductive age was 70 percent. The pace and magnitude of fertility decline is even more dramatic and remarkable: the fertility rate fell by 65 percent between 1968 and 1980.

THE EVOLUTION OF BIRTH-PLANNING POLICY

The Chinese birth-planning programs may be divided into four phases: (1) 1956-58; (2) 1962-69; (3) 1971-79; and (4) 1979 to the present. The organized programs to reduce fertility commenced in the period 1956-57 after the 1953 census revealed a much higher population growth rate than had been expected. The programs were disrupted shortly thereafter, from 1958 to 1961, by the Great Leap Forward and the transition to people's communes. They were reactivated in 1962 and disrupted again from 1966 to 1969 by the Cultural Revolu-

tion. The big push to reduce fertility commenced in 1971, with the issuance of a major policy directive, known as State Council Directive Number 51. In 1979 the one-child policy was initiated.

THE "LATER, LONGER, AND FEWER" CAMPAIGN

State Council Directive Number 51 ushered in the third birth control campaign, known as *wan xi shao*, "later marriage, longer spacing, and fewer births."[2] Prior to this campaign, couples in China, as elsewhere, made their own decisions regarding age at marriage, length of birth interval, and number of children. The implementation of the "later, longer, and fewer" policy in effect socialized these decisions, with all those eligible expected to abide by the reproductive norms officially promoted.

To implement the policy of late marriage, the program emphasized raising the age at marriage to 23 and 25 for women and men, respectively, in rural areas and to even higher ages for urban residents. The age at marriage was controlled by the local authorities—namely, commune or residents' committees—through permits to marry, which for women usually involved permission to change residence as well. During the 1970s it became increasingly difficult to obtain permission to marry at ages younger than the program's specified minimums.

To measure compliance, the program used the late-marriage rate, defined as the percentage of women who marry for the first time during the calendar year in

1. "Communiqué of the State Statistical Bureau of the People's Republic of China on Major Figures in the 1982 Population Census, October 27, 1982," *China Population Newsletter,* 1(1):19-21 (May 1983).

2. Shin Cheng-li, "The Birth Planning Work Since the Founding of the Republic: A Preliminary Discourse on the History of Our Nation's Birth Planning Activities," *Xibei renkou* [Northwest population], no. 2, pp. 33-48 (1980).

question and satisfy the official norm of 23 years of age. According to the one one-thousandth survey, the late-marriage rate was 13.8 percent in 1970 and rose to 52.8 percent in 1980, implying that half of the women married in 1980 were 23 years of age or older. The mean age of marriage was 20.19 years in 1970 and rose to 23.05 in 1980.[3]

To implement the policy of longer birth intervals and fewer births, the Chinese birth-planning programs developed in the course of the 1970s a birth-quota system. Under this system the national government assigned a numerical target for the natural-increase rate to the provinces and expected them to realize it fully or as nearly as possible. The provincial or prefectural authorities in turn translated the targeted natural-increase rate into a planned-birth quota and distributed the quota among the prefectures or counties under their jurisdiction.

A major task for the county birth-planning office each year was negotiating the planned-birth targets up and down the chain of command. This involved converting the county's planned-birth quota into individual certificates of permission to become pregnant and give birth. Each April the county decided at a meeting of all relevant commune or township cadres each commune's or township's planned-birth quota. Each commune in turn distributed its quota among its brigades at a meeting of all relevant brigade leaders. Finally, each brigade held a meeting of all couples eligible under the marriage-age, spacing, and family-size rules in order to assign

3. Editorial Board of Renkou yu jingji [Population and the economy], An Analysis of the National One One-thousandth Sample Survey of Fertility, special issue of Renkou yu jingji, pp. 115-16, 126 (1983).

individual birth permission for the next year.

RULES FOR PREGNANCY AND BIRTH AUTHORIZATION

The prime criteria for eligibility for birth permission were (1) attaining the specified minimum age for marriage; (2) having a four-year interval since the birth of the last child; and (3) having no more than two living children or, toward the end of the 1970s, no more than one.

If the number of families eligible to have a birth exceeded the brigade quota, an appropriate number of families were persuaded to wait a year, or the brigade appealed for an increase in the quota. Negotiations between communes and brigades sometimes required three or four exchanges. Finally, a small, red birth permission certificate was issued to each family approved for a birth in the next year and opened the door to maternity care. All other couples of reproductive age were expected to use contraceptives and to resort to abortion in case of contraceptive failure.

The "later, longer, and fewer" phase saw the introduction of free contraceptive services and incentives to the accepters of contraception.

In the early 1970s, to induce eligible couples to accept the four planned-birth operations, major cities on the coast adopted a system of incentives. Under this system, the accepters of planned-birth operations were awarded leaves of absence with full pay on this schedule: 14 days for early abortion; 30 days for midterm abortion; 21 to 28 days for tubal ligation; 70 days for postpartum tubal ligation, of which 56 days were the standard maternity leave granted to the female employees of government agencies and state factories; 3 to 7 days for vasectomy; and 2 to 3 days for insertion of an intrauterine device (IUD).[4]

During the 1970s this system of incentives was adopted by an increasing number of rural communities. By the end of the decade it was probably instituted in all rural areas. The amount of benefits was decided by the local community and therefore varied from one county to another, one commune to another, and even one brigade to another within the same commune. Generally speaking, the benefits—in paid leaves of absence from collective farming—were as follows: 14 days for early abortion; 7 to 21 days for tubectomy; 30 to 60 days for postpartum tubectomy; 7 days for IUD insertion; and up to 7 days for IUD removal.[5]

THE THREE-TIERED INTEGRATED PRIMARY HEALTH SERVICE

Starting in 1966, China initiated, by way of trial and error, the building of a nationwide network of integrated primary health services in rural areas. By the mid-1970s, such a nationwide network, albeit primitive by the West's standards, was established. Of the innovations borne out of the Cultural Revolution, this is the only one that has survived the death of Mao and the removal of the Gang of Four. The post-Mao leadership not only has not demolished it, but actually has strengthened it by allocating more funds to upgrade the technical competence of the paramedics. Among other functions, its role as the provider of community-based planned-birth services has proved to be indispensable.

At the bottom of the three-tiered health care system is the brigade cooperative medical station. Staffed by two to four barefoot doctors, the station is responsible for providing preventive and simple curative health care as well as contraceptive services to a brigade with 1000 to 3000 persons.

At the middle tier is the commune health center, responsible for the health care of a commune with a population of 15,000 to 50,000. It is staffed by college or vocational medical school graduates, laboratory technicians, and other support personnel. It provides technical training, supports and supervises the barefoot doctors, and treats the cases referred from below.

At the top, or county, level are the county hospital, county maternal and child hospital, and the county epidemic-control stations. Each of these three is responsible for providing training, technical support, and supervision to the commune health centers in their specialized and responsible areas.[6] In addition to these county facilities, there is the county birth-planning office responsible for implementing the "later, longer, and fewer" policy and for coordinating training and the provision of contraceptive services in the county.

4. Pi-chao Chen, "China's Population Program at the Grass-roots Level," *Studies in Family Planning,* 4(8):219-27 (Aug. 1973); Pi-chao Chen and Ann Miller, "Lessons from the Chinese Experience: China's Planned Birth Program and Its Transferability," *Studies in Family Planning,* 6(10): 354-66 (Oct. 1975).

5. Pi-chao Chen, "Rural Health," *Rural Health in the People's Republic of China,* National Institutes of Health pub. no. 81-2124 (Washington, DC: NIH, 1980), pp. 105-27.

6. Pi-chao Chen, *Population and Health Policy in the People's Republic of China,* Interdisciplinary Communications Program, Occasional Monograph Series, no. 9 (Washington, DC: Smithsonian Institution, 1976), pp. 31-74; idem, *Rural Health and Birth Planning in China* (Research Triangle Park, NC: International Fertility Research Program, 1981), pp. 13-33.

By the end of the 1970s, each of the more than 2500 counties had its own county hospital, county maternal and child hospital, and county epidemic-control station. Of all communes, 55,000—or about 90 percent—had their own health centers; and of the nation's production brigades, 700,000—or 90 percent—had their own medical stations. A total of 1.46 million barefoot doctors and trained paramedics were employed at the brigade medical stations by the decade's end.[7]

Contraceptive services have been built into the three-tiered integrated health care system. At least one barefoot doctor in each brigade medical station is female and reportedly trained in IUD insertion and removal. Some of the female barefoot doctors are trained in the use of vacuum aspiration to induce abortion. At least one staff member at each commune health center is reportedly trained in tubal ligation, vasectomy, IUDs, and midterm abortion.

To cope with the perennial shortage of trained medical providers in rural areas, the government has organized urban medical workers into mobile planned-birth surgical teams and has dispatched them to the countryside from time to time. This practice was initiated in the mid-1960s and continues to the present, albeit on a lesser scale.

RAPID RISE IN CONTRACEPTION AND FERTILITY DECLINE

The gradual diffusion and increasingly rigorous enforcement of the planned-birth quota system combined with the nationwide network of community-based contraceptive services to bring about a rapid increase in contraceptive use in the 1970s. At the beginning of the decade, perhaps 5 to 10 percent of the eligible couples, mostly urbanites, were using contraceptives, as indicated by the total fertility rate[8]—5.8 children per woman. Twelve years later, in 1982, of a total of 170 million women aged 15 to 49, 118 million were using contraceptives, achieving a contraceptive prevalence rate of 70 percent (Table 1). In comparison, in 1976 the contraceptive prevalence rate was 61 percent in Japan and 69 percent in the United States.[9]

Of those practicing contraception in China, half were using IUDs, a quarter had had tubal ligations, and one-tenth had had vasectomies. About 8 percent were relying on steroid pills and 2 percent on condoms, with the remaining 4 percent using other methods. The contraceptive prevalence rate was higher in urban than in rural areas: 74 percent versus 69 percent, respectively.

As a consequence of the dramatic increase in contraceptive use and abortion, fertility plummeted. In 1968 the total fertility rate was 6.5 children per woman of reproductive age, ages 15 to 49. It fell to 2.238 in 1980, only to rise to 2.631 in 1981.[10] The fertility decline may be measured in terms of the first-births

7. Pi-chao Chen and Chi-hsien Tuan, "Primary Health Care in Rural China: Post-1978 Development," Social Science and Medicine, 17:1411-19 (1983).

8. Total fertility may be understood as the average number of births a woman will have by the end of her reproductive age if the current number of births by age to women aged 15 to 49 were to continue.

9. Dorothy Nortman and Ellen Hofstetter, Population and Family Planning Programs: A Compendium of Data through 1981 (New York: Population Council, 1982), tab. 21, p. 95.

10. See Lee-Jay Cho, "Population Dynamics and Policy in the People's Republic of China," this issue of The Annals of the American Academy of Political and Social Science, fig. 1.

TABLE 1
CONTRACEPTIVE PREVALENCE RATE (CPR) AND DISTRIBUTION
OF CONTRACEPTIVE METHODS IN USE, 1982 (Percentage)

	CPR	Tubectomy	Vasectomy	IUDs	Steroid Pills	Condoms	Others	Total
Total	69.4	17.6	6.9	34.8	5.9	1.4	2.8	100.0
		25.4	10.0	50.2	8.4	2.0	4.0	100.0
Urban	74.3	15.1	2.1	28.8	14.1	7.2	7.0	
		20.3	2.8	38.9	19.0	9.7	9.4	100.0
Rural	68.6	18.1	7.9	36.0	4.3	0.3	2.0	
		26.4	11.5	52.5	6.3	0.5	2.9	100.0

SOURCE: Editorial Board of *Renkou yu jingji* [Population and the economy], *An Analysis of the National 1/1,000 Sample Survey of Fertility,* special issue of Renkou yu jingji, p. 131.
*Including barrier methods, safety period, and coitus interruptus.

ratio, or first births as a percentage of total births. The first-births ratio was 21 percent in 1971; it rose to 31 percent in 1977 and to 47 percent in 1980.

Like most populations that have experienced reduction in fertility, fertility decline in China began first among the urban residents and then spread to the rural peasants. In 1969, when the secular fertility decline commenced, the total fertility rate in urban areas was already low—3.3—as compared to 6.3 in rural areas. In 1980 it fell by 65 percent, to 1.147 in urban areas and to 2.48 in rural areas. Given China's life expectancy at birth in recent years, a total fertility rate of 2.238—a rate achieved in 1980—may be considered replacement-level fertility.

As in other societies that have experienced fertility transition, fertility decline in China began among teenage and older women. By 1980 the concentration of fertility among women in their mid-twenties and its precipitous decline after age 25 was particularly marked. In 1955, births to women aged 15 to 19 accounted for 7.2 percent of total births. The proportion fell to 4.8 percent by 1965, to 2.8 percent by 1975, and to an incredibly low 2.2 percent by 1980. At the other end of the reproductive scale,

births to women aged 35 and above accounted for a quarter of total births as recently as 1965. By 1980 this proportion had dropped to just 3.6 percent.

The fertility decline has cut across the entire reproductive age span. Births to women in the peak childbearing ages also dropped substantially. Births to women aged 20 to 24 declined by 50 percent in the 1965-80 period, from 289 to 142 births per 1000 women. During the same period, births to women aged 25 to 29 fell by 60 percent, from 311 to 90 per 1000 women.

THE ONE-CHILD CAMPAIGN

In 1979, apparently alarmed by internal population projections, the government shifted the emphasis of its birth-planning efforts in the direction of one child per family.

One internal projection showed that if the total fertility rate remained constant at the estimated 1978 level of 2.3 children, the population would grow to 1.28 billion by the year 2000.[11] This pro-

11. Song Jian, Tian Xueyuan, Li Guang-yuan, and Yu Jing-yuan, "On the Target of the Population Development of Our Country," *Renmin ribao* [People's daily], 7 Mar. 1980.

jected growth is rapid, despite the relatively low fertility that prevailed toward the end of the 1970s, because high crude birth rates up to the mid-1970s produced large cohorts each year. As they reach marital age, these cohorts will swell the number of potential parents in the next two decades. The one one-thousandth survey revealed that women aged 15 to 19 accounted for one-quarter of the women of reproductive age—15 to 49. As these cohorts marry, they will raise the absolute number of births even if each couple has two children on the average.

To overcome this hurdle to rapid transition to zero population growth, regarded as a highly desirable demographic goal by China's political elite since the late 1970s, the government introduced the one-child campaign. The goal was to limit the population size to 1.2 billion in the year 2000. The policymakers frankly admitted that this numerical target, like earlier ones, would be difficult, if not impossible, to achieve. Nevertheless, they believed such targets and the one-child family serve as a focus for their effort.

In the summer of 1979, when she announced the one-child policy on behalf of the government, Vice-Premier Chen Muhua called for the institution of an economic reward-and-punishment scheme to promote the one-child policy.[12] The first draft of a national birth-planning law to provide incentives for the one-child family and disincentives for more than two births was drawn up either before that time or shortly there-

12. M. Chen, "To Realize the Four Modernizations, It is Necessary to Control Population Increase in a Planned Way," *Renmin ribao*, 11 Aug. 1979, trans. Pi-chao Chen, under the title "Birth Planning in China," *International Family Planning Perspectives,* 5(3):92-101 (Sept. 1979).

after. By September 1980, when the National People's Congress—the nominal legislative body that rubber-stamps whatever policy decisions are reached by the supreme Party leaders—was in session, the eighth draft of the law was in circulation at the grass-roots level to gather comments and reaction.

To date, the National People's Congress has yet to pass a national birth-planning law. There are several reasons for this. First, there is the question of the enforceability of the punitive provisions in the draft. If there were widespread noncompliance with the law in rural areas among peasants—who would not stop childbearing until they at least had a son for their support in old age—could and would the punitive provisions be enforced? And with what consequences?

Second, what would be the special provisions for the national minorities, especially the Muslims? Exempting them from the mandatory limit of one child would be an easy way out. In 1982 the minorities constituted 6.7 percent of the population, but numbered 68 million in total—more than the entire population of England or France. If differential fertility were allowed to continue, the minorities as a percentage of the total population would steadily increase over the decades. Is this an acceptable prospect?

Third, the law calls for generous economic and other benefits to couples who pledge to have only one child by accepting a one-child certificate until the child is 14 years old. Delivering those benefits will entail substantial budgetary outlay, which will increase astronomically in the next two to three decades. Where will the funds come from? Would this expenditure cut into funds otherwise available for investment in capital and social overhead projects that promise high return?

Fourth, the army and the women's federation have voiced opposition. The army is concerned with the shrinking military labor pool that the one-child policy would entail. The women's federation has expressed concern about a resurgency of infanticide of female babies in the countryside by peasant families who insist on having at least a son but find their first and only authorized child to be a daughter.

Obviously, there are no easy solutions to these problems. The failure to promulgate a national planned-birth law to date suggests that these and other nagging problems remain unresolved.

Local regulation of fertility

In the absence of a national law, the government encouraged the provincial authorities to issue their own provisional regulations. To date, most provinces have issued and presumably have implemented their own provisional regulations.[13]

13. These regulations are, for Anhui, contents summarized and trans. into English in *Daily Report: People's Republic of China*, 20 Apr. 1979, pp. 01-03; for Hunan, contents summarized and trans. into English in ibid., 26 June 1979, pp. p2-p3; for Beijing, summarized in a Xinhua news release and trans. into English in ibid., 8 Nov. 1979, p. p3; for Guangdong, Guangdong Provincial People's Congress, *Guangdong Provincial Planned Birth Regulations* (Guangzhou, 1980); for Shanghai, "Shanghai Municipal Planned Birth Regulations," *Jiefang ribao* [Liberation daily], 10 Aug. 1981, trans. in *Survey of World Broadcast*, 31 Aug. 1981, pp. FE/6815/B11/1-3; for Shanxi, "Shanxi Planned Parenthood Regulations," *Shanxi ribao* [Shanxi daily], reprinted in *Population and Development Review*, 9(3):554-60 (Sept. 1983); for Sichuan, contents summarized and trans. into English in *Daily Report: People's Republic of China*, 14 Mar. 1979, p. J-1; for

Although the specific incentives stipulated in the regulations vary from one province to another, they are all generous for one-child couples who pledge to have no more children. The regulations stipulate severe economic and other sanctions against those who defy the call to stop at one or two children. Within each province, individual counties, communes, or even brigades may add their own local incentives. The one-child couples are called upon to apply for the one-child certificate, which entitles the holders and their child to various economic and noneconomic benefits.

The benefits and sanctions differ a great deal depending on whether residence is rural or urban. In the urban areas

—the one-child-certificate family will be given a monthly stipend, ranging from 5 to 8 percent of the average worker's monthly wage, or an annual stipend, equivalent to one month's wage. This cash benefit continues until the child is 14 years of age. If the certificate holders break their promise by having a second child, all the cash must be returned;

—space allotted in the future for housing will be the equivalent of the space considered standard for a two-child family, regardless of the number of children the family actually has, and priority for housing allocation will go to one-child families;

—mothers who obtain a certificate upon the birth of the first and only

Tianjin, *Da gong bao* [Da gong newspaper] (Hong Kong), 12 Aug. 1979; for Zhejiang, contents summarized and trans. into English in *Daily Report: People's Republic of China*, 13 Sept. 1979, p. 06.

child will receive at least two extra weeks of paid maternity leave;

—the only child will receive free or subsidized medical care or preferential treatment;

—a 5 percent supplementary pension, over and above that provided for by the existing labor protection law, will be given to certificate holders, and an even more generous pension will be given to childless workers;

—highest priority will go to the only child in admission to nurseries, kindergartens, and schools; and

—highest priority in job assignment will go to the only child.

In rural areas

—the certificate holder is to be allocated extra work points until the child reaches 14 years of age; in some prosperous areas a one-time cash bonus will be offered;

—in the future each family, regardless of its size, will be allocated a four-person housing lot, on which the family will build its own house;

—rural communes will be called upon to guarantee the childless aged person the living standard equal to or higher than the local average, and to begin to build senior citizen houses for the childless; and

—an only child is to be given priority in being assigned jobs in commune-owned factories and sideline activities.

Prior to 1979 there appeared to be no disincentives to providers and supervisors of the planned-birth programs. Since then, disincentives have been introduced to spur the local community and the work unit to exert pressure on individual members to conform. For instance, the Guangdong provincial regulations specifically stipulate that the enterprise units that fail to hold actual births within the assigned planned-birth quota will be assessed a fine equivalent to 2 percent of their profit. In Beijing and virtually all the major cities on the coast, a new collective responsibility system has been instituted. Under this system, if a member of a government office or work unit has a second child in violation of his or her pledge—which is made without any choice in a mass rally—all the rest will forfeit their annual one-child bonus. In places like Beijing and Shanghai, such bonuses can be as much as one month's wages, ¥50 to ¥60.

This collective responsibility system has also been applied to the supervisors of the planned-birth programs, namely the Party and administrative cadres in rural communes. In the past, if the commune or brigade overfulfilled its farm output and delivery quota, its Party and administrative cadres would be awarded a very handsome bonus, which in some areas amounted to as much as a quarter of annual pay. To qualify for the bonus now, the commune or brigade must fulfill two quotas: a farm output and delivery quota and a planned-birth quota. Failure to fulfill either now results in a meager bonus or none at all.

Under the old collective farming system, the team leader assigned peasants to specific farming tasks and remunerated them periodically for the amount of work points credited to their account. Under the production responsibility system, there have evolved several new arrangements. Under one arrangement, the production team allocates farming plots, tools, fertilizers, and plow animals to a household or a group of households for a period of one to three or more years. In return, the household or household group guarantees the delivery of a fixed amount of crops. They are free to dispose of the remaining crops as they see fit, including selling them in the private market. Under a second arrangement, the peasant households are assigned a farming plot and are remunerated in work points.[14] The majority of rural communes has opted for one or another variant of the new production responsibility system.

The experience of the last several years has shown that the production responsibility system has indeed spurred peasants to greater efforts and productivity. The annual growth in agricultural output averaged slightly over 2 percent in the first three decades of Communist rule, and this just barely kept up with population growth. In the last several years, it has averaged at least 5 percent.

The new system, however, has adversely affected the one-child campaign. In the past, the team or brigade cadres rewarded those using contraceptives or holding one-child certificates with extra work points and other benefits. They punished the defiant by deducting work points and denying tangible benefits. In areas where the production responsibility system is now in force, there are no work points to reward or deduct and few tangible rewards to dispense with. Denied the battery of rewards and punishments previously at their disposal and in the absence of a national planned-birth law, some rural cadres have complained that they are powerless to enforce the

planned-birth quota and the one-child policy; they have demanded speedy promulgation of a national planned-birth law.

Confronted with this dilemma, some localities have developed new ways of implementing the planned-birth quota. One such innovation is the so-called double-contract system. Under this system, the peasant household, in exchange for the right to contract out a farming plot, promises to deliver the amount of crops specified by the quota and to refrain from having an unauthorized birth on pain of a severe fine or forfeiting the right to contract farming. In one variant or another, the double-contract system has been put into effect in an increasing number of rural counties.

THE PROGRESS OF THE ONE-CHILD CAMPAIGN

The one-child campaign has progressed fairly well. In 1970, 1 out of 5 babies were firstborn. Since then the proportion has risen to almost 1 out of 3, in 1977, and to almost 1 out of 2—47 percent—in 1981.[15]

According to the one one-thousandth sample survey, at the time of the survey women with one child accounted for 21 percent of all mothers aged 15 to 49; they constituted 33 percent of mothers in urban areas and 19 percent of mothers in rural areas. Of the one-child mothers, 42.3 percent have obtained the one-child certificate. The rate was 77.6 percent in

14. Jergen Domes, "New Policies in the Communes: Notes on Rural Societal Structure in China, 1976-1981," *Journal of Asian Studies,* 7(2):253-67 (Feb. 1982).

15. Editorial Board, *Analysis of the National One One-thousandth Sample,* p. 56; Population Census Office under the State Council, and Department of Population Statistics, State Statistical Bureau, *Major Figures by 10 Percent Sampling Tabulation of the 1982 Population Census of the People's Republic of China* (Beijing, 1983), pp. 26-27.

urban areas and 31.3 percent in rural areas. It also varied by region, ranging from 25 percent in the Central South to 57 percent in the Northeast.[16]

The preference for male children has persisted, as expected. For every 100 females enrolled in the certificate program, 150 males were enrolled. Also as expected, this preference is stronger in rural than in urban areas. In urban areas, for every 100 families with a female only-child enrolled in the one-child certificate program, there were 121 families with a male only-child enrolled. The corresponding ratio in the country-side was 100 to 178.[17]

These statistics testify to the Chinese government's organizational skills and social-engineering capability. Over the last three decades, the government has proved itself capable of penetrating, controlling, and regulating the daily life—including reproduction—of China's vast rural population to an extent seldom seen in history. There are, however, cultural and societal constraints that not even China's government can circumvent.

In today's China, old-age pensions are available to no more than 15 to 20 percent of the population, mostly urbanites and some Party and administrative cadres in rural villages. The peasants, who still constitute over two-thirds of China's population, are not covered by social security of any sort or scope.[18] Like their ancestors, they have to look to their male offspring to take care of them in their old age. The strong male preference, as evidenced by the statistics

cited earlier, is not left over from feudalistic Confucian thought, as the government elite and propaganda machine would have it, but rather is due to pragmatism, pure and simple.

The lack of social security for rural peasants also explains in part the difference in response to the one-child policy. Although urban women comprised only 17 percent of the women of reproductive age in the one one-thousandth sample, they accounted for 44 percent of the total certificate holders. The corresponding figures for rural women were 83 percent and 56 percent, respectively.[19]

The same concern for care of the aged explains the much greater percentage of rural women who changed their minds and proceeded to have a second birth after having obtained one-child certificates. Of the total sample of 15,007 women of reproductive age who have obtained a certificate since mid-1979, 965 had changed their minds and had had a second birth by the time of the survey. Of these 965 women, 98 percent were rural women. For the country as a whole, 6.4 percent of the certificate holders had had a second birth. Whereas 1 out of 10 certificate holders in rural areas had had a second birth, only one-third of 1 percent of the urban women had done so.[20]

Given the biological fact that for about every 106 male babies born there will be 100 female babies born, the government's attempt to prevent about 50 percent of the one-daughter parents from having a second birth is bound to run into massive, bitter resistance, if not outright defiance. The reason is very simple: many peasants hope the second

16. Editorial Board, *Analysis of the National One One-thousandth Sample,* pp. 137-42.

17. Ibid., pp. 143-44.

18. Deborah Davis-Friedmann, "Old Age Security and the One-child Campaign" (manuscript, Yale University, 1983).

19. Editorial Board, *Analysis of the National One One-thousandth Sample,* p. 13.

20. Ibid., pp. 139-40.

birth will result in a son. It remains to be seen whether the government can sustain the one-child campaign over a long period of time.

RAPID AGING OF THE POPULATION AND ITS IMPLICATIONS

Whatever the numerical target—in terms of average number of children per family—eventually achieved, one inevitable consequence will be the rapid aging of the population, entailing a heavy aged-dependency burden and a formidable cost for financing the care of the aged during the next half century and beyond.

A team of Chinese systems engineers under the leadership of Song Jian conducted a series of sophisticated demographic projections. In one scenario, the total fertility rate was assumed to drop to 2 in 1980 and remain constant thereafter, while the death rate would continue its decline at the same pace as in the recent past. With these fertility and mortality trends, the population would grow to 1.222 billion in the year 2000. However, the population would continue to grow even further, thanks to demographic momentum. It would reach 1.542 billion in 2050. Thereafter it would begin to decrease in size: to 1.492 billion in 2075 and to 1.483 billion in 2080.

In another scenario, the total fertility rate was assumed to be 2.3 in 1980—as compared to 2.238 as revealed by the one one-thousandth survey—and remain at that level thereafter. In this case, the population would grow to 1.286 billion in the year 2000 and would continue to grow for at least 80 years. It would reach 2.132 billion in the year 2080.[21]

If the first scenario were to run its course, persons above 65 years of age would increase to 7.7 percent of the total population by 2000, to 27.2 percent by 2050, and to 30 percent by 2080. If the second scenario were to run its course, the corresponding figures would be 7.3 percent in 2000, 22.6 percent in 2050, and 25.2 percent in 2080.[22] In 1982 persons older than age 64 comprised only 4.9 percent of the total population, as revealed by the 1982 census. In 1980 only in four countries did persons older than 64 constitute more than 14 percent of the population: 15 percent in Sweden, West Germany, and Austria and 16 percent in East Germany. The corresponding figure for the United States was 11 percent; for Japan, 8 percent; and for the developing countries as a whole, only 4 percent.[23]

Keyfitz recently did a series of projections for the Chinese population. The age data he used were probably derived from the household registrants of 1978 rather than the census of 1982. In one of his projections, life expectancy at birth was assumed to rise to 72 years over two generations, and annual births were to drop to 16.7 million per year in 1980 and remain at that level thereafter. This projection would result in an ultimate constant, or stationary, population of 1.2 billion.

One of the immediate effects of a drastic drop in fertility would be a favorable ratio of working population aged 15 to 64 to retired population aged 65 and above, as the large cohorts born between 1965 and 1980 attain working age. The working population aged 15 to 64 will continue to increase until 2005.

21. Song Jian, Tian Xueyuan, Yu Jing-yuan, and Li Guang-yuan, *Population Projections and Population Control* (Beijing: Renmin Publishing House, 1982), pp. 181-82.

22. Ibid.
23. "1980 World Population Data Sheet" (Washington, DC: Population Reference Bureau, 1980).

Thereafter, the proportion of retired people would begin to increase sharply. By 2040, when the cohorts born between 1960 and 1979 reach the age of 60 and retire, the ratio of the retired population to the working population would reach its peak: 32 retirees for every 100 workers.[24] In 1982 there were only 12 retirees for every 100 workers.

If the annual number of births were to be kept below 16.7 million, the change in the age distribution would be even more disadvantageous. In another of Keyfitz's projections, an ultimate constant population of 700 million corresponds to 10 million births per year. If the number of annual births decreased to 10 million per year in 1980 and remained at that level thereafter, there would be 50 retirees per 100 workers by 2040. In other words, every working-age couple would have to support one older person. With 20 million births per year, there would be 27 retirees per 100 working-age persons in 2040—still a heavy burden. By comparison, in the United States, the ratio of retirees to workers is projected to rise from about 20 percent in 1980 to 23 percent by 2000, to 33 percent by 2020, to 42 percent by 2030, and to over 50 percent by 2055. In West Germany, the retiree-to-worker ratio reached 45 percent by 1980, probably the highest in the world. It is to rise to 60 percent by 2005 and to about 90 percent by 2030.[25]

CONCLUSION

China's very success in reducing rapid population growth is breeding a second-generation problem. Thanks to rapid fertility decline in the 1970s and the government's plan to suppress fertility at a level well below that of replacement—which is 2.2 children per family—the population will age rapidly in the next several decades. The aging of the population has begun to emerge as a public policy issue challenging the ingenuity and taxing the resources of a growing number of developed countries. Even these affluent countries have found it increasingly difficult to finance care for the aged through taxation or through intergenerational transfer of income. Given the pace at which China's fertility has fallen and will continue to fall, the aging process will be even faster in China than in those developed countries.

In addressing this aging problem, China obviously will be traveling an untraversed path. Just as it innovated its own approach to fertility control, China will have to innovate its own approach to coping with the aging question. The experience of the West, Japan, and the socialist Soviet Union will be of little relevance to China. Needless to say, how China tackles rapid aging will be worth watching closely.

24. Nathan Keyfitz, "The Population of China," *Scientific American*, 250(2):38-47 (Feb. 1984).

25. "Pensions after 2000," *Economist* (London), 19 May 1984, pp. 59-60.

*   *   *

QUESTIONS AND ANSWERS

Q (Fred Greenwald, Norristown, Pennsylvania): When I was in China in 1981, we were told that family planning was augmented by a system whereby if a family agreed to have but one child, that child would get extra rations of clothing and other needs. If they had two children, each would get appropriate amounts for one child each. But beyond that, there was extra taxation, and the taxation increased measurably with each additional child.

A: What you heard is right. There is an incentive for the one-child family. It varies between rural and urban areas. The incentive in the urban area, I think, is critical. In the rural areas, each family with a one-child certificate is eligible for extra work points, credit worth one month's participation in farming, until the child is 14 years of age. In the countryside in the future each one-child family will be allocated a four-person housing lot. The only child will be given priority in admission to school and in assignment of industrial jobs.

COMMENT (S. Goldstein): Realizing that the introduction of the responsibility system to some extent pulls the rug out from under the one-child family system, there has been a movement to introduce a new institution called the double-contract system. When a farm family signs a contract under the responsibility system, in many places they are also expected to sign a contract with respect to fertility, promising not to have more than the number of children that are allowed in that particular location. If they violate that particular contract, then the terms under their responsibility contract are also changed and they may, for example, be relegated to poorer land or to growing a crop that yields less income. The hope is that, by building in a set of rewards and expenses that are tied to the responsibility system, the government will be able to maintain more control over the one-child family policy too.

Sino-Soviet Relations: What Next?

By ALLEN S. WHITING

ABSTRACT: China's three demands for normalization of Sino-Soviet relations are not likely to win Soviet compliance. Only a modest reduction of the 480,000 Soviet troops opposite China is possible, but not removal of the 125 SS-20 missiles and 60 Backfire bombers, which have regional and global strategic significance. No Soviet concessions on Afghanistan or Vietnam-Kampuchea are expected. Ideology is no longer an issue between Moscow and Beijing as during Mao's time, but conflicts in national interest deadlock negotiations. Meanwhile, increased Sino-Soviet trade and travel reflect improved state relations. A further improvement could serve U.S. interests in Korea, Indochina, and arms control without jeopardizing U.S. and allied security interests elsewhere. Sino-Soviet relations are, however, basically independent of American influence and should not determine Sino-American relations.

Allen S. Whiting is professor of political science and director of the Center for East Asian Studies at the University of Arizona. He has held a variety of positions, including senior social scientist at the Rand Corporation, director of the Office of Far East Analysis in the Department of State, and deputy consul general in Hong Kong. His publications include Siberian Development and East Asia *and* The Chinese Calculus of Deterrence.

I N July 1964, Mao Zedong declared to a visiting Japanese delegation,

A hundred years ago they [the Russians] incorporated the territory to the east of Lake Baikal, including Khabarovsk, Vladivostok, and the Kamchatka Peninsula. . . . We have not settled those accounts with them.[1]

This implied claim to 585,000 square miles of territory ceded to Czarist Russia by the Qing empire shocked Moscow into a massive military strengthening of its Siberian and far-eastern regions, which doubled the ground forces there over the following five years.[2]

In March 1969 the Chinese government provoked brief but bloody fighting over a disputed island in the Ussuri River.[3] Sporadic clashes erupted along the 4650-mile frontier during subsequent months. Propaganda campaigns in both countries alerted the two populaces to the threat of war. Meanwhile, President Richard Nixon and National Security Adviser Henry Kissinger publicly moved to deter a Soviet attack while privately signaling their interest in détente with China.[4]

Fifteen years later speculation turns, not on the prospect of Sino-Soviet conflict, but rather on the likelihood of alignment between Beijing and Moscow. Beginning in 1982, the two sides have met four times to probe for détente, in addition to numerous informal exchanges. Visits occur at the level of deputy prime minister, the highest level since 1965. Trade increases have averaged 50 percent annually over the past three years. Delegations traveling between the Soviet Union and China include athletes, scholars, tourists, and technical specialists in various fields.

Yet this past March Prime Minister Zhao Ziyang told visiting Japanese Prime Minister Yasuhiro Nakasone, "The main threat to China's security comes from the Soviet Union."[5] Beijing continues to demand that Moscow reduce its troop concentration opposite China to the 1965 level, including the removal of all forces from the Mongolian People's Republic. It also attacks Soviet hegemony as manifest in the occupation of Afghanistan and support for Vietnam's invasion of Kampuchea. It claims both situations must be reversed if Sino-Soviet relations are to be normalized.

Moscow in turn insists that it desires normalized relations while it steadily strengthens its forces in East Siberia. With more than 120 SS-20 missiles and 60 Backfire bombers there, Soviet nuclear attacks can cover all of China.[6] The expanding Soviet naval and air presence in Vietnam plus Moscow's military support to Hanoi further threaten Chinese security. Last but not least, the Soviet Pacific Fleet is now the largest component in Moscow's navy. This could cut China off from all foreign supplies in the event of war.

    1. Mao Zedong, Speech to Japanese visitors, 10 July 1964, in *Mao Zedong sixiang wan sui* [Long live Mao Zedong thought] (1969; reprint ed., Taipei, 1974), pp. 540-41; for a similar version translated from *Sekai shuho,* 11 Aug. 1964, see Dennis J. Doolin, *Territorial Claims in the Sino-Soviet Conflict: Documents and Analysis* (Stanford, CA: Hoover Institution Press, 1965), p. 44.
    2. Consensus of U.S. intelligence analysis, July 1969.
    3. Chinese responsibility inferred from Neville Maxwell, "The Chinese Account of the 1969 Fighting at Chenpao," *China Quarterly,* no. 56 (Oct.-Dec. 1973).
    4. For my role as an adviser on this matter, see Seymour M. Hersh, *The Price of Power: Kissinger in the Nixon White House* (New York: Summit Books, 1983), pp. 357-59.

    5. *New York Times,* 24 Mar. 1984.
    6. *New York Times,* 30 Jan. 1984.

Given the changing nature of the Sino-Soviet relationship over the past three decades and its central role in world politics as well as American foreign policy, several key questions arise. What constitutes normal Sino-Soviet relations: confrontation or cooperation? Are conflicts of interest so deep-seated as to preclude a real rapprochement? Or can Beijing and Moscow improve relations so as to change the balance of power in Asia and perhaps the world? Finally, how should the United States respond to this relationship? Is China playing a Soviet card to force greater American concessions on technology transfer, trade, and Taiwan? Or do we exaggerate the triangular effect of Sino-American relations on Sino-Soviet relations?

Admittedly, there is little direct evidence to answer these questions. Sino-Soviet consultations began in 1979 at China's initiative, were suspended by Beijing in 1980 because of Afghanistan, and resumed in 1982. No progress has been officially reported by either side on any issue, and no significant leaks have revealed the course of discussion. Fortunately, a thorough recapitulation of these and other interactions, as well as various allusions to them in Soviet and Chinese sources, is amply available elsewhere.[7] To summarize, hints of optimism dropped by both sides in 1982-83 subsequently dissolved into standard statements calling on the opposite number to show sincerity by actions as well as words.

However, the situation is not static by any means. The changing agenda of issues identified by Beijing as characterizing Sino-Soviet differences over the past 20 years provides some measurement of flexibility in China's position. In addition, the nature of those issues permits us to assess whether stalemate or compromise is likely in the foreseeable future. Moreover, despite individual leadership changes, there is sufficient stability in the two regimes for projection from the present over the next five years. This can place the implications of likely Sino-Soviet relations in perspective for U.S. policy.

THE CHANGING AGENDA: TERRITORY AND TROOPS

Despite the far-reaching scope of Mao Zedong's 1964 remark, Beijing subsequently denied it would demand that Moscow return territory taken through "unequal treaties." Instead it called for a Soviet withdrawal from "disputed areas" allegedly occupied in violation of these treaties whose unequal nature need only be so acknowledged by Moscow as a precondition to negotiations. Moscow refused to do so, claiming that such acknowledgment might open the door to a reassertion of Mao's extreme irredentist position. Finally, Beijing apparently abandoned this demand, references to the "unequal treaties" having disappeared in references to the talks.

So far as the disputed areas are concerned, Soviet sources claim they have agreed to give up control over hundreds of islands in the Ussuri River, including the one that triggered the 1969 clashes.[8] But numerous minor points of

7. Donald S. Zagoria, "The Moscow-Beijing Detente," *Foreign Affairs*, 61(4):853-73 (Spring 1983); Banning N. Garrett and Bonnie S. Glaser, *War and Peace: The Views From Moscow and Beijing* (Berkeley, CA: Institute of International Studies, 1984).

8. Interview with M. S. Kapitsa, 17 June 1978.

land remain at issue, according to the Chinese, scattered along the extensive mixture of forest, mountain, and arid plain that constitute the Sino-Soviet frontier. Beijing insists that Moscow must evacuate all such territory before detailed discussions can begin; Moscow refuses.

In addition, two areas of special military interest deserve attention. One is the so-called Pamir knot, a high, populated plateau in the Pamir Mountains adjoining the Soviet Union, Afghanistan, and China.[9] The second involves a pair of large, unpopulated islands opposite the key juncture of Khabarovsk at the confluence of the Amur and Ussuri Rivers. Soviet authorities are adamant on the retention of these two areas because of their strategic location, and Beijing will have to concede at least these points if a border settlement is to occur.

Moscow's military buildup was initially linked to the border dispute and the larger implications of Mao's July 1964 statement. These implications became worst-case possibilities with Red Guard border violence during the heyday of Cultural Revolution anarchy. Thus 22 divisions, nearly half of the total ground forces opposite China, are concentrated in and near the Maritime Province, between Manchuria and the Sea of Japan.[10] They defend the vital rail link between Khabarovsk and Vladivostok, the main base for the Soviet

Pacific Fleet. That railroad runs within 10 miles of the Chinese border for nearly 175 miles along the Ussuri River.

Worst-case contingency planning can make a persuasive case in the Kremlin for this deloyment. Vladivostok is 12 time zones distant from Moscow. The Trans-Siberian Railroad offers the only line of communication by land. It circles Manchuria, where more than 75 million Chinese live, compared with only 11 million inhabitants scattered across East and Far East Siberia. The alternate means, other than by air, is by sea. This requires transiting half the globe through the Suez Canal, the Indian Ocean, the Malacca Strait, the South and East China Seas, culminating in the Tsushima Strait between Korea and Japan, which Tokyo and Washington can jointly obstruct.

To be sure, Beijing's claim of "a million Soviet troops" confronting it overstates the case by a factor of two. Fewer than 500,000 are estimated in the ground forces as against three times that number on the Chinese side. Nevertheless, this is a sizable contingent, requiring a major investment for the supporting infrastructure in a region with a chronic food deficit and low economic development. Moscow is not likely to accede to Beijing's demand that it be reduced to the 15 or so divisions that were there before 1965. The cost of its continued presence is of relatively little consequence as against the initial cost of emplacement.

Over time, Moscow has added air and missile forces with an impressive multiple of retaliatory power to deter Chinese use of a slowly expanding nuclear-weapons inventory. In addition, this buildup permits Soviet power to be projected throughout East Asia, potentially targeting American bases in Korea,

9. For a detailed examination, with maps, of this obscure area, see John W. Garver, "The Sino-Soviet Territorial Dispute in the Pamir Mountains Region," *China Quarterly,* no. 85, pp. 107-18 (Mar. 1981).

10. The distribution of Soviet forces may be found in Shigeo Hiramatsu, "A Chinese Perspective on Sino-Soviet Relations," *Journal of Northeast Asian Studies,* 2(3):60-62 (Sept. 1983).

Japan, and the Philippines, as well as American naval forces in the west Pacific. These regional and global strategic considerations reinforce the utility of SS-20s and Backfire bombers in Siberia and the Soviet Far East, further reducing the probability of any major reduction in force in response to Chinese demands.

The only likely concession to Beijing is a freeze on further deployment in the region, perhaps accompanied by a symbolic transfer of troops from military to civilian assignments associated with Siberian development. Engineering, construction, and timber felling face serious labor shortages, which block exploitation of the region's rich resources. Detailing troops to such work would still leave them available for military duty on short notice, should that need arise.

Of China's three demands for normalized relations, the reduction of Soviet troops is the one most immediately relevant to Chinese security. It is also the only issue readily susceptible to bilateral negotiations. But Beijing's call for the removal of Soviet forces from Mongolia introduces the dimension of a third country, which further complicates the problem. Ulan Bator recently reiterated its 1978 declaration that this troop withdrawal "entirely lies within the internal competence of the Mongolian People's Republic."[11] China's adherence nonetheless to this demand raises doubt as to the seriousness with which it views the larger question, particularly since only three Soviet divisions are in Mongolia facing 10 times that number in north China.

Indeed, there is little in Chinese words or behavior to suggest genuine alarm over the disposition of Soviet military force or its likely use in the near future. On the contrary, for the past 10 years public propaganda and officials in Beijing have played down the immediate threat while professing concern over the long-run implications should Soviet hegemony encircle China.[12] No notable increases in military expenditures have occurred during that time except in connection with the brief attack on Vietnam in 1979. No major purchases abroad of military equipment have taken place up to 1984.

Instead Chinese analyses dwell on Moscow's problems at home and abroad, including Poland, the Middle East, and Afghanistan. In addition, Beijing's deterrent capacity is growing and may be thought invulnerable to a Soviet first strike. At a minimum, Irkutsk, Khabarovsk, and Vladisvostok lie within ready striking range of Chinese missiles. A nuclear attack on any one of the three could cripple the base of Soviet power in the Pacific. After that attack Moscow would have to contend with the largest army in the world backed by a population of 1 billion. These factors justify Chinese confidence in the present balance of power as sufficient, at least for the near future.

Thus territorial and troop issues are not contributing to Sino-Soviet tension as they were a decade or more ago, although they remain important items on the agenda for negotiations. They require concessions on both sides if they are to be resolved. These concessions may be politically difficult in the two capitals, because they involve matters of nationalistic sensitivity as well as na-

11. Mongolian government statement transmitted by Montsame in English, 2 Mar. 1984, in *Daily Report: Asia and Pacific*, 5 Mar. 1984, p F1.

12. Garrett and Glaser, chap. 3.

tional security. But they are not so volatile as to cause an increase in confrontation, much less open conflict.

THE CHANGING AGENDA: IDEOLOGY AND NATIONAL INTERESTS

Long before Mao raised the territorial issue, he accused Moscow of ideological heresy, specifically anathematized as "Khrushchev revisionism." In Beijing's polemic, this alleged betrayal of Marxism-Leninism raged throughout the 1960s and continued until Mao's death in 1976. Then the issue quietly faded from Chinese media. Attacks on the Kremlin leadership ceased to have any domestic content, focusing instead solely on Soviet foreign policy and its threat to world peace.

In part this change of focus followed China's becoming somewhat revisionist itself. Post-Mao economic reforms aimed at stimulating production through material incentives with the virtual abandonment of communes as key decision-making bodies. But contrary to American perceptions, ideology was neither the binding force in Sino-Soviet relations nor the main disruptive agent that split Moscow and Beijing. I addressed this same topic at the American Academy of Political and Social Science in 1958 and challenged the then-existing assumption that a common Communist belief cemented the alliance with common goals. Instead, I argued, "the first decade of the Moscow-Peking axis suggests that in this respect, relations between Communist partners resemble those between capitalist states in the existence of conflicting national interests." [13]

13. Allen S. Whiting, "Dynamics of the Moscow-Peking Axis," *The Annals* of the American Academy of Political and Social Science, 321:103 (Jan. 1959).

Today this observation is commonplace. It is underscored by the fact that among Asia's various points of contention the sharpest are between China and Vietnam, on the one hand, and China and the Soviet Union on the other hand, the two disputes being fused through the Soviet-Vietnamese alliance. There is no better evidence of ideology taking second place to conflicts of national interest; nor is there a more dramatic demonstration of convergent national interests taking priority over ideology than Mao Zedong receiving Richard Nixon in Beijing—unless perhaps it is Premier Zhao Ziyang welcoming President Ronald Reagan.

Of course, ideology was not wholly irrelevant as an issue. So long as it resounded through Chinese rhetoric, it impeded exploration of ways to reduce Sino-Soviet tension through bilateral exchanges. Its disappearance freed the agenda for more tangible matters of national interest. But, precisely because these issues concern concrete national interests, they are very difficult to resolve. When they involve third countries, the difficulty is compounded. Only unilateral concession or third-party participation can bring agreement.

Let us take, for instance, Afghanistan. Can Beijing hope to induce Moscow to withdraw either through negative pressure or positive persuasion? Clearly this demand is of political, not military, importance, regardless of Chinese assertions to the contrary. The narrow finger of Afghanistan known as the Wakhan Corridor adds a minuscule point of access to China for Soviet forces, as against the virtually open sweep possible across the vast Xinjiang and Mongolian borders. As such, Beijing's Afghan demand is not likely to be negotiated, much less won. At a minimum it is a useful polemical club. At most it may be a bargaining chip to be traded for something else.

But if that something else is withdrawal of support for Vietnam's occupation of Kampuchea, as stated by China, agreement seems equally remote. Moscow would lose access to Cam Ranh Bay, that warm-water port that Russian and Soviet leaders have sought for nearly a century. Soviet air and naval projection in South as well as Southeast Asia would shrink to insignificance instead of enjoying the prospect of continual growth. Moreover, Moscow's credibility as an ally would suffer the worst blow since Khrushchev's withdrawal of missiles from Cuba in 1962.[14]

For Vietnam the issue of Kampuchea has transcended all other foreign and domestic priorities. Hanoi resisted Chinese attack in 1979 and threats of a second lesson subsequently. It has rejected annual United Nations resolutions since then. It adamantly opposes proposals from the Association of Southeast Asian Nations that raise the prospect of Hanoi's losing control of Phnom Penh. It continues to field 180,000 troops in Kampuchea and 200,000 opposite China five years after the initial engagements on both fronts. Under these circumstances the prospects of détente between Hanoi and Beijing are bleak in the near future, and concomitantly so are the prospects of agreement between Moscow and Beijing on Vietnam.

PROLONGED DEADLOCK:
NORMALIZED RELATIONS?

Our review of the changing agenda posited by Beijing for the normalization

of relations with Moscow suggests the possibility of minor movement on troop levels, but little else of significance. Border differences could be readily resolved if there were a will to do so; however, they seem locked into the larger conflicts of national interest where no agreement is likely for years to come.

This deadlock is reinforced by domestic factors in both countries. In the Soviet Union the rapid succession from Brezhnev to Andropov to Chernenko inhibits any bold change of policy where national sensitivity and security are so involved with China. Nor is the prospect of longevity and strong leadership enhanced by Chernenko's incumbency. Thus the risks of change encourage playing it safe with past and present positions so far as individuals are concerned. This is probably the way it is argued collectively in the politburo as well.

In Beijing, economic modernization is the highest priority of policy. This requires dependence on external sources of capital and technology. Those sources—whether American, Japanese, or West European—are encourged by assurances that Beijing is not expecting a rapprochement with Moscow. The Americans in particular welcome evidence of China's tilt toward the United States in a tacit, anti-Soviet alignment. Access to external capital and technology is a powerful incentive for recalcitrance on Beijing's three demands on the Soviet Union.

Against these immobilizing factors on both sides, there is an absence of anxiety over the actual state of relations to impel compromise. It is 15 years since the two premiers, Alexei Kosygin and Zhou Enlai, met suddenly in the Beijing airport to halt the escalation of tension that had threatened to erupt into war throughout 1969. Nothing has occurred

14. For Castro's recent criticism of Soviet behavior, see Ted Szulc, "Friendship Possible, but . . .," *Parade*, 1 Apr. 1984, p. 5.

since then to reawaken that level of concern.

On the contrary, Beijing and Moscow seem able to improve state relations despite a deadlock on issues of such moment as disputed territory, troop concentrations, Afghanistan, and Kampuchea. Trade occurs across the Manchurian and Xinjiang borders after 15 years of interruption. The total amount exchanged between the Soviet Union and China is a minor fraction of their global trade, but it is nonetheless steadily increasing in quality and quantity. Of all Chinese students abroad currently, the percentage in the USSR is infinitesimal, but even a token presence represents a symbolic step of some significance. Finally, an apparent moratorium on the mutual denunciation of society and values, replaced with reasonably factual accounts of life across the border, opens the way for a more relaxed relationship as befits two neighbors of such size and ideological similarity.

Seen in this context, the deadlock in Sino-Soviet negotiations takes on the appearance of a normalized relationship. Certainly it is normal for nations, especially major powers, to contest for influence and perhaps control in third countries. It is also normal for them to safeguard against a powerful neighbor by appropriate political and military postures that deter, but do not provoke or invite, attack. For the Chinese at least, it is even normal to engage in prolonged diplomatic exchanges with an adversary without giving in to the other side or to one's own sense of impatience. Fifteen years of Sino-American ambassadorial talks and similarly extended Sino-Indian border negotiations provide ample proof in this regard. Whether they also provide a precedent for Sino-Soviet negotiations remains to

be seen. Moreover, this style of what might be called nonnegotiating behavior is very familiar to Moscow, even if it becomes frustrating at times.

AN AMERICAN CONNECTION?

Reference to the prolonged Sino-American ambassadorial talks provides a reminder that the sharp escalation in Sino-Soviet tensions opened the way for a Nixon-Mao handshake after more than two decades of conflict and confrontation. This union launched the era of triangular diplomacy as successfully exploited by Henry Kissinger and, to a lesser extent, Zbigniew Brzezinski.

It is not surprising, therefore, that signs of improved Sino-Soviet relations raise questions about the role of American policy either in causing that improvement or, preferably, in halting it. The causal connection is often assumed to be Taiwan. Simply put, the more Washington worries Beijing over American intentions concerning Taiwan, the greater Beijing's alleged inclination to seek an accommodation with Moscow. Former President Richard Nixon put this bluntly in commemorating the tenth anniversary of the Shanghai Communiqué,

It would be the height of folly to try to 'save' Taiwan at the cost of losing China. If China slipped back into the Soviet orbit, the balance of power in the world would be overwhelmingly shifted against us.[15]

The implication that the United States has China to lose is as specious now as it was in 1949 when Nixon and others first raised the cry, "Who lost China?" Against that precedent, the irony of Nixon's more recent concern coming

15. *New York Times,* 28 Feb. 1982.

under a Republican administration is worth noting. Perhaps his rhetoric, however inappropriate, deliberately targeted President Reagan's consciousness, much as in 1972 when Nixon won Reagan's support through a similar argument.[16] Yet, setting aside for the moment China's purported weight in the global power balance, are Sino-Soviet relations so simply and directly a function of Sino-American relations as this argument asserts?

Our examination of the changing agenda suggests the contrary. The issues outstanding between Beijing and Moscow, whether bilateral or trilateral, preclude China's slipping back into the Soviet orbit. Moreover, that figure of speech, "the Soviet orbit," with its implications of a stronger power dominating a lesser one, is antithetical to China's experience of the 1950s and Chinese pronouncements of the 1980s.

To take the pronouncements first, Deng Xiaoping employed his uniquely pithy language in addressing the Twelfth Congress of the Chinese Communist party:

No foreign country can expect China to be its vassal or expect it to swallow any bitter fruit detrimental to its own interests.[17]

Secretary-General Hu Yaobang echoed this stance in a somewhat overstated assertion:

In the thirty-three years since the founding of our People's Republic, we have shown the world by deeds that China never attaches itself to any big power or group of powers, and never yields to pressure from any big power.[18]

These declarations have since become the leitmotiv of official statements and academic analyses.

Hu's words to the contrary notwithstanding, the lessons learned from having attached itself to the Soviet Union are precisely what prompt Chinese determination never to repeat that experience. Aside from whatever deterrence and defensive power Moscow may have provided against the early fears of an American-Taiwan attack, the memory and perception in Beijing of that relationship are studded with neglect, if not betrayal, of China's national interests. Foremost, of course, was the failure to acquire Taiwan, initially because the North Korean attack triggered President Truman's imposition of the U.S. Seventh Fleet in the Taiwan Strait. By 1958-59, however, suspicion arose that Nikita Khrushchev placed détente with President Eisenhower ahead of China's goal of territorial unification and final victory in the civil war.

Then Moscow's public stance of neutrality after Sino-Indian border clashes in 1959 similarly put the alliance second to Soviet interests in South Asia. By 1962 the Soviet supply of high-altitude military transport helicopters and negotiations for a MIG jet fighter factory in India convinced Beijing it faced a second opponent as well in its fight with India

16. Helene von Damm, *Sincerely, Ronald Reagan* (Ottawa, IL: Green Hill, 1976), pp. 75-76, quotes a letter from Reagan to M. Stanton Evans: "Stan, let me suggest something about the China visit that unfortunately the President can't say. . . . The President, knowing of the disaffection between China and Russia, visits China, butters up the warlords, and lets them be, because they have nothing to fear from us. Russia, therefore, has to keep its 140 [sic] divisions on the Chinese border; hostility between the two is increased; and we buy a little time and elbowroom in a plain, simple strategic move."

17. *Beijing Review,* 6 Sept. 1982, p. 5.

18. Ibid., 13 Sept. 1982, p. 33.

over disputed territory in the Himalayan heights.

Appreciative as many Chinese were of the availability of Soviet credit, technology, and training when the American embargo sought to strangle economic recovery during the 1950s, the Soviet withdrawal of all assistance, human and material, in 1960 added injury to insult. Following abrogation of the nuclear-weapons sharing agreement in 1959, such a complete withdrawal left a searing memory of how foreign dependence can become a foreign weapon. In the context of economic collapse caused by Mao's ill-fated Great Leap Forward, the Soviet pullout of help from dozens of half-finished factories provided a visible reminder of how little lay behind protestations of Communist unity and monolithic solidarity.

In short, there is nothing in the likely course of American words or actions, now or in the future, which will drive Beijing into the arms of Moscow. The triangular image is wrong to the extent that it depicts a physical object whose respective sides must lengthen or shorten responsively to one another. The atmospherics and tactics of policy can affect the Communist interaction, but in the fundamental sense of strategic orientation implied in the Nixon imagery of an orbital domination, Sino-Soviet relations are not that susceptible to American influence, positive or negative.

CHINA'S STRATEGIC SIGNIFICANCE

Nevertheless, is Nixon right in saying "the balance of power in the world would be overwhelmingly shifted against us" were a Sino-Soviet rapprochement to occur? A recent study by Banning Garrett and Bonnie Glaser calls atten-

tion to the changing calculus of power in different contexts ranging from peace to attack, prolonged war, and a postwar situation.[19] Simplistic images of 1 billion Chinese tying down one-third to one-fourth of Soviet military power suggest that these units of people and power would be turned against the West should Moscow and Beijing patch up their differences.

But just as China will never again make its security dependent on a Soviet alliance, so too the Kremlin will never place its Far East holdings at the mercy of Beijing. As we have already shown, an agreement to reduce forces in mutual confrontation will not demilitarize the Sino-Soviet frontier like its American-Canadian counterpart. The strategic arrangement of Soviet air and missile power will remain, ostensibly justified by the exigencies of the global confrontation with the United States. Such ground forces as might be redeployed elsewhere would be hardly sufficient to impact significantly on local, much less widespread, confrontation.

Nor is China's weight—present and prospective in this decade—a major factor in global power considerations. Its ground forces fared poorly against Vietnam in 1979. Its air and naval power is 20 years behind that of the superpowers. Its power projection is limited to a few hundred miles beyond China's borders. Measured in any dimension of modern military force, the People's Liberation Army is massive in size but minuscule in power except when compared with its immediate neighbors in South and Southeast Asia.

These calculations change drastically, however, in a wartime context. No Kremlin contingency plan for war with

19. Garrett and Glaser, pp. 7-12.

the United States can fail to take account of a possible Chinese attack at some stage after the initiation of Soviet-American hostilities. This will apply whether there is a Sino-Soviet détente or not. The temptation will be great for Beijing to remove, once and for all, its fear of Soviet hegemony by taking advantage of Moscow's vulnerability after a superpower nuclear exchange. The prospect of Beijing passively accepting a possible Soviet victory over the United States, thereby leaving the USSR as the virtual ruler of the world, is remote, to say the least.

It is in this second-stage war and postwar context that China's strategic weight figures significantly, perhaps decisively, in Soviet calculations. But this contingency is independent of Sino-American relations. China's concern over Soviet domination will obtain regardless of how Washington and Beijing manage their political and military relations. How and when China will act on that concern will be a function of Chinese decisions at the time and not of any prior discussions or understandings that might be arrived at with American officials. Just as Chinese security will not rely on Russian promises, so too it will not be linked to American assurances either.

In short, the very fact of China's existence as a potentially hostile neighbor, with a growing inventory of nuclear weapons and inexhaustible reserves of manpower, helps to deter Soviet initiation of global war. This fact will be of increasing importance as Chinese economic and military modernization strengthen Beijing's capacity to exploit that war to its own advantage. It is in this context that U.S. policy should frame its strategic relationship with the People's Republic, rather than tune it to the tactical and transient shifts in Sino-Soviet relations.

IMPLICATIONS FOR U.S. POLICY

It should be clear by now that the United States can influence, but not determine, how Moscow and Beijing will interact. We may have been responsible for the initial Sino-Soviet alliance, although even that is still the subject of historical inquiry and dispute. But we cannot take credit for its erosion in 1959-60. Nor, contrary to the assertions of former White House aide H. R. Haldeman, did we block a Soviet attack on China in 1969.[20]

This does not mean that what occurs between Moscow and Beijing is irrelevant to U.S. policy. On the contrary, we were justifiably concerned with the emergence of the alliance in 1950, with all that portended for the political power, perceived and actual, of communism in what was then known as the Afro-Asian world. The consequences in Korea and Indochina were immediate. Fortunately the impact elsewhere, particularly among the Communist insurgencies of Asia, proved less far reaching.

Conversely, the Sino-Soviet split relieved U.S. military planners of a major threat from coordinated actions by the two Communist powers. More important in practical terms, it opened American policy to the prospect of restored relations with mainland China. This offered a host of political and economic gains in itself, as well as in negotiations with the Soviet Union. The deferral of Taiwan as an issue to be resolved on China's terms occurred primarily because of concern in Beijing

20. H. R. Haldeman with Joseph Dimona, *The Ends of Power* (New York: Times Books, 1978), pp. 93-94.

over a Sino-Soviet conflict. Without that context the Shanghai Communiqué could not have occurred.

Therefore we must assess the prospect for Sino-Soviet relations and how they are likely to affect our interests as well as those of our friends and allies in Asia and elsewhere. But we need not regard the triangular relationship as a zero-sum game wherein any improvement in Sino-Soviet affairs is a gain for Moscow and a loss for Washington or vice versa. On the contrary, we share an interest in reduced tension between the two Communist countries if that reduces the risk of clashes that might escalate. No one will benefit should these massive nuclear powers go to war. A genuine border settlement would be a welcome step in this regard.

To go a step further, the positive side of a mutual force reduction could raise the possibility of Chinese participation in Soviet and American arms-control negotiations. While this is a most unlikely prospect, its essentiality is manifest in the separate positions struck in Moscow, Washington, Beijing, and Tokyo concerning the disposition of SS-20 missiles. So long as the Sino-Soviet confrontation continues, these missiles can justifiably be deployed in East and Far East Siberia, regardless of their threat to Japan or their potential return to European Russia.

Should a Sino-Soviet détente go beyond the issues of territory and troops, third-country matters might be addressed to the advantage of American policy interests. An agreement on the Korean peninsula for cross-recognition of north and south by the respective patrons in Moscow, Beijing, and Washington requires a prior willingness to reduce Chinese and Soviet competition for Pyongyang's favor. Neither Moscow nor

Beijing wants war in the peninsula, both being committed to defend the north under such circumstances. But neither can formalize the status quo on a two-Korea basis so long as both remain rivals for influence in the north, which adamantly rejects the status quo.

An equally intractable but greater strategic problem might prove possible of solution through a *modus vivendi* on Indochina that would remove the Soviet military presence there. This solution is impaled on a third-country relationship. As suggested earlier, such an arrangement would probably require Sino-Vietnamese détente prior to or coincident with Sino-Soviet détente, a highly remote contingency, but one not wholly beyond the realm of possibility.

This is not to suggest that Sino-Soviet negotiations will lead to any of these eventualities, much less all of them. However, in the absence of such negotiations, none of them can occur. Deadlock is not in itself inimical to our interests, but neither is it an unmixed blessing that we should seek to perpetuate by our interactions with either side.

This argument in turn frees us to assess our relations with China in contexts other than the Sino-Soviet relationship. Whether we sell arms to Beijing and what the nature of those arms is should be primarily a function of how our friends and allies in Asia view the situation as China's most immediately concerned neighbors.[21] How we adjust

21. For a thorough examination of this issue from varying viewpoints, see *The Implications of U.S.-China Military Cooperation* (Washington, DC: Government Printing Office, 1981), a collection of papers from a workshop sponsored by the Committee on Foreign Relations of the U.S. Senate and the Congressional Research Service of the Library of Congress; see also *China Policy for the Next Decade: Report on the Atlantic Council's*

our trade balance with China should depend on how that affects our domestic economy as well as China's competitors. How we manage our Taiwan relations should turn on our obligations under agreements concluded with the People's Republic.[22]

Committee on China Policy (Washington, DC: Atlantic Council, 1983).

22. For greater detail, see Allen S. Whiting, "Sino-American Relations: The Decade Ahead," Orbis, 26(3):697-720 (Fall 1982); and idem, "PRC-Taiwan Relations, 1883-93," SAIS Review, 3(1): 131-46 (Winter-Spring, 1983).

Happily, we are past the time of maximum turbulence in the so-called strategic triangle. Sino-Soviet and Sino-American relations are already normalized, Chinese rhetoric to the contrary notwithstanding. This is in the interests of all concerned. We have no reason to fear improvement on any of the triangle's three dimensions. Indeed, peace and stability in Asia and the world may well be served by an improvement in the dimension under immediate examination, the Sino-Soviet relationship.

*   *   *

QUESTIONS AND ANSWERS

Q (Dario Scuka, Library of Congress, Washington, D.C.): Unlike old-fashioned diplomacy, which was conducted in good taste, current relations seem to be conducted with a high-pitched rhetoric that translates into headline banners. What discount would you give to rhetoric from Moscow, Peking, or Washington?

A: I think one has to be very cautious in discounting rhetoric. It tends to be self-confirming and self-convincing. If it is repeated often enough, the agency that puts it out forgets that it was a line and accepts it as reality. It also is something that tends to bind the bureaucracy, so while leaders may "know better" the followers cannot be clued in.

do not expect Sino-Soviet trade to equal Sino-U.S. trade, much less Sino-Japanese trade, which is, as you know, one-fourth of China's foreign trade. I do not expect that there will be 12,000 Chinese studying in the Soviet Union as there are in the United States. I do think that these two neighbors are going to learn to live with each other and make the most of it in trade and other fields of interaction. But as far as competition in third countries is concerned, it has become increasingly intense in North Korea in the last two months. It is certainly at a deadlock in Vietnam. In other words, China and the Soviet Union are major competitors in all of their international relationships.

Q (Murray McLean, Embassy of Australia): What precisely is a normal state of relations between the Soviet Union and China?

A: I would define the present situation as normal: as a portion of their total foreign trade, the trade levels between the two countries are very small. I

Q (Mr. Gilliam, Virginia Military Institute, Lexington): I had the privilege before Pearl Harbor of knowing some army officers who had served in China, who knew the language—they could be referred to as the old China hands. I wonder if there are Americans still left who can really understand what is going on in China. I would like to think there are people in China, like some of the Chinese students who graduated from the Virginia Military Institute a few years back, who would be able to go back to China and advise their government about the United States.

A: I might say that the American corps of old China hands has survived somewhat better than the China corps of old American hands—not much, but somewhat. We do not kill our China experts, we only persecute them, purge them from government jobs, and deny them academic positions. In the 1950s we virtually ostracized them from our society. One of the great survivors of that period, of course, is the now retired professor John Fairbank of Harvard; others are retired foreign service officers O. Edmund Clubb, John Paton Davies, John Stuart Service at Berkeley, Ed Rice in the San Francisco Bay area, and there are others still. But we did a very thorough hatchet job on that China community between 1949 and 1959. On the China side, they literally did elim-inate experts on the United States during the Cultural Revolution. They had some driven to suicide. Some of the experts can still be found, rehabilitated in various institutes; however, their physical and mental powers are not always what they were before. I do not think there is much chance of putting together the alumni of those previous years and reestablishing U.S.-China relations on that ground. In fact, one of the problems is indeed the education of Hu Yaobang and Zhao Ziyang, of a generation of leaders. Zhou Enlai was singular in this regard in that he was one of the few genuine statesmen in the Mao government with a sophisticated familiarity with the world. Deng Xiaoping is certainly not of that same stamp at all. We, in effect, have been learning anew over this last decade, and I appreciate the way Professor Chang emphasized the cycles in the U.S.-Chinese relationship—first the hatred, then the euphoria, and now the realistic balance between the two.

U.S.-China Relations: From Hostility
to Euphoria to Realism

By PARRIS H. CHANG

ABSTRACT: For the leaders in Beijing, the People's Republic of China has no eternal allies or perpetual enemies; only its interests are permanent. This principle has guided China's external relations in the past three decades and has shaped its alignments with the USSR, the United States, and other major powers. Foreign policy of the People's Republic will be influenced by these objectives: containment of Soviet expansionism; acquisition of foreign capital and technology to accelerate China's program of modernization; and Taiwan's reunification with the mainland. The United States is a crucial factor in each of these national objectives; hence Beijing seeks good relations with Washington. For domestic reasons, Beijing has inflated the importance of Taiwan in Sino-U.S. relations, but an agreement in August 1982 has provided a framework to manage Sino-U.S. disagreement about Taiwan. Sino-U.S. relations have improved markedly, as attested by the Zhao-Reagan exchange of visits and increasing economic cooperation.

Parris H. Chang is professor of political science and chair of Asian area studies at Pennsylvania State University. He has visited both the USSR and, frequently, the People's Republic of China. He is the author of Power and Policy in China *and* Radicals and Radical Ideology in China's Cultural Revolution, *as well as numerous articles in* Asian Survey, China Quarterly, Orbis, Problems of Communism, Newsweek, *the* Washington Post, *and other periodicals.*

Who are our enemies? Who are our friends? This is a question of the first importance for the revolution. . . . We must pay attention to unifying with our real friends in order to attack our real enemies.

Mao Zedong, 1926[1]

ALLY OR ENEMY?

To Chinese Communist leaders in Beijing, the People's Republic of China (PRC) has no eternal allies nor perpetual enemies; only its national interests are permanent. In more than three decades after the establishment of the Communist regime, PRC foreign policy has undergone several major shifts as Beijing's perception of external threats has changed and it has redefined enemies and friends.

From 1949 until the late 1960s, PRC leaders were vehemently anti-American. They perceived the United States as China's archenemy; they accused the United States of occupying Taiwan and colluding with the Chinese Nationalist—Kuomintang (KMT)—government to invade the mainland; they attacked the United States for reviving Japanese militarism; and they denounced the United States as the chief bulwark of world reaction and the most vicious enemy of peace. In February 1950 Mao Zedong concluded with Stalin a 30-year Treaty of Friendship, Alliance, and Mutual Assistance. Ostensibly against Japan, the treaty was actually directed against the United States.

The Sino-Soviet alliance did pay handsome political, military, and economic dividends to the PRC. It gave the PRC a protective umbrella, which severely constrained U.S. policy during the Korean War and deterred the United States from directly attacking mainland China. It also enabled the PRC to obtain from Moscow a large amount of modern weapons and military equipment, which were crucial in sustaining Beijing's war efforts in Korea. Through the alliance, Beijing also secured much Soviet material and technical assistance for China's economic development in the 1950s.

The national interests of the two allies were not identical, however; even before the first decade of the alliance drew to a close, Beijing had become disillusioned. In the economic sphere, to Beijing's chagrin, the generosity of the Russian big brother was quite limited. During the Sino-Soviet honeymoon in the 1950s, Moscow provided only two loans—a five-year, $300 million loan in 1950 and another credit of $130 million in 1954—and was unwilling or unable to extend further assistance for China's economic development. Refuting Moscow's subsequent claim of disinterested assistance to China, Beijing pointed out that "far from being gratis, Soviet aid to China was rendered mainly in the form of trade, and it was certainly not a one-way traffic."[2] Beijing also asserted that the prices of many of the Soviet goods were much higher than those on the world market.

Yet the most acute conflict between the two allies centered around their disagreement on the strategy of world revolution, how to handle the United States, and a host of issues that related directly to China's national security. These issues included (1) Moscow's failure to back Beijing more positively during the 1958 Quemoy Crisis in the

1. "Analysis of the Classes in Chinese Society," *Selected Works of Mao Tse-tung* (Beijing: Foreign Language Press, 1967), 1:13.

2. *Peking Review*, 8 May 1964, p. 14.

face of U.S. nuclear threat against China; (2) Soviet unilateral termination in 1959 of a 1957 agreement to assist China's development of atomic weapons; and (3) Moscow's pursuit of détente with the United States, as manifested in Khrushchev's meeting with President Eisenhower at Camp David in September 1959, and in Moscow's decision, in spite of Beijing's repeated protest, to sign the 1963 limited nuclear test-ban treaty with the United States. The treaty was apparently perceived by Beijing as a U.S.-Soviet collusion against China and, to quote the words of an authority on Chinese foreign policy, probably constituted a "point of no return" symbolizing the end, for all practical purposes, of the Sino-Soviet pact as an operative alliance.[3] By then, if not earlier, the PRC leadership had apparently discounted the value and reliability of the USSR as an ally.

Moreover, a series of events between 1968 and 1970 forced Beijing to redefine China's friends and enemies and drastically change China's alignments with major powers of the world. These events were the Soviet invasion of Czechoslovakia; Moscow's proclamation of the Brezhnev Doctrine, which justifies Soviet intervention in other socialist states; the bloody Sino-Soviet border clashes; and the enunciation of the Nixon Doctrine, which foreshadowed U.S. disengagement from the Indochina war.

In the wake of Sino-Soviet military conflict in 1969, Beijing perceived a genuine danger of large-scale Soviet military action against China—including veiled threats of Soviet surgical operation against its nuclear-weaponry facilities—along with America's declining

status as a superpower and its decreased threat to China. These perceptions led most Chinese leaders to agree that a drastic adjustment in relations with the United States and the West would be highly imperative in order to concentrate all forces on the deterrence of Soviet threat and on the opposition to Soviet hegemony. One important result has been China's opening to the West, with efforts at promoting a united front with the United States, Japan, and the North Atlantic Treaty Organization (NATO) against the USSR since the early 1970s.

PLAYING THE AMERICAN CARD

It has been just over 12 years since President Richard Nixon made his dramatic trip to China, during which he met with Mao and Zhou Enlai and signed the now celebrated Shanghai Communiqué. While the trip failed to measure up to the billing of "a week that changed the world," it marked the beginning of Sino-U.S. rapprochement and set in motion the process toward full diplomatic relations—which were consummated in late 1978—and future cooperation between the two former adversaries.

The reconciliation of the PRC and the United States, without any doubt, has been highly beneficial to both parties. Much has already been said about the diplomatic and security benefits that the United States has derived,[4] but there has been relatively little analysis regard-

3. A. Doak Barnett, "Peking and the Asian Power Balance," *Problems of Communism*, 25(4):38 (July-Aug. 1976).

4. See Richard H. Solomon, "The China Factor in America's Foreign Relations: Perceptions and Policy Choices," in *The China Factor*, ed. Richard H. Solomon (Englewood Cliffs, NJ: Prentice-Hall, 1981); Michel Oksenberg, "The Dynamics of the Sino-American Relationship," in ibid.; Strobe Talbott, "The Strategic Dimension of the Sino-American Relationship: Enemy of Our Enemy, or True Friend?" in ibid.

ing what the PRC has gained so far and what additional benefits it seeks.

President Nixon's visit to China alone greatly boosted Beijing's international status and strengthened its diplomacy in Asia and globally. For example, from 1972 onward, dozens of states in Asia, such as Japan; in Europe, such as Germany; and in Africa and Latin America established diplomatic ties with the PRC or switched diplomatic recognition from Taipei to Beijing. The thaw in relations between Washington and Beijing also made it possible for the PRC to develop and expand ties with many nations—Japan and Canada, for example—that may otherwise have been reluctant to move so fast.

The Sino-U.S. rapprochement has also enhanced the security interests of the PRC in a number of ways. For example, it precluded a collusion of the two superpowers against China. It also removed American military threat from the Taiwan Strait and the Pacific and thus enabled Beijing to reallocate its military forces and resources to concentrate on the USSR and, after 1978, Vietnam. In Beijing's calculus of decision, the United States has become a strategic counterweight to the USSR; for example, without normalization of relations, Beijing might not have felt confident enough to launch the punitive war against Vietnam in February 1979. Inasmuch as the Chinese action was taken a few weeks after Deng Xiaoping's tour of the United States, where he openly spoke of teaching Vietnam a lesson, and conveyed a strong impression that the United States was behind such a move, the USSR may have been deterred by China's relationship with the United States. Moscow was, after all, quite restrained in its response to

China's attack on Vietnam, a Soviet ally.

The improvement in Sino-U.S. relations has enabled Beijing to approach Moscow from a position of strength and play the game of balance of power. Without the U.S. connection, the PRC would be at considerable disadvantage in its negotiations on normalizaiton of relations with the Soviets; it would certainly not be in a good position, as it is now, to set the tone of the negotiations.

To succeed in its drive toward modernization—which will have important bearing on the legitimacy and viability of the Deng Xiaoping leadership group and which is therefore a top government priority—China must have access to advanced Western technology. Deng and his associates count on the West, especially the United States, to help train a new generation of Chinese scientists and engineers and hope to use Western capital, technology, and expertise to speed up Beijing's program of four modernizations. Already the PRC has gained a great deal. Currently, more than 12,000 students or researchers from the mainland are in U.S. universities and institutions for advancement and research in the fields of science, technology, and engineering. In addition, since the fall of 1983, the Reagan administration has relaxed controls on U.S. exports and has put the PRC in the category of nonaligned but friendly nations—which also includes Egypt and India—in order to facilitate transfer of technology to the PRC.

BEIJING'S DISAPPOINTMENTS CONCERNING TAIWAN

Ever since President Nixon's trip to the PRC in 1972, Beijing has attempted to use its American connection to isolate diplomatically the Republic of China (ROC) and facilitate Taiwan's return to the mainland. The normalization of U.S.-China diplomatic relations in January 1979 was a major step toward realizing this important objective. Perhaps much to the astonishment and disappointment of some PRC leaders, Taiwan, in spite of diplomatic setbacks, has remained politically resilient and economically prosperous and has persistently rejected Beijing's overtures of peace.

In order to weaken Taiwan's defenses, demoralize its people, and force the KMT authorities to the negotiation table, Beijing has, since 1981, mounted an intense campaign to press the Reagan administration to cut off arms sales to the ROC. For instance, Chinese premier Zhao Ziyang demanded that the United States set a timetable to phase out military sales to Taiwan when he met President Reagan at the Cancun North-South Conference in October 1981. Foreign Minister Huang Hua reiterated the demand during a heated White House meeting not long afterward and threatened to downgrade diplomatic relations if the United States approved the sale of advanced fighters such as the FX, as requested by Taiwan.

Mindful of Beijing's sensibilities, President Reagan made a difficult decision in early 1982, in which he rejected the FX sale to Taiwan, but allowed Taiwan to continue coproduction of F-5E fighter planes. The compromise failed to placate Beijing and in ensuing months, amid threats of diplomatic rupture, the PRC government pushed the United States relentlessly to set a cutoff date for U.S. arms sales to Taiwan.

After 10 months of intense negotiation and hard bargaining—including a special trip to Beijing in May 1982 by Vice-President Bush to hold discussions with the Chinese leaders—the United States and the PRC issued a joint communiqué on 17 August 1982 and momentarily headed off an imminent diplomatic crisis. The communiqué was by no means an American sellout, but it did make new and significant concessions to the PRC, thereby contradicting virtually every campaign promise that candidate Reagan had made on Taiwan less than two years before. While the United States refused to set an explicit cutoff date for its arms sales to Taiwan, it declared for the first time its intention to restrict its arms supplies at current levels of quality and quantity and to reduce the sales gradually, "leading, over a period of time, to a final resolution."[5] Such a pledge softens, hence violates, a firm U.S. commitment to provide Taiwan with "sufficient" defensive capacity as explicitly mandated by the Taiwan Relations Act (TRA).

In return for the U.S. pledge, there was an implicit, ambiguous promise by the PRC to strive for a peaceful solution to the Taiwan question. Like the 1972 Shanghai Communiqué, the 1982 document is essentially also an agreement to disagree—hence its nickname, Shanghai II—because it too contains highly ambiguous provisions that are subject to conflicting interpretation. For example, while U.S. officials, including President Reagan himself, maintained that the U.S. pledge to reduce arms sales to Taiwan would be linked to Beijing's commitment to peaceful resolution of Taiwan's future, Beijing has denied and

5. "Sino-U.S. Joint Communique (August 17, 1982)," *Beijing Review*, 23 Aug. 1982, p. 14.

rejected such linkage.[6] In a speech in New York in January 1984, Chinese premier Zhao Ziyang once again stated Beijing's position, saying China "cannot make a commitment to any foreign country that only peaceful means will be used in solving the Taiwan issue, because this is China's internal affair and within China's sovereign rights."[7]

To display its policy to seek a peaceful settlement of Taiwan's future, Beijing has in the past several years conducted a peace offensive to pressure the KMT into a reunification talk. Since 1981 Beijing has offered to let Taiwan keep its armed forces, autonomy, and socioeconomic system. In his speech in New York on 16 January 1984, Premier Zhao reiterated the proposal to the KMT:

After the country is reunified, Taiwan, as a special administrative region of China, can retain much of its own character and keep its social system and life style unchanged. The existing party, government and military setups in Taiwan can also remain unchanged. The central Government will send no representatives or troops to station in Taiwan.

Using the name of "Taiwan: China," Taiwan may also continue its external economic and cultural exchanges, and foreign investments in Taiwan will be fully protected. Of course, the People's Republic of China alone is to represent China on the international arena. In a word, neither party will swallow up the other.[8]

The response from Taipei has been a resounding no. Not a few KMT officials are aware that Taipei's automatic rejection of Beijing's overtures makes the

ROC look unreasonably recalcitrant, put it on the defensive diplomatically, and could cost the support of public opinion in the United States. On the other hand, however, few among Taiwan's 18.5 million people desire reunification with the mainland under prevailing circumstances, and this very fact has precluded a more flexible response to Beijing's peace offensive. The KMT authorities do not want to undermine the popular support or even risk a possible popular uprising if the people misconstrue any display of interest in negotiation with Beijing as a prelude to a sellout.

Judging from my conversations with people on Taiwan from all walks of life in the past three years, reunification with the mainland is not an aspiration cherished by many. By Asia's standards, most people in Taiwan are doing well economically, much better than in the PRC. They view the three decades of Communist rule on the mainland, which has been punctuated by ultraleft excesses, brutal repression, purges, and large-scale sociopolitical turmoils, with disgust and apprehension. They listen to Beijing's offers for unification with a jaded ear and open derision. Most feel that, if Taiwan and the mainland are reunified, they will have little to gain, and much more to lose: private properties, freedoms, and high living standards.

It is also possible to surmise from my talks with Chinese Communist Party general secretary Hu Yaobang and many cadres at central and provincial bodies that the Chinese leaders do not fully understand the situation in Taiwan. Because of their ignorance, their proposal for reunification is highly unrealistic and unappealing, and their campaign approach is ineffective. For instance, given the public ballyhoo that

6. Ibid., pp. 15-16; see also "Commentary," *People's Daily,* 10 Oct. 1982.

7. *New York Times*, 17 Jan. 1984.

8. Ibid.

Beijing has made about its reunification proposal, it is impossible to tell whether it is interested more in scoring propaganda points or in serious negotiation. Important as reunification is, Beijing tends to treat it as an issue to be settled solely by leaders of the Chinese Communist Party and the KMT; it overlooks the fact that the KMT authorities, unlike the Chinese Communist Party leadership, do have to contend with the views of the people on Taiwan. Due to all of these factors, Beijing's reunification drive has hit a stone wall.

Lack of success notwithstanding, the campaign to reunite Taiwan with mainland China is sure to continue for years to come. For reasons pertaining to China's domestic politics, Beijing has attached exaggerated importance to the subject of Taiwan and has assigned it an inflated role in the Sino-U.S. relations. Inasmuch as the Chinese people are experiencng what the Chinese media call a crisis of belief and because the regime can no longer depend on Communist ideology to elicit popular compliance and cooperation, the regime has to manipulate symbols of nationalism and use appeals to patriotism for popular support. Emphasis on the reunification of Taiwan and, for that matter, of Hong Kong, well serves Beijing's current ideological and political imperatives.

Moreover, despite Deng's political eminence, he has encountered severe challenges from his political adversaries in the past several years, and his power could be jeopardized if he appears to have compromised China's national sovereignty and pride.[9] Thus, whereas it was possible for Mao to tell Nixon and Henry Kissinger in various meetings during 1972 and 1973 that Taiwan was not an important issue, that the issue of international relations was more important, and that "we can do without [Taiwan] for the time being, let it come after one hundred years,"[10] Deng does not seem to enjoy the same flexibility. This is why under Deng the PRC tends to push the United States much harder on the Taiwan question, demanding that Washington phase out the supply of arms and terminate the special ties with Taipei, which in the eyes of some Chinese leaders have impeded PRC efforts to recover Taiwan.

Such pressure has put the United States in a very difficult position and, consequently, has strained Sino-U.S. relations in the past three years. No American president can totally ignore the Taiwan Relations Act—an American law—which commits the United States to provide Taiwan with "such defense articles and defense services in such quantity as may be necessary for Taiwan's defense," and agree to cut off arms sales to Taiwan. Equally important, the TRA has also incorporated a special relationship between the United States and Taiwan; it calls for the United States to "resist any resort to force" against the people of Taiwan and declares that any such use of coercion to effect changes in Taiwan's status would be a matter of "grave concern to the United States." Not surprisingly, Beijing has attacked the TRA for having violated the 15 December 1978 Sino-U.S. agreement and China's sovereign rights.

---

9. For an analysis of the leadership of the People's Republic of China, see Parris H. Chang, *Elite Conflict in the Post-Mao China,* Occasional Papers in Contemporary Asian Studies, no. 2, 1983(55) (Baltimore: University of Maryland, School of Law, 1983), pp. 31-32.

10. Quoted in Solomon, "China Factor in America's Foreign Relations," p. 17.

The agreement between the two nations in August 1982 has defused, for the time being, the arms-sale issue as it has provided a framework to manage their disagreement over Taiwan. Sino-U.S. relations have improved markedly since the second half of 1983, as attested by the exchange of visits between Premier Zhao and President Reagan. Would the PRC be willing to put aside the differences over Taiwan and cooperate with the United States in areas of common and parallel interests? Or, would Beijing resurrect the issue of Taiwan and attempt to push Washington to go beyond the 1982 agreement? The answers to such questions are crucial to Sino-U.S. relations over the coming decade.

STRATEGIC PARTNERSHIP: REAL OR RHETORICAL?

A number of U.S. officials, notably Zbigniew Brzezinski, President Carter's national security adviser from 1977 to 1981, and General Alexander Haig, President Reagan's secretary of state from 1981 to 1982, used to place great emphasis on the strategic component of U.S.-China relations and sought to forge a U.S.-China strategic partnership against the USSR. In Beijing, Deng Xiaoping was known to favor close cooperation with the United States in order to contain Soviet expansionism. In an interview with *Time* in early 1979, for instance, Deng explicitly called for China, the United States, and Japan to "further develop the relationship in a deepening way" and "to unite" in order to "place curbs on the polar bear."[11]

Whereas the United States and China have cooperated on some security matters since 1979, the scope of their co-

operation has been rather limited, and their highly touted strategic partnership has not been consummated. Moreover, because U.S.-China relations were strained in the past few years, both Beijing and Washington have shifted their foreign policy and have deemphasized the strategic aspect of U.S.-China relations. What happened to cause this shift?

Although Beijing has claimed time and again that the Taiwan question is the main obstacle in the growth of Sino-U.S. relations, the reality seems more complicated. The dispute over U.S. support is only one among many causes that have in the past few years impaired the Sino-U.S. relations, and it is as much a symptom as a cause of their differences. The Sino-U.S. rapprochement in the early 1970s was not a marriage made in heaven, but one of expediency. Likewise, a common concern with the Soviet expansionism was the principal motivating force behind the establishment of full diplomatic relations in 1978-79. Once the PRC improved relations with the United States and Japan, Beijing apparently felt strengthened and soon undertook a series of policy reviews to capitalize on its newly acquired position of strength.

The first clear sign of change was underlined by a major speech by Deng Xiaoping on 16 January 1980 to ranking cadres in which he singled out containment of hegemony, reunification of China, and modernization as the three top priorities for leadership for the 1980s, but he placed the emphasis on the third objective as the key to the fulfillment of the other two. To facilitate China's modernization efforts, according to Deng, the PRC would need a peaceful international environment. Thus the first round of talks began in the

11. *Time*, 17 Jan. 1979, p. 34.

fall of 1979 to normalize relations with the Soviets. With a shift in leadership priority, Beijing has no urgency nor strong incentives to forge an alliance with the United States that could provoke extreme Soviet countermoves.

Deng and other Chinese leaders appeared also to have been bothered by what they saw as the absence of a coherent U.S. global strategy and Asian policy. President Carter's unwillingness or inability to rescue U.S. hostages in Tehran, his weak reactions to the Soviet invasion of Afghanistan in 1980, and President Reagan's decision to lift the grain embargo against the Soviets in 1981 despite his tough anti-Soviet rhetoric served to further undermine Beijing's confidence in the U.S. ability or determination to cope with the Russians.

Moreover, Beijing was disenchanted by U.S. attempts to stand on China's shoulders to strike at the Soviet Union and was strongly resentful of Washington's overtly manipulative approach. There was disillusionment in Beijing, according to Secretary Haig's memo to President Reagan,

"at the lack of tangible benefits to China in the technology transfer and economic modernization areas since normalization, and a perception that this administration, like the last, says it wants to further the process but in practice still treats China as an enemy."[12]

Indeed, despite the loud talk of strategic cooperation by officials in the Carter and Reagan administrations, the United States had refused to sell arms to China and took few other actions that would indicate to the PRC that the United

12. Tad Szulc, "The Reagan Administration's Push toward China Came from Warsaw," *Los Angeles Times,* 17 Jan. 1982.

States really wanted such a relationship. Haig's offer of limited arms sales to China when he visited Beijing in June 1981 was instantly and correctly seen as a transparent effort to mollify Beijing while continuing support for Taiwan.

As a result of all these factors, Beijing has sought to pursue an independent foreign policy and has downplayed its strategic cooperation with the United States. Instead, it has reasserted China's identification with the Third World and renewed rhetorical assaults on U.S. hegemony. Meanwhile, Beijing has also taken a less alarmist view of the Soviet threat and has probed the possibility for détente with Moscow, aiming at enjoying greater leverage and flexibility with both superpowers.

On the other hand, despite strong advocates like Brzezinski and Haig in the U.S. government, a policy of alliance with the PRC was never supported unanimously. Furthermore, Beijing's highly cautious reaction to U.S. proposals on joint actions—conveyed by Defense Secretary Harold Brown during his visit to China in January 1980—in the wake of the Soviet invasion of Afghanistan and Beijing's unwillingness to adopt a common stand with the United States during the Polish crisis in 1981-82 did much to discredit the advocates of the alliance policy. Many American analysts inside and outside the government have felt compelled to reexamine more critically various assumptions on U.S.-China security cooperation and the value of China as an ally against the USSR.

Already some China experts who used to work in the National Security Council under Kissinger and Brzezinski have concluded that the "China factor" in U.S. policy is "smaller than life."[13] To some experts, the change in China's policy priorities and an improvement in Sino-Soviet relations have placed limits on the Sino-U.S. strategic relationship. To others, China's modest military budget and relatively backward economic development inhibit its ability to build a modern and effective military establishment, and thus limit China's capabilities and international outreach and lessen its value as a counterweight to the Soviets. Other scholars have cautioned against too close a military alignment with China, lest such cooperation risk provoking extreme Soviet countermoves, such as instigation of North Korea's sense of military adventure. It could also alienate other Asian nations. Some members of the Association of Southeast Asian Nations and India, not to mention Taiwan, have been highly critical of the U.S. decision to sell arms to China.

Coinciding with such a reassessment of U.S.-China relations by experts outside the government, a reexamination of U.S. policy toward China was also under way inside the Reagan administration. Especially since George Schultz replaced Haig as the secretary of state in June 1982, a new U.S. policy toward Asia has gradually emerged. This policy attaches greater importance to a U.S.-East Asia partnership and regards the U.S.-Japan alliance as the cornerstone of U.S. defense policy in East Asia.[14]

This is not to say that the United States has ceased to value China's strategic importance and would forgo the opportunities of security cooperation with China; quite the contrary. Undoubtedly the United States continues to see China as a very important factor in Asia and seeks to cooperate with her and her other allies to enhance security and peace in that region, but unlike in the past, the United States will not chase a rainbow and strive for something unattainable.

Nonetheless, certain strategic ties between the two nations continue. In addition to maintaining regular contacts between their ranking defense and intelligence officials, both sides cooperate to monitor Soviet military moves and share intelligence about the USSR and Vietnam. The United States has also liberalized the transfer of high technology, including civilian-military technology, to China. Furthermore, earnest negotiations on the transfer of U.S. arms to the PRC are underway; it is only a matter of time before such a transfer will actually take place.

One hastens to add, however, that their security ties will remain quite modest. Having gone down a rocky road in the past several years, both sides are sober and realistic enough to know what is feasible and desirable. There are clear indications from the Zhao-Reagan exchange of visits that both sides have chosen to emphasize their economic cooperation.

LESSONS TO BE LEARNED

U.S.-China relations since 1972 have been marked by many ups and downs.

---

13. See Solomon, "China Factor in America's Foreign Relations."

14. See the speech by Secretary of State George Schultz, "The U.S. and East Asia: A Partnership for the Future," *Current Policy* (U.S. Department of State), 5 Mar. 1983; see also Robert A. Manning, "China: Reagan's Chance Hit," *Foreign Policy*, no. 54, pp. 85-87 (Spring 1984).

After two years of deterioration in the early 1980s, there has been a significant upturn. A number of bilateral agreements on trade, industrial and technological cooperation, and economic matters since the summer of 1983 and particularly since the Zhao-Reagan visits underlie the positive trend. Both sides have acquired a better appreciation of the fundamental importance of their friendship, which is not only in the best interests of the two nations, but also in the interests of peace and stability in Asia.

While it is desirable to consolidate the new gains and expand their ties, it is equally important that both sides avoid highly inflated and unrealistic expectations. They also have to realize that, given their different political and belief systems and different foreign policy priorities and commitments, they are bound to differ over many issues and that their continuing disagreements could from time to time affect their relations adversely.

Because the PRC pursues an independent foreign policy, one can expect Beijing to criticize U.S. policy in the Middle East, South Africa, and Central America, as it has done in the recent past. Now as then, the United States will often find the PRC grandstanding to the Third World in the United Nations and other international forums and voting with the other side. Likewise, the United States is a nation of principle and has its own promises to keep. It should continue its policies of promoting human rights, including criticizing human-rights conditions inside China; maintaining close, albeit nonofficial, ties with Taiwan; and supporting the Republic of Korea, even though these policies could upset the PRC leadership.

Just as the periodic presidential elections and American domestic politics will affect U.S. policy toward China and other regions, so the elite conflict and the political dynamics in China's polity will help shape China's policy toward the United States and China's overall external relations. It is important to note that in the next decade China will be run by a group of leaders who, like Party general secretary Hu Yaobang, are in their mid-sixties or older and were either self-educated or educated mostly in party schools or military academies.[15] Standing in the so-called second echelon of the leadership hierarchy today, these leaders have been soldiers and/or administrators for almost their entire revolutionary careers. They see the world very much through their ideological lenses and appear to be quite parochial, inward looking, and xenophobic in their outlook and concerns. Will these leaders some day become so preoccupied with Western spiritual pollution that they will feel compelled to reverse the programs of modernization? Or will they continue China's open-door policy and learn to handle China's interactions with the world? These are important questions, but only time can tell.

Undoubtedly, both Beijing and Washington have much to learn about how to conduct and manage their complex and difficult relations. To begin with, Washington should desist from any crude attempt to manipulate Sino-Soviet relations. Already the increasing contacts between the two Communist states and the modest improvement in their rela-

15. See Parris H. Chang, "Interview with Hu Yaobang," *Problems of Communism,* 32(6):67-70 (Nov.-Dec. 1983).

tions have alarmed Washington, and some analysts have even suggested offering arms or military technology to China so as to entice Beijing away from Moscow. Such an action would be unwise and is sure to be rebuffed by China. Chinese leaders know too well what China's larger interests are, so it would be futile for Washington to forestall, through bribery or trickery, a Sino-Soviet reconciliation if Beijing sees that to be in China's best interests. The Sino-Soviet relationship has evolved independent of interference by third parties in the past and will do so in the future.

Taking into account all the factors affecting Sino-Soviet relations, however, we believe that the détente that could develop would be gradual and modest in scope, and any far-reaching, comprehensive rapprochement seems rather unlikely. We can also predict with reasonable certainty that there will be no return to the Sino-Soviet alliance of the 1950s, inasmuch as the previous U.S.-China hostility and aura of military confrontation are things of the past. Hence Beijing neither needs nor will seek an alliance with the Soviets for protection. Beijing leaders emphasize that China's independent policy does not mean an equidistant policy toward Moscow and Washington. The central fact is that the United States does not threaten China's national security, but for years to come the Chinese will continue to perceive a direct threat from the Soviets.

To underscore a new approach toward China, Washington should no longer treat China as the enemy of our enemy. Instead, China should be viewed as a developing country striving to improve the livelihood of its 1 billion people. Regardless of Beijing's potential value as a counterweight to the Soviets, the United States does have a major stake in China's economic modernization and political stability. The United States can greatly assist that development by relaxing export controls on its high technology. American officials must also resist domestic pressures for protectionist tariffs and quotas that would deny the Chinese access to U.S. markets. Equally valuable would be an open door on the part of American universities and research institutions that gives a new generation of Chinese scientists, engineers, and managers exposure to the best the West can offer.

But Beijing will have to give as well, and the first order of business is to stop haranguing Washington on the subject of Taiwan. In the joint communiqué of August 1982, the Reagan administration went about as far as it could in accommodating Beijing's demands. Reagan has already abandoned his campaign pledge to upgrade U.S. relations with Taipei and has gone beyond his three predecessors in giving a blessing to Beijing's proposal for peaceful reunification of Taiwan and the mainland. If Beijing tries to press Washington to make more concessions, U.S.-China relations could suffer another downturn and major Chinese policy objectives would be severely jeopardized.

In more practical terms, Beijing must begin to understand the ways in which its frequent policy shifts and long delays in decision making have alienated not a few members of the American business community and have discouraged potential investors. The Chinese government can do its share to encourage trade and investment by reducing bureaucratic delays and tidying up government procedures. The success of China's efforts to attract American investment and trade also depends on explicit government regulations and the establishment of an implementation mechanism.

More than 12,000 Chinese researchers and students are in the United States, and they enjoy considerable access to valuable information. Such educational and scientific exchanges, which have benefited the Chinese enormously and almost one-sidedly, can be jeopardized if Beijing is unwilling to observe the principle of reciprocity. American exchange scientists and scholars have complained of the lack of access to their Chinese counterparts and the restrictions placed by the Chinese authorities on library materials, archives, research facilities, and field studies. If these problems persist, support in Congress and academic circles for the exchange programs will diminish.

Last, but not least, to develop a solid and enduring relationship, both sides must cultivate a mutual trust, and each has to learn to appreciate the other's priorities and problems. Unquestionably, differences between Beijing and Washington over Taiwan, Korea, and other issues will remain, but both have far more to gain if they put such differences aside and strive to accent the positive and promote their common interests, as they are doing now.

*   *   *

QUESTIONS AND ANSWERS

Q (Norris Harzenstein, Federal Bar Association): In the past, there was a very strong movement by native Formosans to free their land of Chinese of whatever political coloration. Is there a degree of unification now within the populace of Taiwan so that the people speak with generally one point of view?

A: Most Taiwanese feel strongly that reunification under the Chinese government would not serve their interests. They see it as impossible. Although the Kuomintang government also speaks of reunification—under its own auspices— the people see that as impossible.

In terms of ethnic differences on Taiwan, there are no ethnic differences. The people are all Chinese. There are some differences among them in their political perspective, and they are pressing the Kuomingtang leadership in Taipei to allocate to the Taiwanese, who constitute more than 80 percent of the population, a more equitable share of the political power.

———

Q (Dorothy Solinger, University of Pittsburgh, Pennsylvania, and Association for Asian Studies): I have noticed a few scattered bits of information in the last couple of weeks about U.S. behavior and Chinese behavior with regard to Thailand, and I noticed something similar in early 1979 when Deng Xiaoping was here and China subsequently attacked in Vietnam. Right after Deng left here, I noticed that Thailand's premier came to see Carter almost the same week. Subsequently I heard on the radio that there was a U.S. battleship in the waters near Thailand. Right after that, the Chinese invaded Vietnam. Early in April 1984 China had a border conflict with Vietnam, and in their press releases they made mention of the fact that

Vietnam was attacking along the Thai border. A couple of days after that, we offered military supplies to Thailand, and now Reagan is in China. How does all this fit together?

A (Whiting): There are linkages. In this last instance, the linkage is related to the failure of the Vietnamese to mount their offensive at an earlier point. Foreign Minister Thack was on a mission at the time. Once the mission of Thack was finished, the Vietnamese attacked those bases, spilling over into Thai territory, where the guerrillas find refuge. For the first time since 1979, the Chinese tried to make good their commitment to Thailand by putting pressure on the Vietnamese. The timing of the Reagan visit, however, was arranged many, many months ago, and that is a little coincidence in fact.

Q (Xu Liugen, Mission of the People's Republic of China to the United Nations): The Chinese feel that national reunification is something of paramount importance to everybody. It would be something of paramount importance to everyone if his or her country was divided. There is only one China. Reunification of Taiwan is something that involves the Chinese. I remember remarks by very important American government officials who said that their government would like to stay away from the internal affairs of China. This is welcome. But how can the American Congress justify itself in passing things like the Taiwan Relations Act and the Taiwan Resolution? Since the American government has time and again acknowledged the fact that there is only one

China, and that Taiwan is a part of China, all ideological or political differences between the two sides are differences among Chinese. How can the Congress justify its interference?

A: You are adopting a very legalistic approach, but diplomacy is not conducted purely on legal grounds. In U.S.-Taiwan relations and U.S.-China relations we cannot ignore history, which introduces a note of complexity to this triangular relationship. China's leadership and the Chinese people often talk about reunification as good. Well, good for what? Is it good only for the idea of one China, or is it good in that it enhances people's livelihood, freedom, and prosperity? The people of Taiwan ask about what the government can do for them. They do not see that unification now under the PRC is going to enhance their freedom or their prosperity. If 10 years from now the PRC's economic modernization succeeds to a considerable degree, if there is a greater degree of law and order and democracy, if human rights are observed in China, I think reunification will have greater appeal to people in Taiwan.

COMMENT: Mr. Chang should listen very carefully to what the central government of China has said. The people of Taiwan will, in fact, benefit greatly from unification. For instance, they will get a huge market. Moreover, the central government in Beijing says that everything in Taiwan can be kept intact.

Q (Mr. Gorham, Department of External Affairs, Canada): How do you see Japan's role vis-à-vis China, and how might that relationship affect U.S. or Soviet interests and influence in the area?

A: I think that the relations between China and Japan are quite good, because the two countries feel that they are complementary to each other in many areas. Good China-Japan relations do not bother Washington, which views them as beneficial to stability in East Asia. Moscow, however, is apprehensive that close Beijing-Tokyo relations may turn into an anti-Soviet alliance. Likewise, China distrusts any improvement in U.S.-Soviet relations because it is often very much concerned with a possible collusion by the two superpowers against it. But China does not have such concerns about a Japan-U.S. alliance against China.

Report of the Board of Directors to the Members of the American Academy of Political and Social Science for the Year 1983

MEMBERSHIP

MEMBERSHIP AS OF DECEMBER 31

Year	Number
1973	21,070
1974	19,473
1975	16,923
1976	15,516
1977	14,202
1978	12,816
1979	10,884
1980	10,059
1981	9,874
1982	9,536
1983	8,904

PUBLICATIONS

NUMBER OF VOLUMES OF *THE ANNALS* PRINTED (6 PER YEAR)

1973	132,709
1974	120,397
1975	104,049
1976	101,789
1977	91,367
1978	85,605
1979	71,513
1980	65,153
1981	69,313
1982	74,211
1983	68,236

FINANCES
SIZE OF SECURITIES PORTFOLIO

MARKET VALUE AS OF DECEMBER 31

1973	533,024
1974	371,004
1975	440,450
1976	504,046
1977	451,545
1978	385,795
1979	377,915
1980	368,926
1981	351,886
1982	390,119
1983	485,809

NUMBER OF VOLUMES OF *THE ANNALS* SOLD (IN ADDITION TO MEMBERSHIPS AND SUBSCRIPTIONS)

1973	12,430
1974	13,153
1975	13,034
1976	12,235
1977	6,296
1978	8,124
1979	5,907
1980	8,751
1981	5,884
1982	7,562
1983	5,877

STATEMENT OF INCOME AND RETAINED EARNINGS FOR THE YEAR ENDED DECEMBER 31, 1983

	1983
Income	
Royalty—Sage Publications	$120,000
Sales of review books	2,351
Royalties and reprint permissions	3,887
Annual meeting revenue	7,231
Donations	
Miscellaneous	3,610
Total income	137,079
Operating expenses	
Salaries	77,393
Payroll taxes	9,277
Pension expense	16,178
Employee benefits	1,900
Annual meeting expense	13,701
Depreciation	3,961

Insurance	1,903
Miscellaneous	24,606
Postage	1,891
Repairs and Maintenance	16,770
Supplies	2,121
Telephone	3,302
Utilities	5,815
Total operating expenses	178,818
Loss from operations	(41,739)
Other income (expenses)	
Investment income (net)	25,154
Gain on sale of investments	52,449
Grant administration overhead	10,510
Total other income	88,113
Net income	46,374
Retained earnings—January 1	361,755
Retained earnings—December 31	$408,129

Report of the Board of Directors

During 1983, the six volumes of THE ANNALS dealt with the following subjects:

January — *Housing America*, edited by Wallace F. Smith, Professor, Department of Business Administration, University of California, Berkeley.

March — *Implementing Governmental Change*, edited by Charles E. Gilbert, Professor, Department of Political Science, Swarthmore College, Swarthmore, Pennsylvania.

May — *The Global Refugee Problem: U.S. and World Response*, edited by Gilburt D. Loescher, Assistant Professor, Department of Government and International Studies, University of Notre Dame; and John A. Scanlan, Assistant Director, Center for Civil and Human Rights, Notre Dame Law School, Notre Dame, Indiana.

July — *Health Care Policy in America*, edited by S. E. Berki, Professor and Chairman, Department of Medical Care Organization, School of Public Health, University of Michigan, Ann Arbor.

September — *Nuclear Armament and Disarmament*, edited by Marvin E. Wolfgang, President, The American Academy of Political and Social Science, and Professor, Department of Sociology, University of Pennsylvania, Philadelphia; and Robert H. Kupperman, Executive Director, Science and Technology Center for International Studies, Georgetown University, Washington, D.C.

November — *Robotics: Future Factories, Future Workers*, edited by Robert J. Miller, Professor, Department of Anthropology, University of Wisconsin, Madison.

The publication program for 1984 includes the following volumes:

January — *Paying for Culture*, edited by Patricia A. McFate, President, The American-Scandinavian Foundation, New York City.

March — *Polling and the Democratic Consensus*, edited by L. John Martin, Professor, College of Journalism, University of Maryland, College Park.

May — *The Future of American Unionism*, edited by Louis A. Ferman, Professor of Social Work and Research Director, Institute of Labor and Industrial Relations, The University of Michigan, Ann Arbor.

July — *Gambling: Views from the Social Sciences*, edited by James H. Frey, Associate Professor, Department of Sociology, University of Nevada, Las Vegas; and William R. Eadington, Professor, Department of Economics, University of Nevada, Reno.

September — *Deindustrialization: Restructuring the Economy*, edited by Gene F. Summers, Professor and Chairman, Department of Rural Sociology, University of Wisconsin, Madison.

November — *China in Transition*, edited by Marvin E. Wolfgang, President, American Academy of Political and Social Science, and Professor, Department of Social Systems Sciences, Department of Sociology, and Law School, University of Pennsylvania, Philadelphia.

During 1983, the Book Department published approximately 250 reviews.

The majority of these were written by professors, but reviewers also included university presidents, members of private and university-sponsored organizations, government and public officials, and business professionals. Over 400 books were listed in the Other Books section.

Sixty-five requests were granted to reprint material from THE ANNALS. These went to professors and other authors for use in books in preparation and to nonprofit organizations for educational purposes.

MEETINGS

The eighty-sixth annual meeting, which was held on April 22-23, 1983, had as its subject *Nuclear Armament and Disarmament* and continued the tradition of our gatherings with respect to the diversity of organizations represented by delegates, the size of the audiences and the interest displayed. Eleven embassies sent official delegations, as did twelve United Nations missions and four states, cities, and agencies of the federal government. Delegates were also sent by 78 American and foreign universities and colleges and 48 international, civic, scientific, and commercial organizations. More than 250 persons attended one or more sessions.

The theme of the eighty-seventh annual meeting, held April 27-28, 1984, at the Bellevue Stratford Hotel, Philadelphia, was *China in Transition*. The November 1984 volume of THE ANNALS contains the papers presented at the meeting.

OFFICERS AND STAFF

The Board reelected the following officers: Marvin E. Wolfgang, President; Richard D. Lambert, Vice-President; Rebecca Jean Brownlee, Secretary; Elmer B. Staats, Treasurer. The following Board Members were reelected for three-year terms: Lee Benson, A. Leon Higginbotham, Jr., and Covey T. Oliver.

Respectfully submitted,

THE BOARD OF DIRECTORS

Elmer B. Staats
Marvin E. Wolfgang
Lee Benson
A. Leon Higginbotham, Jr.
Richard D. Lambert
Rebecca Jean Brownlee
Covey T. Oliver
Thomas L. Hughes
Randall M. Whaley
Lloyd N. Cutler

Philadelphia, Pennsylvania
1 September 1984

Book Department

INTERNATIONAL RELATIONS AND POLITICS

DAVIDSON, DONALD L. *Nuclear Weapons and the American Churches: Ethical Positions on Modern Warfare.* Pp. 207. Boulder, CO: Westview Press, 1984. $20.00.

This book, prepared under the auspices of the Strategic Studies Institute, U.S. Army War College, is an examination of how the doctrine of just war is being related to nuclear war. Donald L. Davidson admits in the acknowledgments that in his presentation of material from the churches he includes criticism of some of their points of view. His bias seems to have manifested itself in two ways that are detrimental to the study.

The first is the inclusion of what seems to be irrelevant material. For example, in dealing with the Episcopal church's stance on nuclear issues, Davidson throws in a statement concerning the denomination's stance on U.S. aid to Central America. The selection of material at times seems unusual. For example, in a discussion of a position of the National Council of Churches, he includes material on the criticism of the council by the Institute for Religion and Democracy, rather than the latter's position on the issue at hand.

This relates to the second problem of certain inconsistencies in the book. In discussing a United Presbyterian Church USA's 1981 study guide, Davidson states that the Soviets are "portrayed [as] playing 'catch-up' with the United States." A different implication is given when, in his summary, Davidson states that "the massive buildup over the last fifteen years" has now brought the United States and Soviets into a "rough equality."

One additional weakness has to do with using only a survey letter for collecting the data. In depending on voluntary replies, Davidson limits the scope of the material in the documents used and in the number of churches. Thus in discussing the United Methodist church, basically only an episcopal letter is discussed while the official position of the church is never mentioned. Likewise verification of the major black denominations' positions, or lack of such, would be of value.

The book raises two valuable issues. The first is Davidson's dealing with the development, contemporary forums, and applications of the just war criteria. This summarization draws out points worth considering in any ethical analysis of war. The second is the underlying question of church-state relations and how the responsibilities of each institution affects its world view. Thus while this book has its limitations, it can be of great value in initiating discussion on the ethical dimension of preparation, doctrine, and implementation of modern warfare.

DONALD A. WATT

University of Pennsylvania

Philadelphia

MEARSHEIMER, JOHN J. *Conventional Deterrence.* Pp. 289. Ithaca, NY: Cornell University Press, 1983. No price.

SCHWARTZ, DAVID N. *NATO's Nuclear Dilemmas.* Pp. 263. Washington, DC: Brookings Institution, 1983. $28.95.

The books by Mearsheimer and Schwartz are concerned with how military policy decisions have been made and the implications of those decisions for NATO in Central Europe. Approaching the subject through different venues, each uses case studies to increase readers' understanding of the standoff between the NATO and Warsaw Pact forces. Mearsheimer examines deterrence based on conventional forces in the modern era; Schwartz traces the debates within NATO concerning basing and use of strategic or long-range theater nuclear weapons. The books complement each other, although in the end they draw different conclusions based on varying assumptions of the forces that would be available in a crisis.

Mearsheimer limits his study of conventional deterrence to the mechanized post-World War I period. Although he touches on political considerations for an attack, Mearsheimer largely examines the military strategy in depth. His central work deals with periods when deterrence holds for a time and then breaks down. His first conclusion—that deterrence will break down in a time of political crisis when one side believes it can quickly and decisively obtain its goals—seems self-evident. The second stage of his analysis, however, is of greater value. It asserts that, except in unusual cases—for example, Egypt in 1973—only the *blitzkrieg* will be employed in an attack. His expectation is that in any crisis in the foreseeable future when two armies are massed, the *blitzkrieg* will be the strategy used.

The conclusions Mearsheimer draws from his study for modern warfare in general, and for Central Europe in particular, are subject to question. Mearsheimer touches on the two main weaknesses of his historical analysis, but he does not believe they will effect any great changes. The first is the introduction of precision-guided munitions and their impact on the armor and air forces so necessary for a *blitzkrieg*. Although he analyzes their impact—pro-defense—he does not change his opinion that the *blitzkrieg* as historically constituted will not be outmoded. This is subject to debate.

The second conclusion, concerning the security of Western Europe from a Warsaw Pact attack, also has a weakness in that Mearsheimer assumes the NATO force will be expanded in a time of crisis to optimal levels of 32 divisions in its forward deployment. Although the force ratio of 2 to 1 in favor of the Warsaw Pact is in the proper range, much of his argument on the defensibility of the forward position by NATO rests on the force-to-space ratios in the probable areas of an attack. With fewer than 32 divisions in forward deployment, the probability of a massive breakthrough is greatly increased.

Mearsheimer also neglects the deployment of tactical nuclear weapons and how they may affect deterrence. If neither side wishes to cross the nuclear threshold, and if NATO can position the necessary forces, Mearsheimer's analysis can lend some optimism to the probability of a successful deterrence in Europe.

Schwartz, on the other hand, has a more pessimistic outlook on NATO's ability to raise the necessary forces for conventional deterrence. Through his historical examination Schwartz believes that nuclear addiction has allowed the NATO countries to disregard the provision of adequate conventional forces.

In Schwartz's study of the political considerations and negotiations that met each new proposal, certain elements keep recurring. One is the inability, or unwillingness, of the alliance members to meet the conventional force goals set for NATO. A second theme is the continuing uncertainty in Europe about whether the United States will actually use its nuclear weapons to save Western Europe, and/or if Western Europe might be drawn into a nuclear war through a U.S.-USSR confrontation elsewhere. Schwartz's analysis that the doctrine of flexible response and the deployment of theater, or intermediate range, weapons add to the assurance of Europe is correct. His point that NATO needs to have more possible responses in conventional weaponry is well taken. Without this increase, Schwartz believes, any attack on NATO would necessitate its first use of nuclear weapons, something he finds unpalatable.

Overall, Schwartz gives a good account of the process through which NATO has come in its nuclear weapons policy, with the various dilemmas facing both the European and the North American partners in regard to the policy being documented. His book is worthwhile for its historical overview of this process, as well as the conclusions it draws concerning the interactions of NATO conventional and nuclear forces.

DONALD A. WATT

University of Pennsylvania
Philadelphia

MILLER, JON D. *The American People and Science Policy: The Role of Public Attitudes in the Policy Process.* Pp. xviii, 145. Elmsford, NJ: Pergamon Press, 1983. $22.50.

Here is a compact book that should be useful to anyone interested in the theory of democracy, in public participation, and in the citizen's role, or lack thereof, in the formulation of science and technology public policy. The rich empirical data on which the book is based come from four major surveys of the public's attitude toward science and technology conducted by Miller and his associates between 1978 and 1981. These data are summarized in 71 tables and analyzed in terms of a stratified model that, in the tradition of Gabriel Almond, divides the citizenry into five groups occupying successive layers of a pyramid.

From the pyramid's base to apex, the groups are nonattentive public—nonattentive to science and technology, that is; interested

public; attentive public, which comprises 1 out of 5 adults in the United States and is growing; nongovernmental policy leaders; and governmental decision makers. The existence of an attentive public arises from the information overload on the modern citizen, who is forced to choose a few favorite civic issues to specialize in and give up on all others. Thus there is an attentive public for science and technology, another for foreign policy, another for economic matters, and so on.

The attentive public for science and technology, however, has had little influence over policy. Instead, according to Miller, science and technology policy is very much under the influence of the policy leaders, who are the nongovernmental leaders of the scientific and technological community. Here one wishes that the book had made a clearer distinction between basic science and applied technology, and especially between research and development activities and non-research and development operational activities. Such a distinction was admittedly impractical in the public opinion surveys, but it would be helpful in analyzing the policy process. Thus the influence of policy leaders has traditionally been greatest in certain aspects of basic research policy—for example, the funding for particle accelerators comes to mind—but since the 1960s their influence has usually been negligible in the non-research and development operational policies of such mission-oriented areas as space, energy, resources, and the environment, which account for the bulk of the federal science and technology budget.

This thin volume brings a wealth of empirical data to bear on a hitherto highly speculative subject and makes a definitive contribution to the study of science and technology policymaking and its relationship to the theory of democracy.

BENJAMIN SHEN

University of Pennsylvania
Philadelphia

PADDISON, RONAN. *The Fragmented State: The Political Geography of Power*. Pp. x, 315. New York: St. Martin's Press, 1983. $25.00.

Ronan Paddison is a lecturer in geography at the University of Glasgow. Paddison's book is a treatment of the distribution of power in central, regional, and local governments in a variety of countries in Western Europe and North America, as well as Australia and New Zealand. He might well have dedicated the book to Terminus, the Roman god of boundaries, for this is an extensive review of the literature on boundaries and power, and it reads much like an annotated bibliography.

Paddison has covered a very large territory. He looks at unitary and federal states. He deals at length with local services and local fragmentation, and he reviews the extensive literature of the 1970s on those subjects, American, English, and some others. He ends with a discussion of reorganizing the territorial state.

Paddison has provided undergraduate classes with a valuable reference work on the subject. Teachers of economics, political science, and sociology will find this volume a useful reference and a useful set of auxiliary readings. Geographers may be interested in Paddison's attempt to prove that something called political geography is an important discipline.

I was not familiar with Paddison's previous works. Nevertheless, what is missing from this volume is some considered judgments by the author on the relative importance of the wide variety of topics and opinions that he presents. I suspect he is capable of such discrimination, but that is not evident in *The Fragmented State*.

GUTHRIE S. BIRKHEAD
Syracuse University
New York

TYSON, JAMES L. *U.S. International Broadcasting and National Security*. Pp. xviii, 153. New York: Ramapo Press, 1983. $7.95.

Many Americans are familiar with bits and pieces of the nation's overseas shortwave information distribution apparatus, but few understand the whole picture. James Tyson tries in this brief volume to fit the pieces together into a comprehensible package. In so doing he also assesses their performance in reflecting U.S. policy and their impact on residents of the target areas.

The section dealing with the origins and evolution of the Voice of America (VOA) is particularly useful and will serve as a valuable reference source. The analysis of VOA policy controversies over the years stresses the most contentious of the agency's internal disputes, including one that has never been settled to everyone's satisfaction: should VOA be concerned primarily with objectivity or persuasion? Should it follow a so-called warts-and-all policy in dealing with internal U.S. developments? Or should it try to be purely objective without regard to possible damage that may occur to the image of the United States? Tyson clearly opts for persuasion.

His treatment of Radio Free Europe (RFE) and Radio Liberty (RL) is not as clear or apparently knowledgeable. There is a good reason. The two so-called freedom radios are complex instruments performing a service that is more difficult to define. Their clandestine origins in the nation's intelligence community in the late 1940s makes tracing their early history a complicated process.

The basic difference in goals and objectives between VOA on the one hand and RFE and RL on the other is recognized: namely, that VOA serves essentially as the voice of America abroad, of its culture, its institutions and policies, whereas RFE and RL are charged to function as surrogate domestic radios in the countries into which they broadcast. Tyson is somewhat ambiguous, however, in assessing the extent to which the radios should promote Western values in their programs that are designed primarily to fill the information gap created by censorship. It stands to reason that too hard a sell could lead to an erosion of confidence and credibility.

Tyson is to be commended. His recommendations for government action to strengthen all three services are squarely on target. The list is long and comprehensive, but his most useful service probably derives from the additional light he throws on the critical role played by shortwave broadcasts in crossing international boundaries. If the public's threshold of understanding can be raised just a little, perhaps support from the White House and the Congress will come more easily. The benefits from such support are clear. As Tyson points out, "International broadcasting can be one of the most cost-effective arms of our foreign policy."

SIG MICKELSON

San Diego
California

WILLNER, ANN RUTH. *The Spellbinders: Charismatic Political Leadership.* Pp. 212. New Haven, CT: Yale University Press, 1984. $17.95.

In its institutional aspects charismatic leadership gives rise to three different formations of groups in the social sphere. Well known are the charismatic communities of one leader and a small number of disciples, living together in one household without any family connections. If the leader has political ambitions and gains loyal followers, the small groups multiply and grow into a charismatically led political and social mass movement. Given political support, the leader and followers establish a charismatic rulership in which the government of the state is directed by the leader and the leader's assistants.

In *The Spellbinders*, Willner does not place the leaders and their followers in any such framework of growth. Instead, the reciprocal relationship between leader and followers is seen as the major issue. The core features are examined for their variety, descriptive accuracy, and theoretical significance. The two central chapters of the book deal with heroic and rhetoric leaders. Hitler and Mussolini as well as Roosevelt and Gandhi are lumped together as either heroes or saviors, as if they comprised one uniform type of leadership. The chapter on rhetoric charisma emphasizes a more specific content analysis of the speeches of Roosevelt. The technical underlining of emotive words has the negative effect of excluding Churchill and de Gaulle as well as Lenin and Trotsky from the list of acceptable spellbinders.

A novelty arises from the study of the origin of the exceptional quality of leaders. Sukarno, Castro, and Khomeini are said to derive their claim to charismatic authority either from beliefs in myths or from modeling themselves on the image of a past national leader. For instance, Castro is said to regard himself as the successor of a previous national leader of Cuba. This is certainly a new finding, which differs from Weber's distinction between natural and supernatural origin of the special qualities, except for magic charisma.

An appendix to the book tries to explain why so little of Weber's work has been used in this study. There are two critical arguments. The ideal-typical method is said—correctly—to be inadequate for the analysis of charisma, but nothing is said about the indispensable prototypical method. In using a restrictive definition, Willner correctly rejects Parsons's stress on the normative element of charisma, but this does not justify leaving out the distinction between democratic and dictatorial charisma, which alone permits us to arrive at the constructive and destructive consequences of these two types of charismatic leadership.

ARTHUR SCHWEITZER

Indiana University
Bloomington

AFRICA, ASIA, AND
LATIN AMERICA

CROLL, ELISABETH. *Chinese Women since Mao*. Pp. ii, 129. Armonk, NY: M. E. Sharpe, 1984. $22.50. Paperbound, $11.95.

Elisabeth Croll, in her analysis of the position of women in post-Mao Zedong Chinese society, has managed to present both an optimistic and pessimistic view of the impact of socialist modernization on the female population.

On the positive side, the government has legislated the equality of women, provided for their education and employment, and attempted to raise their status in a society that has consistently undervalued women. Considerable success has attended gender-specific policies that allow women to control their earnings and reproductive capacity.

However, Croll says that gender relationships are still secondary to class relationships in the struggle to form a truly socialist society. Women are still underrepresented in high-paying skilled labor, in important political positions, and among the highly educated. In addition, the economic policies of the government—especially the return of some productive responsibility to individual households at the expense of the collective—creates the danger that women will lose what visibility and public responsibility they had been able to gain.

Croll carefully analyzes the rise of handicrafts and other domestic production in rural and urban households and concludes that the increased intensity and profitability of female labor bodes ill for the future freedom of women. The increased intensity of domestic production, in concert with the still-traditional roles of reproduction and child-rearing, removes women from the more public activities, of both earning and policy-making, of the collectives. The income from this handicraft and private labor being placed in the hands of the head of household deprives the female workers of independence, and their value to the household as workers has frequently created barriers to their free choice of marriage partners. According to Croll, betrothal gifts from the prospective groom, despite their abolition by the government, have become increasingly expensive in order to indemnify the bride's family against the loss of her earning power.

This short essay should be of interest to more than historians of women or of China. It presents a clear statement of the difficulties encountered when government policies in one area ignore or fail to take into account conflicting policies in another area. On a final, optimistic note, Croll reminds readers that the government of China has frequently intervened to help bring about change and suggests that women may yet achieve true equality, not only under the law, but "with the men of their household, their community and their society."

MARY BETH EMMERICHS
University of Pennsylvania
Philadelphia

SHAFFER, LYNDA. *Mao and the Workers: The Hunan Labor Movement, 1920-1923*. Pp. xvii, 251. Armonk, NY: M. E. Sharpe, 1982. No price.

The industrial working class has been virtually ignored in studies of the Chinese revolution. Lynda Shaffer's meticulously researched *Mao and the Workers* is the most important study of the Chinese labor movement to be published in the 15 years since Jean Chesneaux's epic study, *The Chinese Labor Movement 1919-1927*. It is also the first in a wave of scholarly reassessments of workers, industry, and worker movements in republican China, anticipating major studies in progress by Ming Kou Chan, Gail Hershatter, and Emily Honig.

Shaffer persuasively argues for a redefinition of both the Chinese working class and its role in revolutionary processes. Where Chesneaux's narrow definition of a modern working class of 1.5 million led him to exclude from his study the majority of China's urban laborers—self-employed and wage craft workers, shop workers, clerks, and guild members—Shaffer rejects as arbitrary and misleading Chesneaux's use of the distinction between traditional and modern workers. She shows with a wealth of data drawn principally from Hunan Province that such definitions mask the dynamics of the labor movement. For in Hunan protest frequently erupted in the ranks of traditional workers such as miners operating under a contract labor system during periods of destabilizing modernization. Hereafter the study of Chinese labor and labor movements will surely transcend the traditional-modern dichotomy. It will attempt to comprehend the impact of incorporation in the capitalist world system on traditional workers and the relationship between traditional and modern workers in the labor and national movement.

Shaffer illuminates important and little-studied aspects of Mao Zedong's revolutionary role, particularly his important early contributions to the labor movement and his unorthodox—that is, innovative—melding of student and labor protest in his native province, Hunan. If Mao ultimately led a great peasant-based revolution to power, some of his formative political experiences, and those of the Chinese Communist Party, were in worker and student movements in the years 1919-27.

MARK SELDEN
State University of New York
Binghamton

SUTTER, ROBERT G. The China Quandary: Domestic Determinants of U.S.-China Policy, 1972-1982. Pp. xi, 194. Boulder, CO: Westview Press, 1984. $22.50.

The emergence of normal relations between the United States and the People's Republic of China during the 1970s is one of the watershed events of our time. It represents a kind of second stage of the globe's most striking postwar trend: the emergence of three-quarters of the world's people, predominantly nonwhite and poor, from the custody of the metropolitan countries. Stage one was liberation from that custody; stage two, in the case of China, was to have stage one recognized and accepted, so that China could take its rightful place among the nations of the world.

Sutter's The China Quandary deals with precisely these events but omits the context just mentioned. He omits it because Washington officials never raised it; and it is the views of these participants in policymaking that Sutter dutifully follows—he interviewed over 100 of them. This adherence is, at once, the chief deficiency and the chief attribute of his history. What we can find in The China Quandary is something quite useful: a well-documented report on what Washington politicians were doing, saying, and keeping secret during these ten years of China policy reversal. Sutter presents it with restraint: the careful hand of the social scientist qua government consultant, laying out the various sides, making no judgments, offending nobody, and claiming no particular wisdom—small but solid scholarship. Were congressional and State Department officials to read it, they might learn something about the dynamics of gettings things done, a lesson akin to what is taught in organizational development schools of management. Yet at times one wishes that Sutter had pursued this research with more of a thesis in mind, had ventured to share more of his own wisdom and vision. If Washington politicians, as it seems, make decisions about great matters for disappointingly small-minded, pragmatic, political—in its narrowest sense—reasons, then one would hope that at least the historian would offer some guidance. "A scholar is not a thing of use," Confucius once said. Sutter's book is "a thing of use."

Given these limitations, The China Quandary has some positive attributes. Perhaps chief among them is its ability to lay out the interpersonal perceptions between the officials of Congress and those of the executive branch as the Nixon, Ford, and Carter administrations edged closer to the People's Republic of China. Sutter's social scientist's eye for impartiality is most effective when observing, for example, that Carter's "State Department aides were sometimes perceived as arrogant" by members of Congress when in fact it was White House pressures for secrecy that prevented the aides from being frank. Sutter has a feel for diplomacy—which is often needed as much between Congress and the executive branch as between the United States and another country.

On the other hand, parts of the book beg for more in-depth examination by an author with confidence in his own judgment, rather than just reportage of shallow Washington opinions. Was Carter weak and vacillating in his foreign policy or not? Were his policies with regard to Panama, Korea, Vietnam, and Taiwan signs of weakness or wisdom? Sutter merely repeats some opinions about this important question instead of offering an in-depth analysis. Moreover, the opinions that he repeats tilt the balance toward weakness in much the same way that a television newscaster tilts balances, while all the time maintaining "I'm only the reporter."

In another passage Sutter reports opinions on the question of whether or not it is moral to normalize relations with a Communist country at the expense of an old friend. Here again we need in-depth investigation, not just the recounting of opinions. The closest Sutter comes to an investigation is to cite the view of Freedom House, which he calls a "non-partisan" organization. Of course, Freedom House is known to be much closer to, might we say, Ronald Reagan's version of freedom than Martin Luther King's.

Sutter's book should be on library bookshelves, as it represents an important compilation of knowledge. Yet we also maintain the hope that Sutter and others who attempt to write histories will move beyond the timid kind of work that makes scholars subservient to politicians and public opinion. Politicians do not want to raise questions like, "Was our China policy from 1949 to 1972 right or wrong?" Historians and other truth seekers should.

FRANCE H. CONROY

Burlington County College
Pemberton
New Jersey

EUROPE

FUCHS, RACHEL. *Abandoned Children: Foundlings and Child Welfare in Nineteenth-Century France*. Pp. xvii, 357. New York: University of New York, 1984. No price.

One of the ironies of the history of childhood and the family is that we have better evidence for the experience of troubled families and problem children than for the experience of the standard and normal. That is because church and state have kept records of their efforts to help those who seemed to need it. Fuchs shows just how rich those records can be in this study of state provisions for the abandoned children of Paris through the nineteenth century.

Her work, originating as a dissertation, is in the form of an institutional history, but she exploits her material so thoroughly that it expands into a more general social history. She relates her story to the changing values of French society, which governed several policy shifts within the period in question. She shows how Paris's problem involved the rest of France, the typical abandoning mother being a recent arrival from the provinces and the children being returned to nurses in the provinces. And she is able to assess the relative influence of economic factors as against changes in policy in the changing rate of abandonment.

The book is a model of thoroughness, and sometimes the detail becomes slightly clogged, as one expects in monographs. But Fuchs has asked the right questions and has not been sidetracked by an overelaborate statistical method. Nor has she enlisted in the partisan struggles over her subject. Although she is aware that social control is always a concern of policy, she notes that her subject does not fit Foucault's model of institutionalizing misfits. She paints a gripping picture of the Dickensian Hospice, which received the foundlings, and of the awful conditions that tiny infants endured when being shipped around the country. But she is not looking for someone to blame and is fair enough to show how little effect transportation had on mortality. She is also able to show that girls were no more likely to be abandoned and no less likely to be reclaimed than boys. One notes that attitude changes—concern for the child's as well as for the state's welfare—came a generation before the medical knowledge and bureaucratic efficiency of the 1850s and 1880s that made a difference in life chances. The one surprise is a lack of discussion of child mortality as opposed to infant mortality, the index actually confusing the distinction.

C. JOHN SOMMERVILLE

University of Florida
Gainesville

HARRIS, R. W. *Clarendon and the English Revolution.* Pp. vii, 456. Stanford, CA: Stanford University Press, 1983. $39.50.

Edward Hyde, earl of Clarendon, ranks among the most illustrious servants of the English crown. Chancellor of the exchequer under Charles I, implacable adversary of rebellious parliamentarians, companion in exile to Charles II, and chief architect of England's return to monarchical government, Clarendon occupied high office and endured great hardship during one of the most tumultuous periods of English history. Clarendon's own *History of the Rebellion and Civil Wars in England* is a brilliant commentary on the troubled era through which he lived. The earl not only made history, he also recorded it. Intent on exploring both aspects of Clarendon's life, Harris has crafted a biography that reveals more about the royalist policymaker than about the inimitable historian of the English Revolution.

Following the stages of Edward Hyde's progress toward the most powerful offices of the English court bureaucracy, Harris constructs a narrative incorporating topics unduly neglected in studies of the English Civil War oriented toward revolutionary figures and the victories of Parliament. Clarendon's efforts to advise Charles I on politi-

cal strategy and to maintain peace negotiations between the king and Parliament reveal much about the internal workings of the court propaganda machine. Clarendon's service on the Privy Council permits Harris to investigate how the fluctuating military fortunes of royal armies affected the king's ability to raise money and parley with his adversaries. The destruction of the royal forces by Cromwell's army precipitated an exodus of the crown's surviving defenders. Clarendon fled to France and became an advisor to Charles II.

Harris's account of the royalist refugees, their machinations against the commonwealth, and their fruitless attempts to secure assistance from the monarchs of Europe casts new light on the fortunes of those who lost the English Civil War and places the outcome of that conflict in the broader perspective of seventeenth-century European affairs. Harris deftly juxtaposes these chaotic events with Clarendon's stalwart belief in the inevitability of the Restoration.

Yet too often, Harris endorses the assessments of men and events appearing in Clarendon's own writings. Quickly dismissing recent attempts to rehabilitate the character of the rebel John Pym, Harris, like Clarendon, condemns him as the greatest warmonger of the age. Harris also rejects the broader critique of Clarendon's accuracy and objectivity advanced by Ronald Hutton. Perhaps Harris is right not to quibble over minor inaccuracies in Clarendon's magnificent works. However, his reluctance to read Clarendon critically and to probe deeply the motivations for his prose only compounds Clarendon's natural reticence and self-effacing style of discourse. A more trenchant analysis of Clarendon's historical writing would offer the reader greater insight into the character of this noble figure.

KEVIN C. ROBBINS

University of Pennsylvania
Philadelphia

HOPKINS, DONALD R. *Princes and Peasants: Smallpox in History.* Pp. xx, 380. Chicago: University of Chicago Press, 1983. $25.00.

This book explores the historical influence of smallpox with impressive learning and global scope. Hopkins treats his theme geographically: first Europe, then China, India, Africa, and the Americas; and concluding with a final chapter on the traditional red treatment for smallpox and the eradication of the disease in the twentieth century.

As a medical man, Hopkins is cautious about identifying ancient epidemics as smallpox. Even though he personally examined the mummy of Ramses V in Cairo, he refrains from diagnosing smallpox in 1157 B.C. He does seem convinced that the Athenian plague of 430 B.C. was smallpox—an identification that seems unduly precise to me—and occasionally classifies other epidemics as probably smallpox when available descriptions are too vague to make the diagnosis fully convincing. But in general his judgments are careful, and the record of smallpox outbreaks that he has painstakingly assembled makes the reader abundantly aware of the importance the disease had in the past among peasants and princes—and urban folk as well.

As the title indicates, a good deal of Hopkins's attention is devoted to rulers' encounters with the disease. Often the result was a ruler's sudden death, sometimes provoking disputed successions and/or some drastic political change. Such emergencies deflected states as diverse as Austria, Japan, and the Inca empire, for example. Less familiar are occasions on which rulers suffered an attack and still survived—as happened early in Queen Elizabeth's reign, for example, and to Lincoln immediately after his Gettysburg address. By gathering such episodes together into one book, Hopkins certainly shows that smallpox mattered in politics—sometimes.

Yet it must also be said that the book reads choppily and is often dull. Many pages monotonously list epidemics and numbers of victims as reported by one source or another. Similarly, the account of smallpox deities is abstracted from the general religious and social context in an unsatisfactory fashion. I noticed a few minor slips—for example, a mislocation of the Burma road—but the general level of accuracy is very high for a book that roams across so much time and space.

The only major error Hopkins makes is to affirm that "as late as 1600, smallpox was still unheard of among the one-half to two million Indians living in the vast area north of Mexico." A recent book—*Their Number Become Thinned: Native American Population Dynamics in Eastern North America* by Henry F. Dobyns—makes this assertion implausible, to say the least; but Hopkins cannot be faulted, given that his book went to press before Dobyns's work came out.

WILLIAM H. McNEILL

University of Chicago
Illinois

KEIGER, JOHN F. V. *France and the Origins of the First World War.* Pp. vii, 201. New York: St. Martin's Press, 1983. $25.00.

Historians have long debated the origins of World War I. During the war itself, French—and British—historians found Germany and her ally, Austria-Hungary, solely guilty and based the demand for war reparations on this guilt. In the 1920s revisionists placed blame on all the major belligerents, particularly on Russia and France: on Russia for prematurely mobilizing and on France for encouraging her ally to do so, thanks to a festering passion to get back the lost provinces of Alsace and Lorraine. In the 1930s clear Nazi aggression prompted a return to the earlier view. Most recently German historian Fritz Fisher and his disciples have placed emphasis on Germany's willingness in 1914 to risk a European war to secure national objectives.

In a densely written little book, Keiger assesses French diplomatic activity since

1871 and specifically in the establishment of the two alliance systems that faced each other in 1914. He has analyzed the French Foreign Office—the Quai d'Orsay—and has paid special attention to the Frenchman who set his mark on foreign affairs from 1912 through at least the early years of the war, Prime Minister and then President Raymond Poincaré. He closes with a description of the July 1914 crisis, which, unlike previous crises, could not be resolved peacefully.

Keiger concludes that France—and Poincaré—were not guilty of plotting for war; that, on the contrary, the Foreign Office, caught up in wrangling among career officers—the *bureaux*—the ministers, and the ambassadors, was too divided to allow for such a policy; that the so-called nationalist revival preceding the outbreak of war was overstated, represented a minority of the population, and was in any case defensive; that Poincaré, while tightening the bonds of the connection with Britain and Russia and striving to keep it distinct from the other armed camp, worked for peace and even restrained Russia in the Balkans, going so far as to favor German interests in Turkey and not those of Russia; that the absence of French diplomats from their desks in July 1914 showed that France was not plotting war; that Poincaré issued no blank check to Russia during his visit of that month; that at most an impulsive French ambassador—Paléologue—provided excessive assurances; and that, finally, Poincaré could not let Russia fight the Central Powers alone and hence had no choice but to go to war. France, "more than any other power in July 1914 was following events rather than leading them."

This well-argued account of the French position is based on manuscript collections, particularly the Poincaré papers in the Bibliothèque Nationale, on the printed documents, and on such secondary works as J. J. Becker's important study of French public opinion on the eve of the war. The writing, unfortunately, is dry—when Poincaré is not the subject—and the difficulty of reading is increased by the tiniest print I have ever seen in a standard hardbound book.

LESLIE DERFLER

Florida Atlantic University
Boca Raton

UNITED STATES

BOORAEM, HENDRICK V. *The Formation of the Republican Party in New York: Politics and Conscience in the Antebellum North.* Pp. 296. New York: New York University Press, 1983. $39.50.

In this richly textured study, Booraem presents, as he puts it, a "reorchestration" rather than a "radical reinterpretation" of the politics of the 1850s in New York State. His central thesis is that the politics of this era should be examined from the perspective of the county and town leadership of the competing political parties, rather than that of the state and national elites. More broadly, he proposes that American political historians have focused too much attention on the biographical and ideological dimensions of their subject and thus have "divorce[d] political activity from its proper context"—the organizational and symbolic usages that make up "the institutional pattern of the party."

The body of this book is a detailed narrative of New York State politics between 1854 and 1856, three years that saw the breakdown of the Second Party System and the formation of the Republican Party. The first two chapters discuss the splintering impact of the "politics of conscience" on the "traditional loyalties and traditional policies" of the old Whig and Democratic parties in the election of 1854. The third chapter focuses on the continuity between the old Whig machine and the new Republican organization, which emerged from the wreckage of the 1854 election, and the final two chapters examine the politics of 1855 and 1856, focusing on the organizational failings of the Republicans in 1855 and the success of their institutional fusion in 1856.

Booraem's focus on party institutions is seemingly misplaced in an analysis of an era characterized by institutional break-up. In an important sense, his study does not live up to its title: he chronicles the organizational politics of this brief period in loving detail but fails to discuss conscience in more than a cursory fashion. This gap gives the book an ahistorical quality, for it was precisely the dialectic between old-style organizational politics and the new political language of conscience that constituted the engine of change in the 1850s. It is here that a related and central problem with Booraem's construct becomes apparent. The effectiveness of conscience politics was rooted in "a simmering discontent among the voters of New York," yet the focus of Booraem's analysis is on the role of "the local political leadership" in "pressur[ing] the state leadership of the Whig Party into embracing the politics of conscience." While Booraem does an admirable job of dealing with this second issue, he neglects the first. What is clearly necessary is a less constricted view of the political process; one that takes ideology more seriously and that incorporates the explicitly sociological framework that historians such as Lee Benson, Samuel Hays, and Ronald Formisano have long been urging on their discipline. The study of democratic politics should encompass more than "the decisions that politicians ma[ke]."

JOHN BROOKE

Tufts University
Medford
Massachusetts

BURKE, COLIN B. *American Collegiate Populations: A Test of the Traditional View.* Pp. ix, 369. New York: New York University Press, 1982. $35.00.

Burke's monograph is designed to test the accepted theory of the development of higher education in the United States proposed by Tewksbury's 1923 classic, *The Founding of American Colleges and Universities in the United States,* and elaborated in 1955 by Hofstadter's *Academic Freedom in the Age of the College.* These scholars viewed the development of higher education in the United States as dichotomous ideal types. Colleges prior to the Civil War were assumed to be elitist institutions run by local religious dominations that provided normative liberal arts education to a small number of affluent scholars. In contrast, postbellum colleges were viewed as providing vocational and professional education to the sons of the new immigrant populations and served as agents of change, democratizing societal institutions by providing avenues for occupational and social mobility. In this theory, developed by reformist professional educators of the early twentieth century, colleges were seen as independent variables. Changes in their policies and curricula were thought to be effective mechanisms for changing economic, social, and political institutions.

Burke's findings refute these early ideas with data collected from the Library of Congress, college yearbooks, and national biographies. He documents the changes, by decade, from 1800 to 1860 for the founding and mortality of colleges, enrollments, student's social and economic background, and subsequent professional career achievements. Then he tests his findings with post-Civil War statistics. These data indicate that college and university development was a continuous process in which college policies and curricula, rather than being rationally determined independent variables, were dependent on changes in their social and economic milieu. Students both before and after the Civil War made college-entry decisions based on the cost of investment in education, lost income, and the economic benefit to be derived from careers made possible by higher education.

The growth of colleges was a response to increased population growth in different regions, rather than denominational policy. With a fledgling national government unable to support education, it was the denominations that provided resources for education. Colleges were founded in the areas with the least public support, and interstate migration to attend school traced denominational lines. Colleges, which in the colonial period attracted a homogeneous urban elite, came to provide education and upward mobility to broad segments of the American population. Until the bureaucratization of the professions, it was the liberal arts, rather than professional training, that served as gatekeeper to upward mobility through providing entrance to the law, medicine, teaching, and the clergy. Entry into business was limited to urban populations with high social standing and family connections.

Burke was able to revise the assumptions of educational development by testing earlier assumptions empirically. In addition the early reformers made the mistake of using established eastern schools as models for a growing country. As a result they were unaware of the role of the interaction of regional social and economic institutions and students' aspirations in structuring the nature and personality of individual educational institutions. Their view was further limited by focusing on universities and colleges. They failed to notice the popularity of the new vocational school of nursing, business, and education. These nonuniversity educational organizations provided occupational mobility at less cost to sons of low-income families and women whose economic potential could not justify expensive education.

The monograph is important as a model of the role of descriptive research for the development and revision of substantive theory. It is substantively interesting at a time when the value of a university education is again being challenged by alternative providers: industry, professional associations, and community colleges.

CAROLYN R. DEXTER
Pennsylvania State University
Middletown

DELORIA, VINE, Jr. and CLIFFORD M. LYTLE. *American Indians, American Justice.* Pp. xiii, 262. Austin: University of Texas Press, 1983. $19.95. Paperbound, $9.95.

This admirable book analyzes the roots of Indian tribal government and justice and how they have been modified by the American legal system. It asks the important question, How much of Indian self-government and traditional Indian culture and values can survive, given the pressure toward adapting Indian institutions to the values of contemporary American society?

Both authors are lawyer-political scientists and their principal interest is studying the pervasive influence of the white man's political system on the Indian tribes. The federal government has greatly affected tribal institutions; significant Supreme Court rulings provided the basis for the government's absolute power over Indians. Congress has pursued vacillating policies ranging from the treaty-making period through removal and relocation, allotment and assimilation, to reorganization and finally self-determination. Executive branch and paternalistic bureaucratic wardship have weakened tribal institutions.

The story is told in a direct, nonpolemical, but profoundly convincing manner that leads one to the conclusion that federal policy has often been guided by the ethnocentric belief that Indians should be encouraged to adopt the values and civic ethic of white America and that similarity, not diversity, characterizes Indian tribal institutions and values. Federal intrusion into tribal governance has had the effect of rendering tribal self-government dormant, weakening tribal courts, and eroding adherence to tribal customs and religious rituals. In the area of tribal criminal justice, federal preemption of serious crimes has stripped tribes of the authority to deal with much criminal conduct.

Because reservation Indians are subject not only to tribal, state, and federal governments but also to shifting congressional policy and the legalistic maze created by treaties, federal laws, court opinions, and tribal constitutions, the task of rendering complexity to an acceptable level of simplicity and clarity is a major challenge. Deloria and Lytle have succeeded. Subjects such as the concepts of Indian country, tribal criminal and civil justice, and self-government are splendidly described. It is argued that the concepts of tribal sovereignty and Indian country are now merely backdrops against which federal preemption, constitutional rights of Indians, and other policy issues are examined.

Deloria and Lytle not only examine contemporary Indian judicial institutions; they also evaluate their strengths and weaknesses. Other topics dealt with include legal representation and defense of Indian rights, Indian legal interest groups, and current issues regarding voting, criminal defendants' rights, religious freedom, and entitlement to basic educational and social services.

In sum, Deloria and Lytle have compellingly presented a strong case that the weakening of tribal self-government and traditional customs and values has been fostered by the insensitivity and lack of understanding underlying federal policy with respect to tribal governance. Federal policy since 1961 has been somewhat more enlightened. The success of this book is that it untangles the complexities of the evolution of the Indian judicial system in a manner that lay and professional readers will find engrossing.

JAMES R. KERR
Southern Illinois University
Edwardsville

DINKIN, ROBERT J. *Voting in Revolutionary America: A Study of Elections in the Original Thirteen States, 1776-1789.* Pp. x, 184. Westport, CT: Greenwood Press, 1982. $27.50.

In this sequel to his *Voting in Provincial America* (1977), Dinkin examines the electoral process during and after the American Revolution. Tracing changes in both attitudes toward politics and electoral practices, he argues that the colonial political system was profoundly democratized during the 1770s and 1780s; this transformation, which ushered in many of the practices common to modern political systems, provided the underlying conditions for the emergence of a two-party system in the 1790s.

Among the major elements of this political transformation were the following:

— an increase in elective offices, including, most important, the upper houses of the legislatures and in five states the governor;

— a reduction in property requirements for voting, which expanded the electorate from perhaps 60 to 80 percent of free, white, adult males;

— more frequent elections and greater rotation in officeholding;

— greater use of the secret ballot rather than open voice voting, by which wealthy men exacted deference from lesser men they held in clientage;

— reduction of the property requirements for officeholding; and

— the adoption of more strenuous and direct appeals to the electorate by candidates.

These changes were by no means uniform among all the states, but everywhere the direction—if not the degree—of the change was similar.

Collectively, these innovations led to a more open and contested political atmosphere in which men below the elite began to run for office; in which elections became more heated and issue oriented; and in which the electorate grew more insistent that its representatives reflect its interests. Although the war-depleted ranks of the old colonial elite resisted change, the rising political consciousness of the ordinary citizens was steadily translated into liberalized laws governing the political process and into more assertiveness by the populace. The dreaded day had arrived, as one Massachusetts nabob lamented, when "every drabbling dishclout politician, however various their opinions, have all some kind of observation to make upon the times." Thus by the time the first Washington administration began to split into Federalist and Democratic-Republican factions, the rudiments of a modern electoral system had already taken form.

GARY B. NASH

University of California
Los Angeles

ELDOT, PAULA. *Governor Alfred E. Smith: The Politician as Reformer.* Pp. ix, 482. New York: Garland Publishing, 1983. $55.00.

Historians have argued for a long time about the meaning of Al Smith and the nature of his America. Among other things, they have been interested in why such a noteworthy innovator of the 1920s could become such an outspoken enemy of FDR and the New Deal in the 1930s. Was it a question of Smith's changing, some have asked, or was it really more a matter of the changing times? Did a fairly consistent Smith appear liberal in the conservative decade of the 1920s only to seem conservative in the more liberal decade that followed?

Eldot is thoroughly conversant with the historiographical controversies that have swirled around Al Smith, and along the way she recapitulates many of the most important of these arguments as a backdrop to her own study. Eldot herself enters the debate with a book that is highly favorable to Smith.

A refreshing candor marked the entire political career of this man, who never feared to take positions unpopular with his church or the general public, as for example when he defended civil liberties at the height of the Red Scare [p. 222].

Basically what Eldot seeks to show is that Smith, as governor of New York, was a vital link between the progressivism that preceded the 1920s and the New Deal reforms that came later. Thus she seeks to locate him squarely in the American reform tradition. "The following pages will demonstrate that Al Smith, the politician who ran for president, deserves recognition as Governor Alfred E. Smith, the reformer who bucked the conservatism of the age of normalcy" (p. 26). Eldot's procedure for establishing her major point is to take the reader through a meticulously detailed, topic-by-topic treatment of each of the major areas of Smith's activity as governor—restructuring the state government, public finance, the state park plan, housing policy, the conservation of human and natural resources, and so on.

The results are mixed. Although Eldot's research seems commendably thorough and although many of her contentions seem valid enough, there are some problems here—problems, unfortunately, having more to do with form than with substance per se. The book began as a dissertation, and it still has too much of the sound and feel of a dissertation. First, the organizationl structure, though workmanlike, gives a rather plodding quality to the study; and the prose, though readable, is often unexciting. Moreover, at times there is too much detail. Indeed the same basic position could be developed even more effectively in perhaps half the space. Finally, the index that has been prepared for the dissertation's publication in book form is simply not adequate.

This brings us, ultimately, to the question of the serviceability of the volume at hand. It is unlikely that many undergraduates in history or the social sciences would be required to wade through all of it, for the instructors of those undergraduates will probably continue to cover this period of American history by assigning a book such as Oscar Handlin's *Al Smith and His America.* For their part, those advanced graduate students and professors who are in Eldot's field would have been able to avail themselves of Eldot's study in its earlier dissertation form. Given all this—and given the high cost of the book—it would not seem that *Governor Alfred E. Smith: The Politician as Reformer* would have a wide readership.

In sum Eldot has made a substantial contribution to our understanding of Smith's governorship; but it is ironic that that contribution has been put in a form that will make it less usable than it otherwise might have been—less usable, alas, than it deserves to be.

ROBERT P. HAY

Marquette University
Milwaukee
Wisconsin

KEELER, THEODORE E. *Railroads, Freight, and Public Policy.* Pp. xi, 180. Washington, DC: Brookings Institution, 1983. $24.95. Paperbound, $9.95.

This book provides a detailed analysis of government policies as they have affected railroad freight transportation in the United States. It describes the technological and other changes that have occurred during the long period of public regulation of the railroads, leading to the conclusion that policies that earlier may have possessed some merit have long since become outdated and inefficient. Alternative theories of regulation are applied to this regulatory experience, with primary endorsement given to a theory that focuses on the political influence of buyers and sellers in regulated markets.

Chapter 1 establishes criteria for evaluating the financial viability of railroads and concludes that one-half or more of the nation's railroads are unprofitable, pending future regulatory changes. A general history of transportation regulation is provided in chapter 2, dating from its medieval British common-law beginnings, and formal U.S. beginnings in the nineteenth century, to the present time. The third chapter demonstrates the presence of scale economies in the railroad industry, followed in chapter 4 by an evaluation of the social goals of regulation as well as the economic effects of such regu-

lation. Chapter 5 examines recent regulatory reform. Chapter 6 considers various nonregulatory policies that importantly influence the railroad industry. An overview of the topic is presented in the seventh and final chapter, which includes an appraisal of the future outlook for public policy toward the railroads. The text is supplemented by four appendices, numerous tables, and several graphs. The placement of detailed material in the appendices allows for smooth reading.

In all, the book provides a useful analysis of both past and present public policies in the rail freight industry. Moreover, the extensive documentation provides readers the option of pursuing the subject in a more intensive fashion. However, the discussion follows too closely the current wave of deregulatory fervor. As a result it does not adequately reflect the possibility of reaping future benefits from improved regulation as opposed to following a policy of significantly reduced regulation. Furthermore, although the distributional effects of deregulation are considered, they are relegated to a position of secondary importance in line with the usual efficiency emphasis of modern economics. In addition, the long-run perspective that accompanies arguments for deregulation tends to make obscure the short-run but very real transitional costs of deregulation, such as those now being experienced in the airlines and communications industries. This short-run cost can be a high price to pay for pursuing the goal of greater long-run allocational efficiency, the achievement of which is not in itself an inevitable outcome of deregulation.

BERNARD P. HERBER

University of Arizona
Tucson

MATTHAEI, JULIE A. *An Economic History of Women in America: Women's Work, the Sexual Division of Labor, and the Development of Capitalism.* Pp. xiv, 372. New York: Schocken Books, 1982. $29.50.

Matthaei has produced a work of the first order in *An Economic History of Women in America*. The broad sweep of the book, its intellectual richness, and the importance of the phenomena addressed make it significant for economists, historians, women's studies scholars, sociologists, political scientists—indeed for all interested in major transformations in family and economic life.

The panorama Matthaei explores extends from seventeenth-century England through several hundred years of American experience to the present. By tracing the interrelated developments of capitalism, conceptions of womanhood and manhood, and the sexual division of labor across this reach of history, the extent of change becomes clear. Not only are our lives different from those of our parents, a characteristic inhering solely in recent history, but, Matthaei suggests, in the contemporary period masculine and feminine worlds have overlapped and begun a process of interpretation, placing us within sight of a truly new social order.

Certain perspectives shape Matthaei's analysis. She understands reality as socially constructed and, as a Marxist, views history as a process that has its own laws and is progressive. With such analytic tools she examines women's work, beginning with the family economy.

In the first stage examined, economic and family life were merged in the household production unit. Women and men shared a common sphere of activity, but women worked at the private provisioning for family needs while men centered on commodity production. Over time this family economy yielded to the factory system and wage labor. At this stage the family as we think of it came into being, and households became homes. At the same time, women and men began to inhabit different spheres of social life: women's realm was the family and men's was the economy. The sexes were complementary; different but equal. The cult of domesticity distinguished and elevated women's work, which shifted from production to consumption, a shift linked to the develop-ment of capitalism. The cult of domesticity and the idea of womanhood that it involved encompassed inherent contradictions, leading to the breakdown of the sexual division of labor in the twentieth century.

The third part of the book elucidates these increasing contradictions. Here Matthaei discusses "the universalization of needs" within the competitive hierarchy of consumption, a process peculiar to capitalism with many implications. For example, with needs ever expandable within the hierarchy, wealth and poverty cease to have absolute meaning. This "relativity of neediness" led, as did the two world wars, homemakers to enter the paid labor force. A synergetic process was thereby created: as more homemakers worked outside the home, their families moved up the income hierarchy and put pressure on homemakers who stayed home. Further, the more homemakers entered the paid labor force, the more acceptable it became. This, Matthaei argues, represented a crucial transformation of the sexual division of labor, enlarging the wage-earning homemaker's freedom, responsibility, and self-esteem, undermining the either/or choice of marriage versus career, and depreciating the value of the full-time homemaker. In addition this entry has contributed to a breakdown in the sex-typing of jobs:

the more that a woman's labor force career was followed *in addition to* the career of homemaking, the less need she had to affirm or prove her femininity by entering one of the "women's professions" [pp. 290-91].

All these developments have contributed to the "symmetrical marriage," in which spouses, rather than specializing in either family or economic life, participate actively in both spheres. Matthaei argues that the symmetry precipitates yet more fundamental alterations in such areas as child rearing and child development, self-concept, social relations, job structure, and institutions. The book closes with the prospect of these transformations.

This brief review of Matthaei's main line of argument can only hint at the book's depth, insight, and provocativeness. It is a scholarly work, well researched, well written, and well worth reading.

PATRICIA BAYER RICHARD
Ohio University
Athens

McADAM, DOUG. *Political Power and the Development of Black Insurgency, 1930-1970.* Pp. vii, 304. Chicago: University of Chicago Press, 1982. No price.

This book delivers a fresh, rich, and dynamic model to explain the rise and decline of the black insurgency movement in the United States. It portrays this phenomenon within a political process perspective, the core of which is structured around the interaction of four key variables: organizational strength of the insurgents, political opportunities available to challengers, psychological propensity to question extant authorities, and reactive patterns of established powers to a movement. Within this multilayered contextual framework a vast array of information, both historical and contemporaneous, pertaining to the viscosity of black-white relations during most of the twentieth century is given coherence and meaning. Indeed the breadth and depth of analysis is praiseworthy, especially considering that the subject matter regrettably has become far less fashionable to the academic —and political—community these days than it was a decade or so ago. Fault lines, unfortunately, do mar the otherwise solid bedrock of this book.

Without a comparative insurgency movement—say, among women, Chicanos, gays, or farmers—the question of whether the political process model transcends the unique conditions of blacks in white America remains open. Lack of precision in defining key terms, such as "insurgency" and the "structure of political opportunities," is troublesome. There is a tendency to let events provide meaning to major concepts, with the attendant result that conceptual parameters frequently defy location, thus impairing future research along the lines suggested by the political process model.

Further, construction of the political process model occurs at the expense of others. At times the theoretical and empirical critique of counterperspectives is illuminating and constructive, exemplifying the best of knowledge building in social science. Consequently the occasional lapse in both style and substantive argument is annoying and obvious. For instance, McAdam's analysis of the classical tradition of understanding insurgency as a collective psychological response to societal stress moves from eloquence to strained debunking. Treating numerous writers as a uniform lot masks important divergences within this literature. The factual dismissal of this school, presented in chapter 6, is not particularly convincing, especially when some unnecessary juggling of statistical routines appears, as in Table 6-2.

Likewise, the resource mobilization model of insurgency is discounted too prematurely. The data base employed to rule out the possibility that an elite might have fueled black insurgency is insufficient for the task. The treatment of pluralism fails to give due recognition to the fact that many pluralists—especially Robert Dahl—are quite sensitive to the problems that the black experience poses to their notions about the distribution of political power in America. Indeed, a pluralist scholar such as Robin Williams could make a good case that the very factors contained in the political process model are representative of the resources available in a pluralistic system that, when arranged properly, can compel change. Finally, the attempt to link the political process model with a Marxian theory of political power requires sophisticated elaboration or elimination. That this connection is drawn only briefly in the earlier part of the book, failing to reappear even in the concluding chapter, indicates that elimination might have been the wiser choice.

Nevertheless, blemishes and all, the versatility and potential of the political process model in accounting for social movements makes this an important work, worthy of a great deal of attention.

JAMES W. LAMARE
University of Canterbury
Christchurch
England

RAVITCH, DIANE. *The Troubled Crusade: American Education, 1945-80.* Pp. xiii, 384. New York: Basic Books, 1983. $19.95.

Ravitch has developed a fascinating history of American education in the last 35 years. It is a splendid description and analysis of the troublesome problems and endless conflicts, in contrast to the successes and achievements, in the educational community from the end of World War II until today.

It is difficult to summarize and review this long and complex book. Therefore the focus here will be limited to only two examples: the pressures within the educational institution and the social forces outside the schools.

First, beginning with the 1920s and 1930s, the phenomenon of progressive education shaped the pattern of thinking and programming for the schools. In 1945 progressive education was hailed as the acme of educational progress and development. Ten years later this philosophy quietly crumbled and died. What actually happened was a pronounced shift in the objectives of learning. Under progressive education, instead of concentration on intellectual development and mastery of subject matter, the concern focused on social and emotional development and awareness of vocation, health, and family life. Consequently learning was fo-

cused on such areas as how to earn a living, how to get along with other people, and how to stay healthy. However, the reality of Sputnik and the need for concrete knowledge of math and science brought about the downfall of progressive education.

The second influence on education was the problem of racism, or the imbedded belief that variation in the color of skin implied substantial differences among black and white people. Gunnar Myrdal forewarned about this brewing conflict in American society, yet the obvious social gap between the American creed of freedom and equality and the practice of segregation and discrimination was completely ignored. While the battles were fought in the courts, with classic decisions ensuing—such as the 1954 Supreme Court decision that outlawed the doctrine of separate but equal—the main arena for the battles of desegregation and equality was in the public school system. The election of John F. Kennedy to the presidency in 1960 firmly established the civil rights movement to counteract the imbedded racist patterns in American society.

This study surveys the field of education not as isolated academic developments but as dynamic experiences that were intertwined with the social forces of the time. Thus federal aid to education, community control, and black nationalism are discussed as the major social problems in American society but concentrated in the field of education. In fact, the eight chapters of the book might have been published as eight separate studies that explore some specific social problem.

Finally, Ravitch meticulously researched the vast literature in the field and provides each chapter with excellent guiding notes. These notes serve both as an explicit reference to the sources and as a comprehensive bibliography of the vast literature. Some may take issue with Ravitch about the absence of any data used for the study. Ravitch, however, used the existing, scattered literature to develop an extensive analysis of the last three and a half decades. The result is that the field of education has been greatly enriched by this superb study.

MARTIN E. DANZIG
City University of New York
    at Kingsborough
Brooklyn
New York

SABATIER, PAUL A. and DANIEL A. MAZ-MANIAN. *Can Regulation Work? The Implementation of the 1972 California Coastal Initiative.* Pp. xi, 389. New York: Plenum Press, 1983. No price.

LITAN, ROBERT E. and WILLIAM D. NORD-HAUS. *Reforming Federal Regulation.* Pp. x, 204. New Haven, CT: Yale University Press, 1983. No price.

"Governmental regulation." The words stir up complex responses from Americans of all political hues. Regulation is woven into the fabric of our thoughts about political freedom and the proper role of government as a protector. The breadth and depth of governmental regulatory activity encourages widespread discussion and colorful rhetorical excess. Is there a more timely subject for serious scholarship concerning American domestic policy?

Reforming Federal Regulation and *Can Regulation Work?* each provide us with a thoughtful examination of the requisites for successful regulatory activity. Litan and Nordhaus construct a critique of current regulatory policy and concentrate on proposals for improving the accountability, coordination, and cost-effectiveness of federal regulation. Sabatier and Mazmanian provide a rich and careful study of the politics of successfully implementing a single regulatory policy in a state. Together the books cover a wide range of theoretical and practical issues concerning regulation. The scholarly restraint exercised in these presentations may serve to dull the appetite of some casual readers, but the nourishment provided in each serving should sustain anyone.

Litan and Nordhaus argue:

In theory, regulation should arise as a response to market failure. In practice, regulation is more accurately characterized as a government tool for *redistributing* society's resources toward those groups that have successfully enlisted the support of the government on their behalf [p. 34].

As such, regulation must be understood in political as well as economic terms. Analysts who fail to understand that fact are doomed to misunderstand both the benefits from regulation and the problems that beset regulatory efforts. Armed with a proper understanding, however, it is possible to diagnose and prescribe.

The diagnosis is that federal regulatory efforts are systematically flawed by an insufficient degree of political accountability and by "statutory restrictions inhibiting agencies from balancing costs against benefits and from choosing less costly marketlike incentives."

These flaws can be remedied by the introduction of a comprehensive regulatory budget that would force the consideration of regulatory priorities by both the Congress and the president. The language of budgets—dollars—would encourage decision makers to address all regulatory issues in a consistent benefit-cost manner once the costs of regulation borne by the private sector were included in the budget. The budget metaphor carries with it the notion that regulatory activity that imposes costs above an agreed-upon level would be curtailed.

Litan and Nordhaus recognize that such a proposal would place inordinate demands on our present political and economic institutions. But, they argue, such a regulatory budget can be viewed as an ideal, a goal. At a more practical level, a regular calendar of congressional and presidential review of major regulations would accomplish the goals of political accountability and policy coordination.

In this revised form, the proposal by Litan and Nordhaus is unobjectionable to anyone who accepts any proper role for the government as regulator and who sees political accountability as valuable. Cynics might well argue that regulation is too important to be left in the hands of elected officials, but I could not.

My concern with this analysis centers on that intellectual keystone that is allowed to recede in the final proposal—benefit-cost analysis. Litan and Nordhaus claim that policy coherence and accountability demand benefit-cost analysis. Regulatory policy success is implicitly defined in terms of a favorable benefit-cost ratio. Only the political practicality of getting half a loaf now argues for dropping it; but will the drop be temporary?

Yet benefit-cost calculations are notoriously ill suited to certain tasks because they assume that everything of value can be phrased in terms of financial compensation. The calculations are quite sensitive to the accounting rules employed for valuing future goods and services, and the usual accounting rules are well known for systematically understating the costs of producing irreversible damage and diminutions in the quality of life. Nowhere is this point better made than in attempts to assess the consequences of regulations concerning the natural environment.

In an exemplary piece of research on the standards for successful environmental policy implementation, Sabatier and Mazmanian scarcely consider this all too common benefit-cost standard. Rather, implementation success is defined in terms of the stated policy goals of the legislation, and the focus is on the variables that impinge on meeting those goals: the clarity and consistency of the legislative goals, the soundness of the theory that identifies the factors related to the policy objectives, the character of the implementation structures, the skill and resources of the implementation managers, and the presence of organized external constituencies along with a neutral judiciary.

Census and election data, roll calls, public opinion surveys, elite interviews, and archival material are combined with considerable facility to produce a detailed case study of the politics and policies of the California coastal initiative. This is more than a case study, however. Sabatier and Mazmanian have proposed and demonstrated the veracity of a most useful framework for the analysis of public policy implementation.

The utility of the framework is not a matter of speculation. Other scholars laboring in the public policy mines are already using this structure to assist in safe passage to their work site. I have significant quarrels with some of their multivariate analyses, but even there they are on ground solid enough to hold the weight. Suffice to say, this volume will be required reading for some time to come.

The contention of Sabatier and Mazmanian that is of most interest in the context of the larger discussion on regulation is that policies can be implemented successfully only when the goals are related clearly and correctly to the factors that affect those goals. It would seem that policy success does not simply depend on a favorable benefit-cost ratio if the policymakers did not set that as a goal. Rational and successful policy is that which gets the job done. Ultimately, regulation is a political question amenable to political, not economic, analysis. Sabatier and Mazmanian have remembered that. Litan and Nordhaus have not.

ROMAN HEDGES
State University of New York
Albany

SELEY, JOHN L. *The Politics of Public-Facility Planning.* Pp. xiv, 236. Lexington, MA: D. C. Heath, 1983. $23.95.

Seley's *Politics of Public-Facility Planning* is well titled. This immensely readable volume combines analysis with case studies in an integrative and comparative framework. The cases are diverse in terms of type of facility, characteristics of siting controversies, perceptions of impacts, and implications of outcomes, but they are held together by an ingenious method for integrating the case material that should be readily applicable to a wide range of public-facility siting attempts. The siting controversies include cases involving urban renewal, an urban expressway, group homes for the mentally disabled, the disposal of radioactive waste, and recombinant DNA research facilities.

Of potentially greatest value to the reader is a highly original chapter on the methodology of case studies. Seley explains and then demonstrates the framework for organizing case study material according to dimensions of the siting process. He also proposes scaling units for these dimensions and methods for recording the changes of the dimensions over time. The procedure allows the investigator of a new case to approach his or her study with a ready-made checklist of 150 variables found to be relevant across the cases Seley examined. In the same chapter there is also a valuable synopsis of the life cycle of siting controversies and their variations.

Following the case studies and methodology chapters is an extensive section on impact assessment that highlights the issues of socioeconomic impacts and the difficulties in their identification and measurement. Seley reviews the shortcomings of conventional cost-benefit and risk-benefit analyses and proposes a number of optional approaches that incorporate the results of social science research on facility impacts.

An imaginative chapter follows that discusses a number of innovations for bringing those affected by the siting process into the negotiations. A summary section reviews some of the major approaches being used for resolving siting controversies, including use of the courts, mediation, arbitration, and compensation. The 28 pages of bibliography will provide readers with an immensely useful catalogue of cases and methodological source material.

I heartily recommend this volume to social scientists, policy analysts, and planners. The problems of siting valuable but unwanted public facilities is presented in a format that is rigorous and thorough, yet highly readable. The book is an important contribution to a very significant problem.

JULIAN WOLPERT

Princeton University
New Jersey

TUCKER, ROBERT W. and DAVID C. HENDRICKSON. *The Fall of the First British Empire: Origins of the War of American Independence.* Pp. ix, 450. Baltimore, MD: Johns Hopkins University Press, 1982. $24.00.

Tucker and Hendrickson have written a book that attempts to shift responsibility for the advent of the American Revolution away from the British and in the direction of the colonists. Their interpretation, although differing in general and in particular from my own, raises provocative questions about the years between 1763 and 1776 and should produce some rethinking of issues during this period.

According to Tucker and Hendrickson, the conclusion that British policy initiated Anglo-American friction rests on the inclination of post-World War II historians to spotlight events immediately preceding the American Revolution. Such historians are able to fault the alleged innovations of the British only by accepting the limited and inaccurate definition of the status quo advanced by the colonists. It was, in fact, the Americans who disturbed the status quo by gradually undermining the imperial connection. Even their assumed willingness to allow parliamentary regulation of trade was more apparent than real. The British, on the other hand, were merely trying to preserve some semblance of order, and the measures adopted between 1763 and 1775 aimed only at the continuance of a status quo that the colonists had seriously undermined.

Tucker and Hendrickson argue that the great war for empire was fought largely to defend the colonies, and victory brought the metropolis increased responsibilities. When the British took steps to accept this responsibility, however, they were thwarted by colonies willing to grant the form but not the substance of authority. The Rockingham, Chatham, Grafton, and even the North ministries wanted to avoid military conflict and so encouraged colonists in their claims with a decade of appeasement. But when, in 1774, it became clear that British authority in Massachusetts Bay was virtually nonexistent, the North administration was forced either to accept American independence or to take steps to reassert British control.

The British government, according to Tucker and Hendrickson, had no viable alternative. The First Continental Congress offered no concession and confidently stood its ground in the expectation that the mother country would once more capitulate. The North ministry believed—correctly—that such capitulation meant loss of the colonies. The government also believed—incorrectly— that such a loss would reduce Great Britain to a secondary position in world affairs. This view, "accepted as an article of faith by virtually every significant political group in the country," would simply not permit the government to concede independence.

So we seem to have come full circle. The measures adopted by Britain were not incursions on the status quo—redefined—and were thus defensive in nature. The maneuvers of the colonists actually did intrude on the status quo—redefined—and were thus offensive in nature. " 'When *I* use a word,' Humpty-Dumpty said, in rather a scornful tone, 'it means just what I choose it to mean—neither more nor less.' "

In the final analysis Tucker and Hendrickson have written consensus history. They find agreement among both the colonists and the British, although their respective positions were, as John Shy has noted, quite incompatible. They may also be attempting a parable for our time: appeasement leads to loss, but one should not overemphasize the importance of what one is losing. If they play with words and overstate their case too often, they have nevertheless reminded us that all interpretive overviews lead to distortion. If they have passed over the fears of the Americans too easily, they have accurately noted that the British did, after all, have an empire to run, and what was it we expected them to do?

DAVID AMMERMAN
Florida State University
Tallahassee

UNDERWOOD, JAMES E. and WILLIAM J. DANIELS. *Governor Rockefeller in New York: The Apex of Pragmatic Liberalism in the United States.* Pp. xvi, 335. Westport, CT: Greenwood Press, 1982. No price.

Throughout the course of American history, hundreds of politicians have contracted White House fever. But in our own time few have had a more obvious or celebrated case of that republican malady than Nelson Rockefeller of New York. Because the closest Rockefeller came to his goal of being elected president was his appointment as Gerald Ford's vice-president, in his own mind Rockefeller had to regard his long political career as having an element of failure about it. After all, as he himself made clear, he "never wanted to be vice-president of anything."

This is a detailed examination of the 15-year governorship that Rockefeller had expected to be his springboard to the presidency. Specificially, Underwood and Daniels seek to evaluate Rockefeller as an example of the modern, pragmatic, problem-solving, liberal politician. To this end they establish a set of 11 criteria for pragmatic liberalism, and then they judge Rockefeller's career as New York's fifty-third governor by this model. The subtitle of the book makes clear their conclusions about how well Rockefeller measured up to the norms.

Indeed, as Underwood and Daniels see it, Rockefeller personified these norms. Thus Rockefeller's departure from the scene, they further insist, was nothing less than a reflection of the waning of pragmatic liberalism in general.

When he no longer had the means to function as an effective problem solver in the pragmatic liberal style to which he had become accustomed, he left the office of Governor of New York State. More than any other event, his departure symbolized a decline in the currency of pragmatic liberalism in America [p. 255].

One of the strengths of this study is its striking characterization of the man and its emphasis on how his political style manifested his character. Rockefeller had once gone to a John Dewey-type school, and life for him was problem solving. He had a monumental capacity for work and rarely did anything purely for pleasure. Business was pleasure for him. He regarded himself as an ideas man, so that others were to attend to the day-to-day details of administration. He spent his own money lavishly. He presented Henry Kissinger with a gift of $50,000 in 1969 and gave more than $.5 million to the United Jewish Appeal in the years before 1974. He also spent the state's money lavishly and was charged with having mortgaged its future in the process. He could be combative, determined, and persistent. He could rarely admit defeat.

Finally, when all tactics failed to produce success and the legislature or public balked, Rockefeller proved adept at shifting the conflict to a new arena or finding a novel way to circumvent those who opposed his proposals [p. 151].

Although this collaborative study is based on thoroughgoing research and although there is much to be learned from it about the man and his methods, some substantial questions can be raised. To begin with, models are just that—models—and there is a certain arbitrariness about them, as we all know. Not everyone would agree with Underwood and Daniels's criteria for pragmatic liberalism. That aside, however, what is worse is that the model they choose eventually gets in the way of their telling the Rockefeller story. One sometimes finds oneself wishing that Underwood and Daniels would simply deal with the man as the unique person he was without worrying so much about how he met some arbitrary norms previously established. Moreover, there is a considerable amount of jargon in the study, and there are numerous occasions when the mode of expression detracts from the essential message. One example will perhaps suffice.

Seeing the proper role of the president as the activist problem solver, a role that should only be filled by an activist leader such as himself, and being committed to the ultimate exercise of his life strategy as president, he could not, and would not, abandon the rhetoric or behavior appropriate to this conception and commitment [p. 81].

Obviously, what Underwood and Daniels are trying to say here could be said twice as well in perhaps half the words.

Even with these problems, however, this book still makes a decided contribution to our understanding of Nelson Rockefeller.

ROBERT P. HAY

Marquette University
Milwaukee
Wisconsin

SOCIOLOGY

ADAMSON, WALTER L. *Hegemony and Revolution: A Study of Antonio Gramsci's Political and Cultural Theory.* Pp. x, 308. Berkeley: University of California Press, 1983. $28.50. Paperbound, $8.95.

Since at least the 1970s Antonio Gramsci, a founder-leader of the Italian Communist Party, has increasingly been considered one of the most important—if not the single most important—Marxist theorists since Lenin. Among the few book-length studies of his thought that have recently become available, Adamson's recently published study—the hardcover was published in 1980—is clearly one of the best.

In his analysis of Gramsci's political and cultural theory, Adamson consistently seeks to place it in the intellectual currents and political events of the time. Thus Gramsci's writings are examined in chronological order, and Adamson seeks to bring out carefully the evolution of his ideas. He attempts "to present the overriding continuities in Gramsci's political understanding... to avoid any mechanical confrontation between the 'early' and 'late' Gramsci," which Adamson dismisses as "figments of the interpretative imagination" of those scholars, mostly Western Marxists, who posit such a difference by contrasting his mature *Prison Notebooks* with the early writings.

In this study Adamson squarely places Gramsci in the group of Hegelian-Marxist theorists considered to be in the Western Marxist tradition, as distinct from the more orthodox Marxist-Leninists including Lenin himself. Intriguingly, the author cites Merleau Ponty's definition of Western Marxism and ignores Perry Anderson's major work, *Considerations on Western Marxism,* published in 1976, although the latter's book is to date the most definitive study formulating such a distinction. Indeed, Anderson's book is not even cited in Adamson's otherwise comprehensive bibliography.

In any case, the inclusion of Gramsci in the Hegelian-Marxist tendency, not to speak of the Western Marxist tradition, is problematic. In his admiration for Hegel, Gramsci was no more Hegelian than Lenin himself, who, in his *Philosophical Notebooks,* praised Hegel very highly. Surprisingly, Adamson refers to Gramsci's knowledge of this text, or at least of the "crucial chapter," "On the Question of Dialectics," which was published in March 1925, only in a footnote. Even in his criticism of Bukharin's mechanistic Marxism, Gramsci held a position similar to that of Lenin, who in his late December 1922 letters—the so-called Lenin Will or Testament—argued that Bukharin had never properly understood dialectics. It is therefore not sufficient to assert, as Adamson does, that "Gramsci's notion of the state subsuming both civil and political society resembles nothing so much as Hegel's conception of the state as the historical moment of civil society canceled and preserved." The Hegel-Marx-Lenin-Gramsci relationship is more complex than Adamson makes out, as recent commentators like Buci-Glucksmann, Anne Showstack Sassoon, and Eric Hobsbawm have shown.

At this stage, it is necessary to point out an apparent shortcoming in this fine study. The *Prison Notebooks*, Gramsci's major and last work, were written in Fascist Italian prisons and were therefore written in a particularly elliptical and allusive style so as to escape the censors. And at least from early 1933, as his biographer Giuseppe Fiori has noted, "Gramsci was already slowly dying" of tuberculosis, arteriosclerosis, and Pott's disease, to mention only the more major diseases that afflicted him at the time. These factors, of which Adamson is doubtless aware, make interpretation of the fragmented and unfinished *Notebooks* extremely difficult, yet he does not appear to take them into account. This is a serious lapse for a scholar so aware of the need to examine an author's works against the background of his life, even though he has cautioned readers that he has "not intended this as biography or even intellectual biography."

Despite these drawbacks Adamson's treatment of the *Notebooks* is illuminating. Above all, his analysis of what Hobsbawm has called Gramsci's "pioneer work on a Marxist political theory" merits serious consideration. Development of the concepts of hegemony, historical bloc, and the relative autonomy of politics is carefully scrutinized and evaluated, even though readers may differ with Adamson's conclusions.

This book must be considered necessary reading in the growing corpus of interpretive studies of perhaps the most exciting Marxist theorist since Lenin.

KAMAL A. MITRA CHENOY
Columbia University
New York

HAAG, ERNEST VAN DEN and JOHN P. CONRAD. *The Death Penalty: A Debate.* Pp. xiv, 305. New York: Plenum Press, 1983. $16.95.

There are points that are positive and edifying about *The Death Penalty: A Debate.* In an effort to cover more completely its many controversial dimensions, van den Haag and Conrad argue the merits of capital punishment, as a deterrence especially. Van den Haag argues for the retention of the death penalty even though there is little evidence that it deters. Conrad's position is against executions because they are wrong, regardless of whether they deter or not. Van den Haag and Conrad extensively debate the relevant data—although not much data are given—the constitutional and legal questions, and the justice and equality issues.

Some of the more enlightening exchanges are over the morals and meanings of capital punishment—for example, natural rights, sanctity of life, or the biblical bases. Each author calls on many historical figures in philosophy or politics to substantiate his side. These include Mill, Kant, Beccaria, Jefferson, and especially J. S. Stephen, who was a leading proponent of capital punishment in nineteenth-century Britain. Among other labels, Conrad identifies himself as a retributivist—believing that proper punishment is proper for the guilty—but also as an abolitionist. Van den Haag is identified as a utilitarian—believing that crime is prevented by intimidation, while execution deters would-be killers—and as a retentionist or advocate.

Just what audience the book is relevant to is not clear—perhaps the informed public. The reader should prepare for effort because of the sometimes obscure language with, for example, many legal Latinisms—not always defined—and tangents on what constitutes theory. But van den Haag is defensive here. The audience, he seems to fear, is college educated and therefore composed of already committed abolitionists. He advises us that "education does not necessarily produce judgment or stability." It is better to "heed the common people," or it is "common sense to presume that the more severe punishment is more deterrent," and the general or common sentiment for capital punishment is often "judicially sabotaged." Although couched as democratic, all this is unconvincing.

And what is Conrad's "maturing society"? Is it a more humane, advanced, educated, and European one? Do "standards of decency . . . evolve [progress?] as a civilization matures"? To Conrad, capital punishment is indecent and so perhaps are those who advocate it, now apparently including most Americans. This is not convincing either.

The book can be quite tedious and distracting. Conrad uses many high-blown characterizations of his "imperious opponent." Van den Haag "wherefores" us extensively and occasionally name calls; for example, his opponents are "uninformed do-gooders." Both authors make a number of unsupported assertions, while Conrad especially "postpones discussion till later." He does, however, eventually address most of van den Haag's points. The latter does not or perhaps cannot do the same to Conrad's. One example in particular is the case of the hit-man killer who is rarely caught and thus not punished. Capital punishment is irrelevant here.

Some other distractions include unnecessary appendices to several of the chapters. They are placed after the chapters, rather than at the end of the book, and merely continue the argument instead of, for example, providing empirical support. Second, there are too many getting-in-the-last-word occasions. Many chapters end with a series of short restatements of each position and an attack on the opponents. Finally, there are numerous points of agreement, of which we are told unnecessarily and often.

I do not believe this book will persuade many fence-sitting readers. Those already committed to whichever position may find some ammunition here. As for the rest, they could obtain information, especially on the history and background of capital punishment, but they will probably be unconvinced by the arguments of the book—if, in fact, they even read it.

WILLIAM BRIDGELAND
Michigan State University
East Lansing

HEKMAN, SUSAN. *Weber, the Ideal Type, and Contemporary Social Theory.* Pp. ix, 213. Notre Dame, IN: University of Notre Dame Press, 1983. $19.95.

Hekman's book is a serious but vexing effort on an important topic. Max Weber's methodological writings, sprawling and unfinished, remain the most sustained, deepest reflection by a practicing social scientist on the principles of inquiry of his own discipline. These writings have stimulated a library of commentary by three generations of authors from each of the major nations of the West—from Alexander von Schelting in Germany in the 1920s and 1930s to Toby Huff in the United States in the 1980s. Some part of this commentary, not least by the aforementioned scholars, has a pertinence and force that exceeds much contemporary discussion of questions that continue to plague social theory. The most eminent social scientist since Weber to have taken his methodology seriously, if critically, was Talcott Parsons, who wrote hundreds of pages on the topic over a 40-year span, from the late 1930s to the late 1970s—pages in which the general issues of concern to Hekman are discussed in considerable detail.

The book is vexing on two counts. First, hardly anyone other than Weber—and, of course, Rickert—appears to have existed for Hekman before 1965. If this is merely another instance of a too common historical myopia, it is not for that reason any more forgivable. Second, the work of the one scholar who has clarified many of the most difficult issues with which Hekman grapples—namely Parsons—has been utterly ignored. The reasons Hekman gives for ignoring Parsons's commentary, which perhaps also apply to the other commentary mentioned, are unconvincing. Parsons, she says, has not figured prominently in contemporary discussion. This is undeniably true if contemporary discussion is taken to have begun in the late 1970s. Yet Althusser, to whom she devotes attention as a representative of the structuralist and objectivist positions, had begun to fade from view precisely in the late 1970s and with the exception of Hekman's scrutiny is no longer much noticed. Further, Hekman observes that the recent resurgence of interest in Weber has repudiated Parsons's interpretation. Again true, but Hekman is highly, and I think justifiably, critical of much of the recent view of Weber. In a less creditable effort these inexplicable silences would be sufficient to dismiss the book as another tedious case of an ignorant scholar's muddlings.

Hekman's analysis is in the main forceful. She is particularly good at exposing several epistemological and logical inadequacies in the positions of Winch, Althusser, and the earlier Habermas. In part, however, she has set up something of a straw man by selecting to criticize two weak versions—namely Winch's and Althusser's—of the theories she wishes to integrate. The methodology and epistemology implied in the work, say, of Gadamer, Geertz, or Bellah, more powerful representatives of subjectivist theory, or in the work of Levi-Strauss, Needham, or Leach, whose structuralism is richer and suppler than the few hardened forays of Althusser, would have been more central to her concerns.

Hekman's discussion of Schutz's methodological views in relation to Weber's is suggestive but cursory. There remains unresolved the issue of the scope of Weber's ideal types and of whether in Schutz's view these types can be applied as well to the present as to the past. There is also the issue of the cognitive bias in Schutz's view of the world—doubtless due to his primary interest in epistemology—and whether this bias foreshortens the things to be included in any ideal-typical synthesis of social action. There is, finally, the meaning of intersubjectivity—crucial to Hekman's effort at synthesis—which is insufficiently developed in her discussion.

Nevertheless, within its limits Hekman's discussion is rewarding, rigorous, and fair minded. She concludes by drawing on the philosophical reflections mainly of Wittgenstein and Toulmin to clarify and strengthen Weber's conception of the logical status of social scientific theory. The discussion is too fleeting but fertile in its implications.

Hekman's conclusion points to an interesting question. If partly through her efforts social theories are synthesized, will we not yet be left with a further task of synthesis? Separately synthesized theories must themselves be brought together or we will have another version of the dilemma Hekman has set out to resolve. Intersubjectivity, the sharing of thought, is not achieved by fiat, but precisely through synthesis, which must remain an ongoing effort. Perhaps Weber will again prove helpful. And not least Parsons. Hekman is a promising young scholar. I look forward to reading her future work.

HAROLD J. BERSHADY
University of Pennsylvania
Philadelphia

STUB, HOLGER R. *The Social Consequences of Long Life.* Pp. 278. Springfield, IL: Charles C Thomas, 1982. Paperbound, $16.75.

OLSON, LAURA KATZ. *The Political Economy of Aging: The State, Private Power, and Social Welfare.* Pp. 272. New York: Columbia University Press, 1982. Paperbound, $12.50.

Both of these books have appeared at a time when growing old in American society has prompted politicians to take greater interest in the cost of growing old and in limiting the institutional victimization of the elderly. As I was reviewing these two books, the Los Angeles City Council decided to take emergency measures to curtail the increasing number of evictions among the elderly in the city. The city was quick to realize that the coming of the Olympics would be the right opportunity for landlords to optimize their rental fees. After all, once the Olympics are over, those same units can be converted into condos and sold to the up-and-coming young professionals.

The Social Consequences of Long Life is a social psychological and sociological analysis of increased life expectancy in everyday life. The book examines how changing conceptions of life expectancy have been associated with social transformations of the past two centuries. By examining life expectancy as a cumulative process, Stub asserts that it is possible to understand the impact of increased life expectancy on the structural expansion of modern society. For example, Stub argues that advances in the treatment of disease during the last century have increased the life expectancy of individuals, and, as a result, society has had to develop the necessary structural arrangements, such as increased schooling of the young, to accommodate individuals with a long-range perspective on life.

Stub's book is interesting, well written, and amply documented. Some of the questions he raises—"At what point does a society become aware of the social consequences from increased life expectancy? What effect does increased life expectancy have on social relationships and the structure of social opportunity?"—permit the reader to view long life as an issue that requires greater social definition, a greater presence in the educational process, and a stronger role in the political implementation of its meaning. By institutionalizing the presence of increased life expectancy in modern society, Stub clearly demonstrates, the problems of the old are transformed from moral concerns to technical concerns.

The Political Economy of Aging is an extremely concise analysis of the social and political problems associated with the uses of old age in a capitalist society. Olson's perspective is that old age has become a necessary instrument in a capitalist society's quest for capital formation. The social and political problems of the old are therefore bureaucratic creations that mystify the real social problems faced by the elderly—victimization, poverty, homelessness, disease.

What is most interesting about this book is Olson's use of population data for the 65-and-over population in the United States from 1900 to the present, coupled with an examination of federal expenditures for the elderly to contrast the following viewpoints: the free-market conservative who advocates more solutions from the private sector for the public problems of the elderly; the liberal accommodationist who argues for more public programs to confront the everyday dilemmas of old age; and the radical who advocates a revolutionary change in the state's conception of old age.

Second, Olson's use of demographic data, together with an analysis of private and public pension plans for the elderly, clearly communicates the instrumental role of old age in a profit-oriented environment: capital investment in longevity secures greater profits and diversifies the nature of investments while at the same time limiting the amount of cost on the source of investment. In other words there are big bucks to be made from the elderly because the elderly will never be in a position to recover their total investment in such things as pension plans. To facilitate matters, Olson argues that pensions plans have maximized their investment of pension funds by attaining a high level of collaboration from the medical sector, which seeks to stabilize, rather than to improve, the health status of the elderly. That is, the medical sector in society also recognizes that stabilizing the health status of the elderly guarantees higher profits than does actual improvement of their health status.

As a whole, these books complement each other quite well. Where Stub examines the social presence and meaning of long life, Olson analyzes the capitalistic manipulation of long life for profit and capital formation. Where Stub calls for greater recognition of the meaning of increased life expectancy, Olson calls for less exploitation of the elderly. In short, both books demonstrate in a clear manner that the elderly are valuable to society but relatively meaningless in their recognition by society.

ADALBERTO AGUIRRE, Jr.
University of California
Riverside

TAYLOR, LARRY. *Dutchmen on the Bay.* Pp. xviii, 206. Philadelphia: University of Pennsylvania Press, 1983. $12.95.

Dutchmen on the Bay is an anthropological account of the Dutch shellfish industry community of West Sayville, Long Island. Taylor's account covers the period from 1730 to the present but focuses on the period between 1880 and 1910, when the oyster industry was at its height and key changes were taking place in the Dutch immigrant community.

Taylor makes no pretense of covering every aspect of the culture of this Dutch immigrant community, but rather focuses attention on what he calls the contractual community—the social world of Calvinism— marked by extreme tension between the individual and the society as a whole. The Dutch community of West Sayville is perhaps one of the most ideal places to explore this question. It was dominated by two warring congregations dedicated to repressive Calvinistic dogmas; it was inhabited by Baymen and shellfish shippers, who, like many fishermen, are highly entrepreneurial and independent. Conflict was inevitable, not only between individuals and the congregations to which they belonged but between fishermen and Baymen and the shippers, who controlled their means of livelihood.

Taylor argues that the constant conflict and confrontation, rather than fragmenting the community, served to integrate it. Following Simmel, Taylor asserts that West Sayville was a community of confrontation. If members of the community disagreed, at least they agreed on what the conflicts were about and the rules by which the game was to be played.

Dutchmen on the Bay, however, is more than an ethnography of a small, unique ethnic group. The relationship between the individual and the society has long been a key issue for the social sciences as a whole. If Taylor offers no definitive answers or startling theoretical breakthroughs, he does add another case study that makes a clear contribution to the literature. He also adds another dimension to our understanding of the Protestant ethic and the nature of capitalism.

Taylor's book sheds light on aspects of U.S. history and American society in chronicling the experience of an immigrant group that made a unique adaptation—aquaculture—to the environment in which it found itself; he illustrates the way the community changed in response to the changes in the fishing industry, in technology, and in trends in American history as a whole.

The book also contributes to the study of maritime societies. The cultured oyster industry was one of the first commercially successful aquaculture operations in the New World. This industry, which depended on techniques brought with the immigrants from the Netherlands, is described in some detail by Taylor. Taylor gives his description of the 1902 strike against the oyster shippers an interesting twist. Most strikes in this period are presented as confrontations between capitalists and workers; Taylor suggests this one might better be seen as a reaction to an enclosure of the commons that occurred when a change in the legal system allowed leasing of the oyster beds—a change that Dutch entrepreneurs were quick to take advantage of.

Nothing in *Dutchmen on the Bay* will strike American readers as bizarre or unusual. Dutch culture and American culture are two variants on Western European culture. They differ in degree, not in kind. But the ordinariness of the West Sayville ethnography should not obscure the contribution Taylor has made. He has ventured to examine and explain a variant of his own culture—a most difficult task for an anthropologist.

If anything, Taylor's book is perhaps too ambitious. In a book of under 190 pages he attempts to cover everything from the ethnography of present-day West Sayville and the immigration of the Dutch to Long Island to the history of the oyster industry and the religious schisms that rocked the Dutch community. At times descriptions of important events and techniques seem inadequate and truncated. No quantitative data are offered. I suspect Taylor, in common with historians, was able to gather some data on a vast number of topics, but not enough on any one to do a complete analysis.

Dutchmen on the Bay is unusually well written. Taylor handles the English language with wit, élan, and precision. The book should be of great interest to those interested in maritime communities, European immigration into the United States, and the relationship between the individual and society.

JAMES M. ACHESON
University of Maine
Orono

ECONOMICS

APPLEBY, JOYCE. *Capitalism and a New Social Order: The Republican Vision of the 1790s.* Pp. x, 110. New York: New York University Press, 1984. $16.50.

This excellent little book is part of a distinguished series of studies, each of which developed out of the Anson G. Phelps Lectureship on Early American History. This volume attempts "to uncover how the market economy influenced the way people thought about politics and the human potential for purposefully reordering social institutions." Appleby's specific focus is the manner in which growing economic commercialization influenced the world view of many Americans, especially the Jeffersonians. During the 1790s, they "coalesced around a set of ideas—radical notions about how society should be reorganized." This vision, institutionalized during the early nineteenth century, stimulated the continued development of American capitalism.

Appleby convincingly locates the creation of a new economic and political point of view in the transformations that occurred in the American and English economies. In the subsistence economies of sixteenth-century England and early New England it was expected that the government had a moral obligation to intervene in daily economic affairs for the public good, in order to ensure the distribution of life's necessities to everyone. Correspondingly, the notion of the existence of limited social wealth meant that one person's material advance came at the expense of another's decline. Thus morality and economic activity were intimately intertwined; to charge more than a just price in order to maximize profits was to offend social standards.

The economic structure of seventeenth-century England and eighteenth-century America grew increasingly commercialized, drawing into its web not just merchants but artisans and farmers as well. The outlook of many people changed to sanction their new economic behavior. A new conception of sustained prosperity and the possibilities of unlimited social wealth meant that individual material improvement was not necessarily detrimental to the physical condition of others. Not only did the idea of innate human motivation based on self-interest receive wide acceptance, but the government's role in the economy also was redefined. A self-regulated economy operating on the natural principle of individual self-interest was harmed, not aided, by government intervention.

Contrary to the popular image of Jeffersonians as backward-looking agrarians who hoped to retard economic development, Appleby argues that because they adopted this new economic vision, they shaped American institutions to facilitate the growth of capitalism. Eschewing the traditional Federalist ideas of deference and hierarchy, the victors of the Revolution of 1800 adopted self-interest as a radical means to establish their fundamental belief in democracy and equality.

Appleby offers both a valuable explanation of the development of a capitalist ideology and a needed corrective for the traditional image of the Jeffersonians. However, like many revisionists, she may push her argument too far. Too much has been uncovered about their fear and loathing of the common people and their belief in a natural aristocracy to totally embrace Appleby's new image of the Republicans as radical democrats committed to a classless society. This caveat aside, this is an excellent book, written in a lively style and particularly well suited for classroom use.

BILLY G. SMITH
Montana State University
Bozeman

HANKEL, WILHELM and ROBERT ISAAK. *Modern Inflation: Its Economics and Politics.* Pp. 222. Lanham, MD: University Press of America, 1983. $23.50. Paperbound, $10.25.

This is a good book, with a well-stated central argument, sprinkled with insights into the modern inflationary process. It is a book dealing with modern inflation. It relies heavily on the central role of inflationary expectations and analyzes inflation mainly as an integral part of the entire socioeconomic-political process of growth and claims on income shares in modern participating democratic societies. It has no rigorously stated model to be subjected to mathematical econometric testing of the kind so dominant in modern macroeconomics. It is in the tradition of Schumpeter, Wicksell, and Hayek. Thus the book will probably be highly criticized, or disregarded—I think, incorrectly—by many modern economists who are interested mainly in rigorous theoretical models that can be econometrically tested.

In this brief review, it is impossible to state the sophisticated, intricate reasoning the authors use in building this picture of modern inflation and problems it raises for us. Let me list instead merely a few typical propositions, which I hope will give some flavor of the book.

1. Modern inflation arises out of the process of economic growth and change and can be understood only as part of these processes.

2. Entrepreneurship and investment play central roles in the process of growth and expansion in the modern economy; thus the behavior of entrepreneurs and investors is crucial to understanding real growth and the development of inflationary pressures in society.

3. Aggregate monetary demand in excess of real supply accounts directly for much of the immediate inflationary pressure in modern market societies. But the excess demand is fundamentally explainable by the income demands of different groups. Hankel and Isaak suggest that these demands can be illuminated partly by grouping people into four ideal types: entrepreneurs, defeatists, free riders, and maintenance men. The titles convey some flavor of the attitudes and behaviors of the different groups.

4. Modern industrial, political-democratic societies are inflation inclined. Excess income claims press governments to spend more than they collect in taxes. The political process makes it substantially impossible to

check the expansion of money that is needed to finance the inflationary growth.

5. In the modern Western world, t¹ growing importance of international money, called xeno credits, has produced a way of satisfying the increased demand for money substantially outside the effective control of individual nations. The growth in xeno credit thus plays a crucial role in setting off and maintaining inflationary spirals.

6. The welfare state plays a central role in this process because individuals and groups come to believe they are entitled to more. How long the illusion of inflation succeeds in fooling the public is crucial to the continued life of big inflation. Economics, politics, and sociology are intricately interwoven.

Hankel and Isaak have written a somewhat old-fashioned book as far as methodology is concerned. They have, however, made a serious effort at interdisciplinary analysis of an obviously interdisciplinary phenomenon, weaving it into the whole economic-political-sociological milieu of modern participating democracy. And in emphasizing disputes over income shares as central to the whole dynamic process of growth, inflation, and conflict resolution, Hankel and Isaak have seen a very important issue that is given all too little attention by most writers on inflation.

G. L. BACH

Stanford University
California

HOPKINS, ANNE H. *Work and Job Satisfaction in the Public Sector*. Pp. x, 146. Totowa, NJ: Rowman & Allanheld, 1983. $27.50.

Hopkins, an associate professor of political science at the University of Tennessee, Knoxville, has written an interesting little study about job satisfaction among a group of public employees. Hopkins developed a questionnaire, sent it to a cross section of public employees in five state capitals, and achieved a 65 percent return rate. Her book essentially consists of an explanation of the development of her survey and an exposition and interpretation of the answers.

Hopkins notes that by the early 1970s, at least 2000 studies of job satisfaction had been conducted. She argues that her study improves on the normal model in three ways: she considers unionization as a variable, she includes questions about job environment as well as job characteristics, and she uses a multivariate method to analyze her findings.

Most of the employees who answered the Hopkins survey were fairly satisfied with the intrinsic job characteristics of their positions, whereas a somewhat smaller number were pleased with their job environment. For Hopkins, job environment includes such factors as income, civil service status, mobility, promotions, size of work place, unionization, discrimination, and supervision. Hopkins concludes that efforts to increase worker satisfaction will yield their best results if the job environment, as well as the more narrow intrinsic job traits, are modified.

The research survey and its interpretation are well thought out. Hopkins sees and notes the limitations of her data. She also explains, in a clear, convincing fashion, why questions were asked and how her conclusions were arrived at. No sooner had I raised a question about her analysis than it was answered in the text.

The major weakness was precisely the extremely narrow research scope of the study. What we have to work from as data are the answers to one survey. As Hopkins notes, "Our description of the work situation lacks a certain vitality or texture." At the least, some historical account of the civil service status and unionization history of each group of workers would have given the book a little more substance.

I recommend the book to social scientists interested in the question of job satisfaction and to students of and workers in the field of public employee labor relations.

MARK McCOLLOCH

University of Pittsburgh
Pennsylvania

PERETZ, PAUL. *The Political Economy of Inflation in the United States.* Pp. 268. Chicago: University of Chicago Press, 1983. $28.00. Paperbound, $14.00.

Paul Peretz addresses the perennial political science issue of whether a pluralist, an elitist, or a Marxist model best describes the American political system. His refinement of these hypotheses is applied to the problem of controlling inflation. The failure to contain inflation often has been laid at the clay feet of the American pluralist-democratic system. The models have different implications for those sufficiently powerful to forge economic policies and for what those policies might be.

Peretz surveys the economic theory of inflation; public perceptions of inflation, based on survey research; the translation of perceptions—or misperceptions—into political demands; and the power nodes of policymaking. Finally, he appraises the performance of the three models. The survey of economic theory is accurate, save for minor slips. His own statistical estimate of the distributional effects of inflation on real income is seriously flawed by identification and collinearity snafus. Peretz gets back on track with a superb review-interpretation of the public opinion surveys. Although most of those surveyed dislike inflation, the respondents do not understand its actual effects because of income illusion and demand transference, in which financial situations deteriorating for reasons unrelated to inflation nonetheless are blamed on inflation. So much for economists' theory of rational expectations!

We go deeper into the quagmire of perception as Peretz addresses political demands. The policies people seem to want would not, according to conventional economic theory, be anti-inflationary. Peretz finds that elites influencing the Federal Reserve, the White House, and key congressional committees determine economic policy while broad segments of the population are safely ignored. In addition to the power of the nonelected groups such as the Federal Reserve, the elected officials do not always get what they want, and when they do, the economy does not always respond as anticipated.

In a society in which interests are inaccurately perceived, not represented, or, where represented, wrong-headed but often ineffective, the pluralist model appears hopelessly flawed. Do elitist and Marxist models fare any better? Peretz claims that the failure of perception is consistent with the false consciousness or general ignorance seen as normal in these models. After three decades of inflation, people do not seem to know which policies slow inflation. Moreover, the views of the general public and the policymakers, as well as the goals of organizations and their membership, diverge. Of the models' variants, Peretz finds the competing elites model most reliable.

It is difficult to know what to make of a society in which people are ignorant and elites are wrong but ineffective. Certainly people cannot be blamed if economists cannot correctly diagnose, much less prescribe. What we do reap is massive economic mismanagement: the evidence since 1968 is there for all to see. The real problem is found in one table in Peretz's book, a matrix of occupations and attitudes toward anti-inflation policies in 1969 (p. 193). Non-wage-earners would raise income, but laborers would not; shareholders would raise interest rates but laborers would not; laborers would have price and wage controls but shareholders would not. Everyone would reduce government spending. Ideology rules; the divisions are not so much along class lines as along the lines of free market versus government planning. Government spending becomes the convenient scapegoat for the entire society because the safest recommendation is the one that we know will never be implemented.

Peretz fills a major gap in the literature: he ties economic theory to policymaking through the skillful use of public opinion polls. Even where his diagnosis is wrong, he sheds light.

E. RAY CANTERBERY
Florida State University
Tallahassee

OTHER BOOKS

ALDERMAN, GEOFFREY. *The Jewish Community in British Politics.* Pp. xiii, 218. New York: Oxford University Press, 1983. No price.

ANDREWS, WILLIAM G. *Presidential Government in Gaullist France: A Study of Executive-Legislative Relations, 1958-1974.* Pp. xiii, 304. Albany: State University of New York Press, 1982. Paperbound, no price.

BADEAU, JOHN S. *The Middle East Remembered.* Pp. 271. Washington, DC: Middle East Institute. $25.00.

BAHMUELLER, CHARLES F. *The National Charity Company: Jeremy Bentham's Silent Revolution.* Pp. xi, 272. Berkeley: University of California Press, 1981. $25.00.

BAKKEN, GORDON MORRIS. *The Development of Law on the Rocky Mountain Frontier: Civil Law and Society, 1850-1912.* Pp. 200. Westport, CT: Greenwood Press, 1983. $29.95.

BALL, NICOLE and MILTON LEITENBERG, eds. *The Structure of the Defense Industry.* Pp. xi, 372. New York: St. Martin's Press, 1983. $27.50.

BANAC, IVO, ed. *The Effects of World War I: The Class War after the Great War: The Rise of Communist Parties in East Central Europe, 1918-1921.* Pp. xv, 282. Boulder, CO: East European Monographs, 1983. Distributed by Columbia University Press. $27.50.

BARADAT, LEON P. *Political Ideologies.* 2nd ed. Pp. xiv, 336. Englewood Cliffs, NJ: Prentice-Hall, 1984. Paperbound, $15.95.

BARNETT, ANTHONY. *Iron Britannia.* Pp. 160. New York: Schoeken Books, 1982. $5.95. Paperbound, no price.

BIDWELL, ROBIN. *The Two Yemens.* Pp. xvii, 350. Boulder, CO: Westview Press, 1983. No price.

BOARDMAN, ROBERT and JAMES KEELEY, eds. *Nuclear Exports and World Politics: Policy and Regime.* Pp. xiv, 256. New York: St. Martin's Press, 1983. $26.00.

BOISOT, MAX. *Intangible Factors in Japanese Corporate Strategy.* Pp. 55. Paris: Atlantic Institute for International Affairs, 1983. Paperbound, no price.

BRACKEN, PAUL. *The Command and Control of Nuclear Forces.* Pp. xii, 252. New Haven, CT: Yale University Press, 1983. $19.95.

BRYANT, RALPH C. *Controlling Money: The Federal Reserve and Its Critics.* Pp. xii, 155. Washington, DC: Brookings Institution, 1983. $18.95. Paperbound, $7.95.

BULLOCK, PAUL et al. *Building California: The Story of the Carpenters' Union.* Pp. xi, 371. Los Angeles: University of California, 1982. Paperbound, no ning: A Critique. Pp. xiv, 335. Boulder, CO: Westview Press, 1982. No price.

CAMPBELL, COLIN. *Governments under Stress: Political Executives and Key Bureaucrats in Washington, London, and Ottawa.* Pp. x, 388. Toronto, Canada: University of Toronto Press, 1983. $24.95.

CEAUSESCU, ILIE, ed. *War, Revolution, and Society in Romania: The Road to Independence.* Pp. vi, 298. Boulder, CO: Social Science Monographs, 1983. Distributed by Columbia University Press. $27.50.

CHAMPAGNE, ANTHONY and ROSEMARY N. DAWES. *Courts and Modern Medicine.* Pp. xi, 260. Springfield, IL: Charles C Thomas, 1983. $29.75.

CHEREVIK, E. and Y. SHUY-ROKOV. *An ABC of Planning*. Pp. 247. Moscow: Progress, 1982. $6.45.

CHUBB, JOHN E. *Interest Groups and the Bureaucracy: The Politics of Energy*. Pp. xiii, 319. Stanford, CA: Stanford University Press, 1983. $29.50.

CLINTON, CATHERINE. *The Plantation Mistress: Women's World in the Old South*. Pp. xix, 331. New York: Pantheon Books, 1982. $19.95.

COHEN, JEAN L. *Class and Civil Society: The Limits of Marxian Critical Theory*. Pp. 264. Amherst: University of Massachusetts Press, 1982. $22.50.

COLE, PAUL M. and WILLIAM J. TAYLOR, Jr., eds. *The Nuclear Freeze Debate: Arms Control Issues for the 1980s*. Pp. xix, 245. Boulder, CO: Westview Press, 1983. Paperbound, $20.00.

COLLINS, JOHN M. *U.S. Defense Planning: A Critique*. Pp. xiv, 335. Boulder, CO: Westview Press, 1982. No price.

CRANSTON, MAURICE and PETER MAIR. *Language and Politics*. Pp. 218. Brussels: European University Institute, 1982. No price.

CRYSTAL, STEPHEN. *America's Old Age Crisis: Public Policy and the Two Worlds of Aging*. Pp. vii, 232. New York: Basic Books, 1982. $16.50.

D'ANTONIO, WILLIAM V. and JOAN ALDOUS, eds. *Families and Religions: Conflict and Change in Modern Society*. Pp. 320. Beverly Hills, CA: Sage Publications, 1983. $25.00.

DAHL, ROBERT A. *Modern Political Analysis*. 4th ed. Pp. xiv, 157. Englewood Cliffs, NJ: Prentice-Hall, 1984. No price.

DRELL, SIDNEY D. *Facing the Threat of Nuclear Weapons*. Pp. x, 120.

Seattle: University of Washington Press, 1983. $10.00. Paperbound, $4.95.

EDDY, WILLIAM B., ed. *Handbook of Organization Management*. Pp. 576. New York: Marcel Dekker, 1983. $99.75.

ELYANOV, A. Y. *Economic Growth and the Market in the Developing Countries*. Pp. 277. Moscow: Progress Publishers, 1982. $7.45.

FAGEN, RICHARD R. and OLGA PELLICER, eds. *The Future of Central America: Policy Choices for the U.S. and Mexico*. Pp. xii, 228. Stanford, CA: University Press, 1983. $20.00. Paperbound, $11.95.

FELD, WERNER J., and ROBERT S. JORDAN with LEON HURWITZ. *International Organizations: A Comparative Approach*. Pp. xxii, 332. New York: Praeger Publishers, 1983. No price.

FORBES, IAN and STEVE SMITH, eds. *Politics and Human Nature*. Pp. x, 198. New York: St. Martin's Press, 1983. $25.00.

GINSBURG, HELEN. *Full Employment and Public Policy: The United States and Sweden*. Pp. xix, 235. Lexington, MA: Lexington Books, 1983. $24.95.

GORDON, DAVID C. *The Republic of Lebanon: Nation in Jeopardy*. Pp. xiv, 171. Boulder, CO: Westview Press, 1983. $18.50.

GUILLEMARD, ANNE-MARIE, ed. *Old Age and the Welfare State*. Pp. 265. Beverly Hills, CA: Sage Publications, 1983. $28.00. Paperbound, $14.00.

GUTTENTAG, MARCIA and PAUL F. SECORD. *Too Many Women? The Sex Ratio Question*. Pp. 336. Beverly Hills, CA: Sage Publications, 1983. $27.50. Paperbound, $12.95.

HEIDENHEIMER, ARNOLD J. et al. *Comparative Public Policy: The Politics of Social Choice in Europe and America.* Pp. xvi, 367. New York: St. Martin's Press, 1983. $16.95. Paperbound, $10.95.

HILGARTNER, STEPHEN, RICHARD C. BELL, and RORY O'CONNOR. *Nukespeak-The Selling of Nuclear Technology in America.* Pp. xiv, 282. New York: Penguin Books, 1982. Paperbound, $6.95.

HINKSON CRAIG, BARBARA. *The Legislative Veto: Congressional Control of Regulation.* Pp. xviii, 176. Boulder, CO: Westview Press, 1983. Paperbound, $16.00.

HOLLANDER, PAUL. *The Many Faces of Socialism: Comparative Sociology and Politics.* Pp. viii, 355. New Brunswick, NJ: Transaction Books, 1983. $29.95.

HOUT, MICHAEL. *Mobility Tables.* Pp. 93. Beverly Hills, CA: Sage Publications, 1983. Paperbound, $5.00.

HUDSON, JOHN. *Inflation: A Theoretical Survey and Synthesis.* Pp. xii, 171. Winchester, MA: Allen and Unwin, 1982. No price.

HURWITZ, LEON, ed. *The Harmonization of European Public Policy: Regional Responses to Transnational Challenges.* Pp. xviii, 264. Westport, CT: Greenwood Press, 1983. $37.50.

INOZEMTSEV, N. N. et al., eds. *Peace and Disarmament.* Pp. 486. Moscow: Progress Publishers, 1982. No price.

JACKSON, ELMORE. *Middle East Mission: The Story of a Major Bid for Peace in the Time of Nasser and Ben-Gurion.* Pp. 124. New York: W. W. Norton, 1983. $12.95.

JENKINS, JOHN J. *Understanding Locke: An Introduction to Philosophy through John Locke's Essay.* Pp. xviii, 256. Edinburgh, UK: The University Press, 1983. Paperbound, no price.

JOSEPH, JOHN. *Muslim-Christian Relations and Inter-Christian Rivalries in the Middle East.* Pp. xviii, 240. Albany: State University of New York Press, 1983. No price.

KAMINSKAYA, DINA. *Final Judgment: My Life as a Soviet Defense Attorney.* Trans. Michael Glenny. Pp. 364. New York: Simon and Schuster, 1982. No price.

KEEFE, WILLIAM J. *Congress and the American People.* 2nd ed. Pp. xii, 237. Englewood Cliffs, NJ: Prentice-Hall, 1984. Paperbound, $12.95.

KEGLEY, CHARLES W., Jr. and EUGENE R. WITTKOPF. *Perspectives on American Foreign Policy.* Pp. x, 544. New York: St. Martin's Press, 1983. Paperbound, $9.95.

KINCADE, WILLIAM H. and CHRISTOPH BERTRAM, eds. *Nuclear Proliferation in the 1980s: Perspectives and Proposals.* Pp. xiv, 272. New York: St. Martin's Press, 1982. No price.

KLINE, HARVEY F. *Colombia: Portrait of Unity and Diversity.* Pp. xv, 169. Boulder, CO: Westview Press, 1983. $18.00.

KOFAS, JON V. *Authoritarianism in Greece: The Metaxas Regime.* Pp. x, 244. Boulder, CO: East European Monographs, 1983. Distributed by Columbia University Press. $20.00.

KUEHL, WARREN F., ed. *Biographical Dictionary of Internationalists.* Pp. xvi, 934. Westport, CT: Greenwood Press, 1983. $75.00.

LENGLE, JAMES I. and BYRON E. SHAFER. *Presidential Elections: Readings on Nominations and Elections.* 2nd ed. Pp. x, 405. New York: St. Martin's Press, 1983. Paperbound, $11.95.

LINDBOM, TAGE. *The Tares and the Good Grain: Or the Kingdom of Man at the Hour of Reckoning.* Trans. Alvin Moore, Jr. Pp. x, 143. Macon, GA: Mercer University Press, 1983. No price.

LISTOKIN, DAVID. *Landmarks Preservation and the Property Tax.* Pp. xxvi, 229. Piscataway, NJ: Center for Urban Policy Research, 1982. $20.00.

LODGE, JULIET, ed. *Institutions and Policies of the European Community.* Pp. xv, 264. New York: St. Martin's Press, 1983. $32.50.

LUNDQUIST, LENNART. *The Party and the Masses.* Pp. 336. New York: Transnational Publishers, 1982. No price.

MacPHERSON, STEWART. *Social Policy in the Third World: The Social Dilemmas of Underdevelopment.* Pp. 220. Totowa, NJ: Allanheld, Osmund, 1982. Paperbound, no price.

MANDEL, RUTH B. *In the Running: The New Woman Candidate.* Pp. xxv, 280. Boston, MA: Beacon Press, 1983. Paperbound, no price.

MARTIN, J. PAUL and LOUIS HENKIN, eds. *Human Rights: A Topical Bibliography.* Pp. xii, 299. Boulder, CO: Westview Press, 1983. $30.00.

MINSKY, HYMAN. *Can "It" Happen Again?: Essays on Stability and Finance.* Pp. xxiv, 301. Armonk, NY: M. E. Sharpe, 1982. $35.00.

MINTZ, JEROME R. *The Anarchists of Casas Viejas.* Pp. xvi, 336. Chicago, IL: University of Chicago Press, 1982. $20.00.

MORRIS, MICHAEL A. and VICTOR MILLAN, eds. *Controlling Latin American Conflicts: Ten Approaches.* Pp. xiii, 272. Boulder, CO: Westview Press, 1983. Paperbound, $22.50.

NEFF, DONALD. *Warriors at Suez: Eisenhower Takes America into the Middle East.* Pp. 477. New York: Simon and Schuster, Linden Press, 1982. Paperbound, $8.25.

PARNES, HERBERT S., ed. *Policy Issues in Work and Retirement.* Pp. vii, 286. Kalamazoo, MI: W. E. Upjohn Institute for Employment Research, 1983. Paperbound, no price.

PHILLIPS, KEVIN P. *Post-Conservative America: People, Politics and Ideology in a Time of Crisis.* Pp. xxvi, 261. New York: Random House, 1983. Paperbound, no price.

PIPER, DON C. and RONALD J. TERCHEK, eds. *Interaction: Foreign Policy and Public Policy.* Pp. 235. Washington, DC: American Enterprise Institute, 1983. Paperbound, no price.

POLLAK, OTTO and NANCY L. KELLEY. *The Challenges of Aging.* Pp. xiii, 128. Croton-on-Hudson, NY: North River Press, 1982. $9.95.

POLLOCK, DAVID. *The Politics of Pressure: American Arms and Israeli Policy Since the Six Day War.* Pp. 328. Westport, CT: Greenwood Press, 1982. $35.00.

RABINOWITZ, HOWARD N., ed. *Southern Black Leaders of the Reconstruction Era.* Pp. xxiv, 422. Urbana: University of Illinois Press, 1982. $27.50. Paperbound, $9.95.

REYNOLDS, CLARK W. and CARLOS TELLO, eds. *U.S.-Mexico Relations: Economic and Social Aspects.* Pp. vii, 375. Stanford, CA: Stanford University Press, 1983. $25.00.

ROBBINS, WILLIAM G. *Lumberjacks and Legislators: Political Economy of the U.S. Lumber Industry, 1890-1941.* Pp. xiv, 268. College Station,

TX: A & M University Press, 1982. $22.50.

ROSENBLATT, ROGER. *Children of War*. Pp. 212. Garden City, NY: Doubleday, Anchor Press, 1983. No price.

SASSOON, DONALD. *The Strategy of the Italian Communist Party: From the Resistance to the Historic Compromise*. Pp. xi, 259. New York: St. Martin's Press, 1981. $25.00.

SBRAGIA, ALBERTA M. *The Municipal Money Chase: The Politics of Local Government Finance*. Pp. xii, 251. Boulder, CO: Westview Press, 1983. $25.00. Paperbound, $12.50.

SCARROW, HOWARD A. *Parties, Elections, and Representation in the State of New York*. Pp. ix, 142. New York: New York University, 1983. Distributed by Columbia University Press. $25.00. Paperbound, $12.50.

SCHMIDT, STEFFEN W. *El Salvador: America's Next Vietnam?* Pp. vii, 217. Salisbury, NC: Documentary Publications, 1983. $19.95.

SEALANDER, JUDITH. *As Minority Becomes Majority*. Pp. xiii, 201. Westport, CT: Greenwood Press, 1983. No price.

SHULL, STEPHEN A. *Domestic Policy Formation: Presidential-Congressional Partnership?* Pp. xv, 218. Westport, CT: Greenwood Press, 1983. No price.

SMYTH, HOWARD M. et al., eds. *Documents on German Foreign Policy 1918-1945*. Pp. lxxxi, 1140. Washington, DC: Government Printing Office, 1983. No price.

SOLOMON, SUSAN GROSS, ed. *Pluralism in the Soviet Union: Essays in Honor of Gordon Skilling*. Pp. xiii, 179. New York: St. Martin's Press, 1983. $22.50.

SOLOVYOV, BORIS. *The Turning-Point of World War II*. Pp. 207. Moscow: Progress Publishers, 1973. $5.95.

STEWART, ANGUS. *Contemporary Britain*. Pp. x, 262. Boston, MA: Routhledge and Kegan Paul, 1983. Paperbound, $10.95.

STIVERS, WILLIAM. *Supremacy and Oil: Iraq, Turkey, and the Anglo-American World Order, 1918-1930*. Pp. 207. Ithaca, NY: Cornell University Press, 1983. $19.95.

SYMMONS-SYMONOLEWICZ, KONSTANTIN. *National Consciousness in Poland: Origin and Evolution*. Pp. ix, 68. Meadville, PA: Maplewood Press, 1983. $7.95.

TOMLINSON, JIM. *The Unequal Struggle? British Socialism and the Capitalist Enterprise*. Pp. 160. New York: Methuen, 1982. Paperbound, no price.

TOURAINE, ALAIN et al. *Anti-Nuclear Protest: The Opposition to Nuclear Energy in France*. Trans. Peter Fawcett. Pp. 202. New Rochelle, NY: Cambridge University Press, 1983. No price.

TOWLE, PHILIP. *Arms Control and East-West Relations*. Pp.187. New York: St. Martin's Press, 1983. No price.

TSIPIS, KOSTA and SHEENA PHILLIPS. *Annual Review of Military Research and Development: 1982*. Pp. x, 171. New York: Praeger Publishers, 1983. $24.95.

VARDY, STEVEN BELA and AGNES HUSVAR VARDY, eds. *Society in Change: Studies in Honor of Bela K. Kiraly*. Pp. xii, 680. Boulder, CO: East European Monographs, 1983. Distributed by Columbia University Press. $27.50.

VON BEYME, KLAUS. *The Political System of the Federal Republic of*

Germany. Pp. xiii, 209. New York: St. Martin's Press, 1983. $25.00.

WALLER, ROBERT. *The Almanac of British Politics.* Pp. 608. New York: St. Martin's Press, 1983. Paperbound, $19.95.

WYNOT, EDWARD D., Jr. *Warsaw between the World Wars.* Pp. viii, 375. New York: Columbia University Press, 1983. $27.50.

YERGIN, DANIEL and MARTIN HILLENBRAND. *Global Insecurity: A Strategy for Energy and Economic Renewal.* Pp. xiii, 427. New York: Viking Penguin, 1983. Paperbound, no price.

ZUCKERMAN, SOLLY. *Nuclear Illusion and Reality.* Pp. xiv, 153. New York: Random House, 1983. Paperbound, $2.95.

INDEX

Of Special Interest...

BEYOND METHOD
Strategies for Social Research
edited by GARETH MORGAN, *York University, Toronto*

Is "social research," a neutral, technical discovery process through which researchers reveal latent truths? **Beyond Method** supports a radically different view: that researchers make knowledge as a result of the assumptions that guide the research process. Twenty-one varying research perspectives are juxtaposed to highlight significant links between assumption and method. The authors all make persuasive cases for engaging in their favored research modes, while Morgan discusses the implications of their conflicting claims for the conduct and evaluation of research. Because the volume reframes understanding and debate about research practices in a way that goes beyond consideration of method alone, it will interest applied social scientists and theorists, as well as students of organizational behavior, psychology, sociology, anthropology, and education.

CONTENTS: Preface // **I. Introduction** // 1. Research as Engagement: A Personal View G. MORGAN / 2. Research Strategies: Modes of Engagement G. MORGAN // **II. The Research Strategies** // 3. Studying Organizational Structure and Process D.S. PUGH / 4. The Case for Configuration D. MILLER & H. MINTZBERG / 5. Quasi-Experimentation T.D. COOK / 6. Action Research: A Sociotechnical Systems Perspective G.I. SUSMAN / 7. Organizational Learning D. SCHON / 8. Interpretive Interactionism N.K. DENZIN / 9. Life History Methodology G.R. JONES / 10. Studying Organizations as Cultures L. SMIRCICH / 11. Uncovering Cognitive Maps: The Self-Q Technique M.G. BOUGON / 12. Studying Organizations Through Levi Strauss's Structuralism S. TURNER / 13. The Other: A Model of Human Structuring R. COOPER / 14. Dramatism and the Theatrical Metaphor I.L. MANGHAM & M.L. OVERINGTON / 15. Critical Theory and Organizational Analysis J. FORESTER / 16. Antimethod as a Counterstructure H.T. WILSON / 17. Synthesism: A Case of Feminist Methodology L.M. GLENNON / 18. Initiating Collaborative Inquiry W.R. TORBERT / 19. Transformational Theory O.F. WHITE, Jr. & C.J. McSWAIN / 20. Organization and Praxis W.V. HEYDEBRAND / 21. Toward a Realist Perspective W. OUTHWAITE / 22. A Dialectical Method J.K. BENSON / 23. Class Analysis and the Study of Social Forms C. CARCHEDI // **III. Conclusions** // 24. Toward a More Reflective Social Science G. MORGAN / 25. The Significance of Assumptions G. MORGAN / 26. Knowledge, Uncertainty, and Choice G. MORGAN / 27. Exploring Choice: Reframing the Problem of Evaluation G. MORGAN / 28. We Meet Ourselves in Research as in Conversation G. MORGAN // Bibliography

1983 / 424 pages / $29.95 (h) / $14.95 (p)

SAGE Publications, INC.
275 South Beverly Drive
Beverly Hills, California 90212

SAGE Publications, LTD.
28 Banner Street
London EC1Y 8QE, England